Radicalizing Educational Leadership:
Dimensions of Social Justice

EDUCATIONAL LEADERSHIP AND LEADERS IN CONTEXTS
Volume 2

Series Editor
Tony Townsend and Ira Bogotch
Florida Atlantic University, Boca Raton, FL., USA

Scope

The series, *Educational Leadership and Leaders in Contexts,* emphasizes how historical and contextual assumptions shape the meanings and values assigned to the term leadership. The series includes books along four distinct threads:

- *Reconsidering the role of social justice within the contexts of educational leadership*
- *Promoting a community of leadership: Reaching out and involving stakeholders and the public*
- *Connecting the professional and personal dimensions of educational leadership*
- *Reconceptualizing educational leadership as a global profession*

Perhaps to a greater extent than ever before, today's educational leaders find themselves living in a world that is substantially different from what it was just a decade ago. The threads of social justice, community leadership, professional and personal dimensions, and globalism have added contextual dimensions to educational leaders that are often not reflected in their local job descriptions. This book series will focus on how these changing contexts affect the theory and practice of educational leaders.

Similarly, the professional lives of educational leaders has increasingly impinged upon their personal well-being, such that it now takes a certain type of individual to be able to put others before self for extended periods of their working life. This series will explore the dynamic relationship between the personal and the professional lives of school leaders.

With respect to communities, recent educational reforms have created a need for communities to know more about what is happening inside of classrooms and schools. While education is blamed for many of the ills identified in societies, school leaders and school communities are generally ignored or excluded from the processes related to social development. The challenge facing school leaders is to work with and build community support through the notion of community leadership. Thus, leadership itself involves working with teachers, students, parents and the wider community in order to improve schools.

As for the fourth thread, globalism, school leaders must now work with multiple languages, cultures, and perspectives reflecting the rapid shift of people from one part of the world to another. Educational leaders now need to be educated to understand global perspectives and react to a world where a single way of *thinking and doing* no longer applies.

Radicalizing Educational Leadership

Dimensions of Social Justice

Ira Bogotch
Florida Atlantic University

Floyd Beachum
University of Wisconsin-Milwaukee

Jackie Blount
Iowa State University

Jeffrey Brooks
Auburn University

Fenwick English
University of North Carolina-Chapel Hill

With critical commentary by Jonathan Jansen

SENSE PUBLISHERS
ROTTERDAM / TAIPEI

A C.I.P. record for this book is available from the Library of Congress.

ISBN: 978-90-8790-414-2 (paperback)
ISBN: 978-90-8790-415-9 (hardback)
ISBN: 978-90-8790-416-6 (e-book)

Published by: Sense Publishers,
P.O. Box 21858, 3001 AW
Rotterdam, The Netherlands

Printed on acid-free paper

TABLE OF CONTENTS

SERIES PREFACE

Radicalizing Educational Leadership: Dimensions of Social Justice is the second book in a new Leadership Book Series edited by Tony Townsend and Ira Bogotch for Sense Publishers.

The series will emphasize how historical and contextual assumptions shape the meanings and values assigned to the term leadership. The series will include books along four distinct threads:

- Reconsidering the role of social justice within the contexts of educational leadership
- Promoting a community of leadership: Reaching out and involving stakeholders and the public
- Connecting the professional and personal dimensions of educational leadership
- Reconceptualizing educational leadership as a global profession

Perhaps to a greater extent than ever before, today's educational leaders find themselves living in a world that is substantially different from what it was just a decade ago. The threads of social justice, community leadership, professional and personal dimensions, and globalism have added contextual dimensions to educational leaders that are often not reflected in their local job descriptions. This book series will focus on how these changing contexts affect the theory and practice of educational leaders.

For example, in terms of social justice, governments ask education to provide opportunities for people to make their way in the world, yet it appears that the gap between those well-off and those not so well-off has never been wider, both in schools and in societies. How can the educational leader provide both the environment and the learning needed to ensure a more socially just world? More pointedly, how can educational leaders contribute to making a material difference in the everyday lives of people around the world?

In this volume, we strived to meet two important editorial objectives: (1) confronting and challenging traditional and generic notions of leadership in order to re-consider how cultures, communities, teachers, as well as students, influence and act as educational leaders; and, (2) engaging new authors and new voices alongside those who have shaped the field for the 21st century.

We hope you enjoy reading it.

Tony Townsend

Ira Bogotch

PREFACE

The authors of *Radicalizing Educational Leadership: Dimensions of Social Justice* have taken varied approaches to the study of social justice in relationship to educational leadership. Each stakes out a different and original theoretical position across social science disciplines and political, social, and ethical philosophies. What you will not find in this book, however, is a consensus on a single definition or meaning for the term social justice.

Not only have we not arrived at a single definition of social justice, we have deliberately introduced new ideas and theorists to educational audiences. Our approach extends beyond the small world of educational leadership and school improvement researchers. Thus, alongside the more familiar names of John Dewey, Ivan Illich, Paolo Freire, Jerome Bruner, Maxine Greene, Deborah Britzman, William Foster, and Michele Fine, etc. are the ideas of Cornel West, Michael Dyson, Michael Mann, Jared Diamond, John Rawls, Frederick Hayek, Iris Young, Kwame Appiah, and many others writing outside the fields of education. Their inclusion here puts an added responsibility on us as authors and on you as readers. For us, we have to be concise and precise as to why non-educators and their theories are relevant to education and educational leadership; for readers, you have to be critical of our choices and the ideas contained in this book.

Two points of emphasis: we all agreed from the beginning on the need for theory when discussing social justice; and, we have been respectful of our differing, if not contradictory, theoretical positions.

HOW THIS HAPPENED MAY BE OF INTEREST

From the beginning, the idea behind taking an extended period of time to develop our ideas on social justice across three academic conferences was deliberate. Some emerging lines of inquiry disappeared while others re-emerged, at times with just minor revisions, at other times with extensive shifts in thinking incorporating different literatures and arguments. Regardless, the authors remained committed to this process believing that what would emerge would be stronger theoretical approaches in connecting social justice to educational leadership.

We first came together in collaboration in preparation for the 2005 University Council of Educational Administration (UCEA) conference under the symposium title *Beyond Whining and Protesting: Towards a Theory of Social Justice*. At the time, we had thought to organize our ideas around two concepts: diagnosis and treatment. We debated this electronically through e-mails and over the phone.

> We don't want to become part of the problem. The dilemma is that as we have tried to incorporate social justice in our educational leadership program, [but] it's mostly protesting this and that across courses and encouraging our students to be "activists"– but I don't see anywhere a solid, empirical, model

by which as "activists" they could use to get inside schools and change them to do anything else but reproduce the social structure...Right now, there is no solid theory for social justice. We have only critical racial theory or queer theory. In order to unlock schools and keep them unlocked from reproducing the social order we need to have a better understanding of how they locked it up in the first place. A good theory would do that. It would point out where to start to make a difference beyond what we are doing now for social justice. That was my thinking. What do you all think about the two step process? Diagnosis: "What's wrong?" and Treatment: "Here's how to fix it?" Fenwick English

Floyd Beachum responded:

[W]e barely can define its [i.e., social justice] components and as I said before political correctness has people regurgitating the rhetoric instead of refining it into a reality. Thus, this effort becomes a substantial effort into unpacking and examining the internal components of social justice and pushing the theoretical boundaries beyond the existing philosophical silos.

Out of our convictions to understand social justice better came a second symposium for the 2006 American Educational Research Association convention (AERA) titled: *Confronting the riddle of the social justice sphinx: Is a theory of social justice possible as a research base?*

Between conferences, there were more e-mail conversations:

I worry about the same fate befalling social justice–will it be a buzzword for the in-crowd of researchers that will soon be replaced by another, sexier, term? Our work here gives me hope that we can build a more solid theoretical foundation from which future inquiry can build. To extend that metaphor, our "raw" building materials are planks borrowed from philosophical, historical, critical, and social theories. Now, please don't misinterpret that to think I am suggesting that work done to date is useless or that we shouldn't pursue certain lines of SJ inquiry. On the contrary, I think Ira [Bogotch] is dead-on in suggesting that the foundation can grow and grow and grow. I just think that our effort, which is in part to attempt to provide theoretical weight to important and loosely- coupled lines of inquiry, holds a lot of promise and is an important contribution. Okay...now I need another coffee! Jeffrey Brooks

Every step toward the goal of justice requires sacrifice, suffering, and struggle; the tireless exertions and passionate concern of dedicated individuals. Without persistent effort, time itself becomes an ally of the insurgent and primitive forces of irrational emotionalism and social destruction. This is no time for apathy or complacency. This is a time for vigorous and positive action. Floyd Beachum

These thoughts are changing as we speak (in terms of theoretical insight and philosophical depth). Floyd Beachum

Our words took on a decidedly radical and critical stance of our own field of educational leadership. We came together around the need for changes in research questions and methods, graduate leadership preparation, and school-wide practices. At the same time, we did not limit ourselves to the worthy pursuits of ethical schools, democratic school leadership practices or equitable opportunities of teachers and students. Our theories looked past the artificial walls of schooling and entered into the daily lives of people regardless of where they lived.

[M]y take is that educational researchers are too often stuck in a conceptual rut because rather than building on solid work already completed with increasingly sophisticated and theoretically-dense analyses, we have a self-defeating tendency to rename phenomena and act as though we have discovered something new, when in fact, what people mainly do is refine and test theories and phenomenon. Could it be in part due to the entrepreneurial bent that so much educational leadership literature/research exhibits? I don't know, but anyway, that's where I am today...and that's the paper I am planning to work toward. Jeffrey Brooks

Embedded in our conversations were continuing concerns about how to organize our presentations. How would the original metaphor of diagnosis-treatment evolve? How should we connect philosophy with contemporary ideas? In a personal communication with a colleague outside the narrow field of educational leadership, we read the following:

Is it possible to connect the writing on the philosophers to the "problems" [of social justice]? Coming at this from a Freirean perspective (I don't know that he even uses the term social justice), I find this historical journey rather puzzling, quite unconnected to what I do. So please connect it. Give me a reason for why I need to be interested in taking the journey into what these dead white men had to say about social justice. (I find 'justice' to be a very different thing!!). Dilys Schoorman

Such criticism is not at all surprising. In fact, how theory – any theory – connects to the lives of school administrators and teachers in a meaningful way must be addressed. And it is. For Jackie Blount, her cogent response calls for the necessities of historical understanding when pursuing social justice work. Her histories and biographies speak to the lived experiences inside of school practice. For Jeffrey Brooks, there is a need for educators, particularly researchers, to step back from immediate problems in order to re-discover our fundamental mission as both educators and educated citizens. For Floyd Beachum, the dominant discourses reveal double-edged swords of justice and injustice which require a transformation constructed from the margins of society. For Ira Bogotch, the failings of both social theories and educational theories require that education itself be re-invented and then inserted as valid theories into social justice. For Fenwick English who argues that while history may be accidental, neither injustices nor our educational leadership responses to them can be anything but deliberate. Each of the five authors finds a way to build a social justice theory from intimate educative experiences that connect explicitly to larger social forces.

But, alas, even that was not enough to bring this book to you. The Series co-editor, Tony Townsend read our completed first draft. His response:

> Each of the 5 authors has written essays that look at social justice from his/her own [theoretical and North American] viewpoints. I have read the chapters they have written and believe that a responsive chapter written by someone from a completely different context would make the book more whole – a chapter that puts what has been said into an international context.

The name Jonathan Jansen came immediately to mind. Fortunately, he accepted this challenge. Thus, a book which was considered finished and whole was put onto the shelf awaiting critique.

Jansen's critique comes after the five essays. It complements the text. He pushes the argument to make the abstract terms of justice, social justice, and injustice even more concrete – not just with adverbs, direct objects, and prepositions, but with the realities of educators inside of educational institutions and outwards into all societies. He extends the book's critiques of social theory and social science and personalizes the consequences for all of us as educators and citizens. In short, he completes the book by speaking of leadership and leadership theory as concrete and action-oriented, highlighting that the enemies of social justice have us all pointing fingers at ourselves and at others in ways that existing theories cannot explain. Why are we so complicit and compliant?

Collectively, we conclude not with a consensus on a concise definition of social, but with acknowledging that there are no utopias on planet earth and that all educational struggles for social justice – including this book – remain unfinished and incomplete. We readily acknowledge our limitations and the many holes in our arguments. We certainly could not speak on behalf of the entire international community. But that is also our promise to you; for if the essays here do not capture your unique situation, then you, too, are obligated to bring forth your subjective theories of justice. As educators, we hold positions of relative status and privilege while also having a minority voice in social theory debates. By adding your voices as educational leaders, we may all become stronger.

MEET THE AUTHORS

[in alphabetical order]

Floyd Beachum is an Associate Professor in the Department of Administrative Leadership at the University of Wisconsin-Milwaukee. He is on the editorial board of the *Journal of Cases in Educational Leadership*. His research has been published in the *Journal of Negro Education, Educational Forum, Multicultural Learning and Teaching*, and *Values and Ethics in Educational Administration*. Floyd has co-authored an edited book titled *Urban Education for the 21st Century*.

This book is dedicated first to my wife Katerri Stacks-Beachum for her continued love and support. It is also dedicated to my entire family who keeps me focused and grounded. Lastly, this book is dedicated to teachers and scholars everywhere who struggle for a social justice discovery, definition, and destiny.

Jackie Blount is currently a Professor of Historical, Comparative, and Philosophical Studies in Education and also Associate Dean of the College of Human Sciences at Iowa State University. Her work has been published in the *Harvard Educational Review, Review of Educational Research*, and *Educational Administration Quarterly*. She also has written *Destined to Rule the Schools* (1998) and *Fit to Teach: Same-Sex Desire, Gender, and School Work in the Twentieth Century* (2005). Currently, she is writing a biography of Ella Flagg Young.

I have drawn intellectual support from more persons, both known and unknown, than I could ever adequately acknowledge. The persons whose ideas have most significantly affected my scholarship have been Ella Flagg Young, John D'Emilio, Kate Rousmaniere, David Tyack, Fen English, Cheryl Achterberg, and Jared Diamond. Personally, BeJae Fleming has profoundly influenced all of my thinking. Overall, I have endeavored to find links between my scholarship and my own social justice work, making them one and the same where possible.

Ira Bogotch is currently a Professor in the Department of Educational Leadership at Florida Atlantic University. He has served as the School Leadership Program leader at both FAU and at the University of New Orleans. His interest in social justice dates back to the Vietnam War era and the many protests needed to end that war. Ira is the Associate Editor of the *International Journal of Leadership in Education* and currently serves on the editorial boards of *Urban Education, The Professional Educator*, and *Educational Administration Quarterly*.

My first publication on the topic of social justice appeared in the *Journal of School Leadership* in 2002. I have been rethinking that article ever since. Along the way, I was encouraged to keep *beginning again* by many colleagues, most notably Luis Miron, Spencer Maxcy, Scott Bauer, Fenwick

English, Fran Kochan, Carolyn Shields, Robert Kottkamp, and Gail Furman. My FAU colleagues, Pat Maslin-Ostrowski, John Pisapia, Jennifer Sughrue, Dilys Schoorman, Daniel Reyes-Guerra, Michele Acker-Hocevar, and Tony Townsend have all criticized my works. Thank you. Yet, in all of my years writing, I wonder if I will ever be able to communicate so that Rochelle, Sara, and Ari would consider reading. That's my motivation.

Jeffrey Brooks is an Associate Professor in the Department of Educational Foundations, Leadership, and Technology at Auburn University. His research focuses on socio-cultural and ethical aspects of educational leadership practice and preparation, with specific emphases on teacher leadership, school reform, and issues of race and gender. These lines of inquiry include both domestic research conducted in the United States, and more recently international studies in the Philippines. He is author of the book, *The Dark Side of School Reform: Teaching in the Space between Reality and Utopia* (2006, Rowman & Littlefield Education).

> I owe a debt of gratitude to my collaborators in this book for initiating this endeavor, inspiring me, and urging me to push my thinking about social justice. We have not arrived at the goal equitable schooling, but as the Buddha pointed out: the journey of a thousand miles begins with a single step. I am proud to have taken a step with each of you. I also thank Catherine Marshall, Catherine Lugg, Linda Tillman, Gail Furman, Ernestine Enomoto, Margaret Grogan, Jerry Starratt, Joan Shapiro, Jackie Stefkovich, John Merrill, and Michael Dantley and many other authors I cited in this work for guidance through their scholarship. While many others undoubtedly deserve my gratitude, I acknowledge the particular contributions of my friends and colleagues Jeffrey Ayala Milligan and Anthony H. Normore for their constant support and honest critique. Most importantly, I thank my wife Melanie and daughters Holland, Bronwyn, and Clodagh for their love and support during the development of this book; the four of you are my personal and professional foundation, and I love you dearly.

Fenwick English is currently the R. Wendell Eaves Senior Distinguished Professor of Educational Leadership in the School of Education at the University of North Carolina at Chapel Hill. Formerly he served as a program coordinator, department chair, dean, and vice-chancellor of academic affairs, the latter two positions in the Purdue University system at Fort Wayne, Indiana. As a K-12 practitioner, he has been a superintendent of schools in New York, an assistant superintendent of schools in Florida, and a middle school principal in California. He also had a stint as an associate executive director of AASA and served as principal (partner) in Peat, Marwick, Main & Co. (now KPMG Peat Marwick) where he was national practice director for elementary and secondary education, North America. Dr. English created the curriculum management audit process which has been in use since 1979. He is the author or co-author of over twenty books in education, many of which are used as texts in college courses today.

Jonathan Jansen is currently Rector of University of the Free State, South Africa. He recently was a Fulbright Scholar at Stanford University. Prior to that he was Dean of Education at the University of Pretoria. In 2007, Dr. Jansen delivered a keynote address at the University Council of Educational Administration in Alexandria, Virginia. Other keynotes include the International Conference on School Effectiveness and School Improvement and the Annual Conference of the Association for Supervision, Curriculum, and Development. A 2006 article, Leading Against the Grain: The Politics and Emotions of Leading for Social Justice in South Africa, explored the work of school principals who promote social justice against the grain of public expectations. Employing a biographical lens, Dr. Jansen's work focuses on how race, gender, history, and institutional culture intersect, often in the volatile context of South Africa. He explains his own leadership as a negotiated transition of Black leadership inside of the dominant White institutions by means of balancing tensions of affirmation and inclusion, retention and restitution, caring and correction, accommodation and assertion, and racial reconciliation and social justice.

[handwritten annotations: framework: justice has roots in other disciplines, and school leaders would do well to base equitable practices on a broader understanding of justice]

[handwritten: Brooks]

INTRODUCTION

[handwritten: purpose: to explore how justice has manifested in disciplines like philosophy, politics, and sociology]

Educators have much to learn from social science debates on social justice. Conversely, social scientists engaged in social justice research have much to learn from education. In this Introduction, we have approached social justice from both perspectives. *[handwritten: see pages 8-9 for links to ed. practice]*

PART ONE: WHAT CAN SOCIAL JUSTICE EDUCATORS LEARN FROM THE SOCIAL SCIENCES?

Jeffrey Brooks

I contend that a more deliberate and meaningful connection to the social sciences could ultimately help provide a foundation for radical innovation in both the research and practice of educational leadership—it could also be the intellectual scaffold on which a theory of social justice is ultimately built. As you read further, I will endeavor to provide support for these assertions and discuss how formal and informal educational leadership can be a force for the creation and sustenance of more equitable and just schools. Before I provide rationales and evidence for these contentions, it is important to note at the onset of this phase of the investigation that I am not calling for any particular "focus" or narrowing of research on leadership and justice. On the contrary, this is a call for an explosion of thoughtful and interconnected activity; I am in favor of a proliferation of approaches to the way scholars and leaders-in-the-field go about their work. I *am* suggesting that by learning from, and building on, already rich veins of scholarship, educational leaders can understand and enact justice in a more deliberate and reasoned manner. Cohen (1986) summarized this sentiment when he noted that:

> Whatever its initial (and perhaps, disciplinary) foundation, an understanding of justice and injustice will require attention to concerns that are psychological, economic, sociological, and philosophical. Failure to recognize this may lead those working in this area to substitute unacknowledged and therefore unexamined, assumptions based on their ignorance of work in related disciplines (p. 3).

One of my great hopes is that educational leaders are destined to become social rights leaders in a new era of equity and equality (Scheurich & Skrla, 2003); my great fear is that these same leaders are doomed to repeat individual and collective behaviors that contribute to school systems that have at times been rightly characterized as "evil"—hegemonic, discriminatory, unjust, and unfair. In the subsequent section, I briefly and broadly review specific lines of justice-related inquiry in philosophy, economics, political studies, sociology, psychology, anthropology, and public policy. Building on this foundation, I then discuss how these concepts have been (and have not been) extended into research on educational leadership before finally discussing the implications of these connections, and disconnections, for scholarship and practice.

Ira Bogotch et al. (eds.), Radicalizing Educational Leadership: Dimensions of Social Justice, 1–15.
© *2008 Sense Publishers. All rights reserved.*

JUSTICE: PERSPECTIVES FROM THE SOCIAL SCIENCES

It is important first, however, to point out certain assumptions that under gird this multidisciplinary review of research on justice. *First, justice* (like freedom, see Brooks pp. 61ff in this volume) *is both individual and organizational.* It is not by accident that I refer to justice, rather than *social* justice throughout this essay. This exigency was prompted by the recognition that justice has both personal and collective dimensions, and that it can be enacted and experienced as one person and as a collective or sub-collective. Accordingly, while educational leaders can (and should) be conceived as advocates for social justice, especially those with positional power and formal influence, it is also appropriate to consider leaders as advocates for individual justice. *Second, justice has both conceptual and empirical qualities.* While research on justice often necessarily begins with abstract concept-ualizations, it can also be manifest as tangible and observable activities and behaviors. Thus, it follows that justice can be studied through a variety of methodological approaches. Depending on the epistemological and/or methodological orientation of a study, justice may be a measurable or observed event, a purely theoretical construct, or more likely a combination of the two.

PHILOSOPHICAL STUDIES OF JUSTICE

Philosophers have long been interested in the concept of justice. While it is certainly possible to trace justice studies to Plato's *Republic* and throughout many Eastern traditions, Western philosophers have tended to concentrate on a few central themes. Among these is the issue of whether justice is properly conceived as retributive and/or distributive. Retributive justice holds that

> "...the guilty are to be punished, not in order to deter others from committing similar offenses, nor to satisfy the desire for revenge or otherwise contribute to social utility, but simply because wrongdoing as such ought to be punished, regardless of the consequences of doing so" (Buchanan & Mathieu, 1986, p. 13).

Distributive justices, on the other hand, are "those principles that are designed to regulate social and economic inequalities" (Buchanan & Mathieu, 1986, p. 13). Recently, philosophers have argued that this distinction is not salient due to the fact that retributive justice is more correctly one of many criminal justice theories.

Philosophers also differentiate between justice as a comparative and non-comparative phenomenon. That is, should justice be meted out on the principle of equity (comparative) or equality (noncomparative)? This fundamental question has inspired hot debate among philosophers for thousands of years and is wrapped up in several conflagrated issues. The first of these issues is consideration of the material principles of justice, or put differently, we must decide which concepts and charac-teristics should determine the distribution of justice. For example, Rescher (1972) suggests that "there are seven common material principles of distributive justice recognized today: equality, need, ability, effort, productivity, public utility, and supply and demand" (Buchanan & Mathieu, 1986, p. 20). In a sense, the relative weight and distribution of these characteristics, and others such as institutionalized discrimination and hegemony, can be said to indicate a kind of equation of justice:

Equality + Justice = Equity

If this is the case, it follows that a consideration of just procedures and just outcomes must necessarily accompany any such formula.

While there is much debate among philosophers as to which concepts are relevant to a discussion of justice, Rawls (1971, 1999) is frequently cited as a modern point of departure. His theory of justice rests on three principles:
- The principle of greatest equal liberty: Each person is to have an equal right to the most extensive system of equal basic liberties compatible with a similar system of liberty for all.
- The principle of equality of fair opportunity: Offices and positions are to be open to all under conditions of equality of fair opportunity—persons with similar abilities and skills are to have equal access to offices and positions.
- The difference principle: Social and economic institutions are to be arranged so as to benefit maximally the worst off (Buchanan & Mathieu, 1986, p. 27).

Certainly, these principles are only a place to begin the conversation of how to operationalize justice, and philosophers have debated the utility of Rawls' position, as do my co-authors in this book, but these principles lay an excellent foundation for the purpose of this review.

ECONOMIC STUDIES OF JUSTICE

Economic studies of justice can be thought of emanating from four distinct strains of thought. The first is Aristotelian, and entails

> "an effort to differentiate three kinds of social obligations, those relating to (a) distributive justice, which has to do with the divisions of honors, money, or other goods among participants in a common enterprise; (b) rectificatory justice, which takes account of injuries done one private individual to another; and (c) exchange, or commutative, justice, which provides norms for the regulation of voluntary transactions between private individuals" (Worland, 1986, p. 47).

A second strain is rooted in Adam Smith's notion of the disembedded place of economics as a part of the larger social system. That is, particular institutions, such as school systems, develop their own idiosyncratic norms of interaction and exchange. This position particularly prompts an analysis of microeconomic activity *in situ* at the school or classroom level, rather relying on larger (say, federal but also possibly even state and district level) indicators as a measure of just distribution. This strain of inquiry begs the questions: Which children have what? Why do they have it? And how have educational leaders influenced, by omission or commission, this distribution? Strain three of economic justice is rooted in the thinking of Karl Marx. Marx's labor theory of value suggests abolition of personal property and a redistribution of goods and services based on an overriding socialist

3

principle that calls for value to be determined by the relative amount of labor required for production. Put differently, Marx places a premium on production, with supply and demand and market forces taking a back seat. To be sure, I am painting with broad strokes here. There exist myriad economic distinctions that extend far beyond these simplistic explanations. For the purpose of this review, the key point I wish to make is that there are many ways to conceive of the distribution of goods and services in a just manner; there is no *one* way to fairly distribute the products of an economic system. Educational leaders would do well to continually interrogate the reasons and manners in which they influence the distribution of goods, services, and resources.

POLITICAL STUDIES OF JUSTICE

Political studies of justice center, broadly, on the relationship of an individual, sub-group, and/or a political plenum to other individuals, political sub-groups, and/or political plenums. Social contract theorists such as Hugo Grotius, Thomas Hobbes, John Locke, and Jean Jacques Rousseau explored the nature of this relationship. Grotius, writing in the 19th century, argued that whether or not an individual or group retains or abdicates sovereign authority over their actions is the essential aspect of political life and the quality that makes political systems possible (Schacht, 1970). The social contract, as conceived by both Hobbes and Locke, is entered into when an individual refrains from single-minded pursuit of their own good if the means of achieving their goals impinged on another member of society's pursuit of their own good. The social contract, then, allows competing (yet possibly tempered) visions of the good life to co-exist, provided that individuals respect others by agreeing to absolve some rights and ends for the good of society. Hobbes deemed this a useful and necessary arrangement: "society is constructed for the sake of the individual, and it seeks only to preserve singular interests and accommodate singular needs" (Wiser, 1983, p. 194). Famously, Hobbes characterized natural life, that is, life before or without the social contract as "solitary, poor, nasty, brutish, and short" (Wiser, 1983, p. 199 quoting Hobbes' *Leviathan*). Locke's political theory differs to some degree, as he placed greater emphasis on punitive action against adjudged violators of codified doctrine, yet retains the central focus of resigning certain freedoms to others as a foundation of society. Both Hobbes and Locke asserted that individuals stand to gain a great deal more than they lose in this arrangement in that co-existence allows for exchange of goods and services unequalled by a solitary existence (Schmitt, 2003, p. 17). Others, such as Rousseau, believed that such an arrangement exacted too great a toll on the individual, instead suggesting that such a contract is debilitating. To Rousseau, the quality of life in modern civilized societies compared unfavorably to that of a solitary (and somewhat fictive) "natural man," whose life was characterized by authentic pride and self-love (Schmitt, 2003, pp. 16-18). Although his notion of natural man was abstract and archetypal, he used the construction as a romantic alternative to the contemporary "civilized" man. Thus equipped with a theoretical counterpoint, Rousseau used natural man as a means to critique the extant relationship of individual to society. Rousseau believed that "alienation is

Social Contract: giving up some freedoms for the sake of the collective, greater good (Hobbes + Locke). Rousseau believed the individual was more important.

INTRODUCTION

rampant because people, [who] instead of trying to be themselves, succumb to the demands of society and arrange their lives to meet fashion's demands" (Schmitt, 2003, p. 19). Therefore, as people enter into a social contract that allows them to cohabitate, personal values give way to normative processes and the discrete individual melts into an aggregate political plenum. In such an arrangement, justice becomes a protean negotiated concept, realized as a function of norms and mores. Rousseau believed that people give up too much of themselves to become citizens. Individuals, as natural beings, are unrecognizable within the social contract and are instead infected with extrinsic and intrinsic conformity and sanction, whose inescapable symptom is alienation. Educational leaders would do well to (re)examine the ways they shape the social contract in their schools.

Contemporary political studies also center on concepts such as differentiations between "old" and "new" forms of liberalism and conservatism (Di Quattro, 1986), relative vs. normative justice, the role of market values and institutions as a vehicle for the administration of natural justice, and the notion that as closed and/or open political systems, justice is variously effected by extra-institutional forces, actors, and agents.

SOCIOLOGICAL STUDIES OF JUSTICE

To sociologists, "justice is more often an implicit theme rather than an explicit object of study in sociology" (Rytina, 1986, p. 117). To some extent this is due to the focus of sociology as a hermeneutic discipline, since the "concept is often relative to a particular point of view of a participant in a particular set of social arrange-ments" (Rytina, 1986, p. 117). As such, while there is much research that could be characterized as related to justice, there is little work directly focused on the issue as such, and even fewer sociologists hazard a definition of the phenomenon. Instead, the issue is often explained in terms of social arrangements. As Rytina (1986) explains:

> "The question of justification of inequality is one of distributive justice or fair rules or procedures or processes for the allocation of advantage and disadvantage. Ideally, the issue is not whether a particular arrangement is fair, but whether or to what degree it is accepted as fair by those who live under it" (p. 117).

Sociologists have evoked conflict theory and various forms of critical theory to explain justice-related issues. Conflict theory

> "uses the same general systems analysis as does functionalism but focuses on conflict, change, and inequality, which it views as a consequence of unequal resource distribution within society. Conflict theorists believe that conflict, rather than equilibrium, is natural and inherent to social systems and that it in fact contributes to the healthy adaptations of social systems" (DeMarrias & LeCompte, 1999).

On the other hand, critical theories have been defined in different ways by various theorists. However, DeMarrias and LeCompte (1997) offer a broad overview. They explain that critical theory

useful explanation

> "asserts that existing social structures derive from historically generated patterns of domination and subordination. Many critical theorists state that patterns of oppression derive from inequities in the distribution of economic resources; others focus on the unequal distribution of knowledge and skill in society. These theorists are concerned with the power of language and the control of information, and so they often give particular attention to curriculum. Still others emphasize asymmetries such as race, gender, religion, age, gender preference, and region. Critical theorists make two different critiques of the existing social order. The first views the hegemony of the existing order as inescapably rigid and inegalitarian, dooming most of the human race to slavery or rule by autocrats. The second and less pessimistic critique emphasizes human "agency" or self-determination in the face of institutional rigidity. The latter provides a basis for social transformation insofar as it uses social critique as a way to escape the control of the dominant classes" (p. 34).

These theories offer powerful and well-articulated perspectives that can help researchers and educational leaders alike understand socially constructed justice-related phenomena such as inequity, bias, discrimination, and stereotyping.

PSYCHOLOGICAL STUDIES OF JUSTICE

Like sociologists, psychologists have refrained from advancing germinal definitions of justice. Psychologists have also engaged in a running debate about how to measure justice (Furby, 1986). However, a great deal of work has developed around a distinct cluster of phenomena, which are commonly grouped together as a domain of inquiry. This cluster includes (at least) research on equity, equality, procedural justice, distributive justice, and the sense of injustice (Furby, 1986). Psychologists have sought to refine their understanding of each of these phenomena and more recently have begun to explore the relationship between these psychological concepts. Historically speaking, research on justice grew out of social exchange theory, which "emphasizes the role of distributional or exchange considerations in shaping the dynamics of interpersonal interactions (Furby, 1986, p. 154). However, this perspective has grown in obtuse directions over the past sixty years, which has led to advances in psychological thinking about a panoply of topics, including cognitive developmental stage theories of justice, multiple standards theory, and research on fulfillment of expectations, entitlement, and interpretations of justice.

ANTHROPOLOGICAL STUDIES OF JUSTICE

While rarely dealing with justice as a formal subject of inquiry, anthropologists still make some interesting assertions about the phenomenon. For example, Nader and Sursock (1986) claim that

- justice beliefs and behaviors and the justice motive are universal phenomena
- the meaning of justice will vary with different social and cultural settings
- different forms of justice may exist within one sociocultural setting and often in societies with ranked or stratified social structures.

The authors continue by asserting that these three points need empirical study, but offer evidence in support of their claims. The contention that justice beliefs and behaviors are universal phenomena stems first from psychological studies of child development data (Nader & Sursock, 1986, p. 206) and was generalized even further by Lerner and Whitehead (1980) who argued that "considerations of justice shape the way people interact with one another in every encounter, especially where there is a common endeavor or resources to be allocated" (p. 242). Conceived in this way, the idea of justice "encompasses what people's expectations are in relation to the mechanisms of justice, what they feel they deserve, and the decision-making processes that are used in arriving at outcomes" (Nader & Sursock, 1986, p. 206). These concepts urge empirical studies to consider justice as an *in situ* construct that is both individually and institutionally perceived and enacted in conceptual and empirical domains.

Certain anthropological methods and epistemological orientations may yet yield important findings in the study of educational leadership for justice. For example, anthropologists "have often presented polar types whose usefulness lies not so much in their accuracy as in their illumination of salient ideological values or social features" (Nader & Sursock, 1986, p. 208). This technique has already yielded important and useful findings about justice among indigenous populations (e.g. Evans-Pritchard, 1940; Gibbs, 1987) where justice dichotomies such as individualistic/holistic, paternal/matriarchal, compensatory/therapeutic, etc. have paved a path for subsequent inquiry. This technique has already led to insightful research that investigated trenchant ideological values in schools, school districts, and communities (e.g. Brooks & Jean-Marie, 2007; Wolcott, 1999) but may ultimately yield important advances in understanding justice as a leadership-specific phenomenon.

Anthropological explanations of justice-related phenomena have also produced interesting findings that need further exploration and clarification. Among these are the concepts of justice as a social exchange (reciprocity), the way individuals and cultures justify events (luck, fate, desert, etc.), the way social (in)justice is manifest as mundane behavior and overlooked cultural norms, and the social structures erected around concepts such as multiculturalism and pluralism.

PUBLIC POLICY STUDIES OF JUSTICE

Soltan (1986) argues a point familiar to educational researchers, but from the perspective of public policy:

"..Public policy analysis, together with management theory and legal theory, are areas in which intellectual work in the social sciences most directly impinges on practical questions. In all three of these areas the unity of theory and practice is not a slogan of a revolutionary party but the need of everyday (and quite unrevolutionary) experience. This determines the form that interest in justice takes in the policy sciences" (p. 235).

Justice is both an abstract "big" idea and also a concrete "little" idea in that it permeates the norms of practice in professional fields. This basic assertion should not be taken as an inseparable rift between theory and practice, but rather as a tension to be negotiated.

Public policy researchers' work in justice has largely taken place at the systems level, and concerns objectivity of standards, normative pluralism, and investigations of the complexity of said pluralism. Accordingly, a genuine concern of public policy researchers has been just development and application of policies that meaningfully address and reconcile *systemic* inequities. Corollary to this primary concern is interest in measurement and objectivity in analysis of justice. Traditionally, objectivity and direct measurement were the norm in this area of research, but more recently the field has accepted that "indirect" and "imprecise" measures may offer the most important and useful insights into justice-related phenomena such as willingness to pay and sacrifice (Soltan, 1986).

Soltan (1986) characterizes public policy research on justice as existing on a continuum between utilitarianism on the one hand and normative pluralism on the other. In a sense, this frames the debate on justice as a struggle between whether or not characteristics such as race, class, gender, sexual orientation, etc. should weigh into public policy debates.

HOW DEEP AND HOW WIDE? EDUCATIONAL LEADERSHIP AND SOCIAL JUSTICE

Over the past two decades, justice has become an area of interest among educational leadership practitioners and researchers (See Marshall and Oliva, 2006 for an outstanding collection of this literature). Scholars have developed vibrant conceptual lines of inquiry and have engaged in an ongoing conversation on, particularly, social justice. This work is promising, and has lead to insightful commentary and critiques of:

- *The knowledge base(s) that under girds our understanding of educational leadership.* In what ways is the "base" biased? What questions have been historically obscured, ignored, and suppressed?
- *The methodologies used to understand justice as phenomena in educational leadership.* The interrogation of both qualitative and quantitative methods as viable tools for addressing systemic inequity. Should new techniques be developed (e.g. equity audits)?
- *The relationship of the researcher to the researched.* Should researchers be "public intellectuals" (Dantley & Tillman, 2006) or "bridge people" who assume an activist and/or advocate stance toward issues of justice?

While each of these questions is fodder for academic debate, a more substantive question looms; what comes next?

My contention is that the field might consider taking a step backward in order to take several forward. That is, educational leadership researchers might re-examine freedom and justice, both in terms of social and individual dynamics and as disciplinary-specific, multidisciplinary and interdisciplinary phenomenon. By adopting this approach, we can connect and extend long-established lines of conceptual and empirical inquiry and thereby gain insights that may otherwise be overlooked or assumed. This holds great promise for generating, refining, and testing theories of social justice in educational leadership and will help strengthen already vibrant lines of inquiry. That is, rather than citing a single, or a few, works out of their disciplinary context it might be more fruitful to situate educational leadership for social justice research in their respective traditions. This could be carried out by extending extant lines of inquiry I have discussed in this Introduction into educational leadership research, and then incorporating lessons gleaned from this work into innovative practice. For example, why not more clearly establish lines of educational leadership and justice research into the Philosophy of Social Justice, Economics of Social Justice, Political Studies of Social Justice , Sociology of Social Justice, Anthropology of Social Justice, and the Public Policy of Social Justice as focused and discrete areas of inquiry? This inquiry might begin with the following questions:

- How have the concepts of justice and injustice emerged in the theoretical and practical history of the discipline?
- What are the major controversies that have emerged from this history and that characterize current discussions of justice in the discipline?
- What are the crucial issues one might propose as an agenda for work in the discipline in the immediate future?
- What specific aspects of this agenda would require work conducted primarily from the perspective of other disciplines in the social sciences, and how much would such work contribute to advancing the understanding of issues on that agenda? (Cohen, 1986)

Once this new orientation toward the knowledge base of justice and educational leadership is laid, we might then seek to explore some of the natural connections between traditions before ultimately investigating justice in educational leadership through a free association of ideas as the worlds of practice and research co-construct a "new" language they can use to discuss educational leadership. Such an endeavor *may* demand reconceptualization of both the processes and products of collaborative research and the communication of findings, but it *will* demand a breaking-down of methodological and epistemological biases and a more meaningful level and type of engagement between primary and applied knowledge bases.

The implications of the interdisciplinary orientation I am proposing are as much of interest to practitioners as it is researchers. Faculty teaching in educational leadership preparation programs might, for example, create an interdisciplinary strain of justice research or organize program curricula, course content, and student experiences on this framework. P-12 educational leaders might consider that freedom and justice, as I have described them here, entail both: (a) a sensitivity toward and understanding of the ways these concepts are theoretically and empirically manifest in educational settings, and, more importantly; (b) an understanding of how to influence change in each of these domains. It is simply not sufficient to identify achievement gaps using standardized testing data, although that is certainly a useful point of departure. Instead, I would argue that practitioners should be attuned to the various disciplinary manifestations and conceptualizations of justice and be trained in techniques that allow them to positively influence these phenomena, such as *satyagraha* (non-violent resistance) and critical consciousness. Only then will we begin not only to rethink the way theories of justice and practice inform educational leadership, but also to reconsider how leaders can influence systems and practices to offer a new vision of freedom and justice for their students.

PART TWO: WHAT CAN SOCIAL SCIENCE LEARN FROM THE STUDY OF EDUCATION?

Ira Bogotch

Jeffrey Brooks argued that educational researchers might profit from taking a step backwards in order to move forward on the topic of social justice. But what if we reversed the question? What if social theorists grounded in the social sciences, humanities and philosophy paid *more* attention to educational theories and practice? The evidence I will present here seems to indicate that social theorists and philosophers have tended to ignore educational theory and practices or have viewed education instrumentally as a byproduct of the global society, or, at best, as developmental processes rooted in the cognitive sciences or developmental psychology (see for example Rawls, 1999, p. 430).

For many intellectuals, education is delimited to institutionalized structures of schooling, a defined place in time for children, primarily, and thus, disconnected from the dominant social forces that propel and constrain the peoples and nations of the world. In spite of evidence that schooling correlates not only with economic well being, but also with the quality of one's life, there are those who simply do not see education having a central role in the accumulation of wealth or the exercise of power across continents, else why would governments and their leaders not provide quality educational opportunities to all citizens?

Why has education been ignored or devalued as a generative social theory? Instead, education is equated with grade levels and subject areas measured by standardized tests which translate into accountability systems that compare performances of children and adults across cultures and continents. Issues of achievement, equity and excellence have been subsumed under the assumptions of centralized authorities, politically and economically. Educational artifacts and coherent policies align measures of student achievement with testing, textbooks, promotions, and graduation around the world. It is nothing short of the globalization of state mandated education. Thus, there is no necessity to hear from educators on professional issues of pedagogy, research or leadership. The field has been folded into already pre-conceived ideas regarding the foreseeable future.

Educators themselves have not given political or business leaders viable alternatives that might disrupt the governance or practice of schooling. Educators

Bogotch:
purpose is to place ed. practice at the forefront of
other disciplines rather than drawing on other
disciplines to inform practice, as Brooks does

INTRODUCTION

themselves tend to underestimate the power of education as theory and social practice to transform individuals, communities and whole societies. If this is so, then we are confronted by a reciprocal problem: that is, social theorists eschew the constructive and necessary role of educational institutions and processes, especially pedagogy and leadership, in building a just community; while, educators eschew the influences of macro and micro social theories. If we are to succeed in clarifying social justice issues and problems of contemporary educational leadership, it will happen only when educators, at all levels, fully embrace the intellectual, political, social, and ethical challenges they face everyday. The majority of educators today look to centralized authorities, local, state, and national agencies, to tell them "what matters" in our schools, not *vice versa*. Therefore, before we can demand respect from social theorists regarding the theories of education, we ourselves need to be self-educated with respect to history, cultural studies, and philosophy. On this point, Brooks is correct. Still, I want to look at the other side of this same coin. Our vocation is about educating educational leaders.

The emergence of social justice as an educational leadership theme for organizing school practices and educational research holds out new hopes for educators. But this contemporary movement is still young, and the ideas too fragmented to cause any ripple in global mindsets or markets. Nevertheless, social theories themselves have not been able to explain successfully how global phenomena emerge or develop (see Hayek, 1976). Global phenomena are readily evident from the fall of communism, the rise of nationalism, the commodification of music, art, and blue jeans to technological advances in virtual and real time communications, etc. Despite the lack of an explanatory social or political or economic theory, education has not been elevated to a place at the social justice policy table. This absence of educators and educational theory should not be troubling just to educators. It should be troubling to social theorists, too, who have presupposed the possibilities for social justice without understanding pedagogical and leadership theories [of liberation] or acknowledging the power of the most dominant social institution throughout the world – i.e., educational institutions – for either social justice or social ills. It is not naive to be asking the question: How can social justice become a reality without acknowledging the power of teaching, learning, and leading around the world?

While it is true that aspects of education can be found inside of a number of social justice theories (Bojer, 2000), I will demonstrate first, in this introduction, that educations' inclusion has been inadequate, and then expand upon these foundational ideas later in the text (see Bogotch, pp. 79ff). My thesis is that education belongs inside every social justice debate, not as a byproduct, but rather as a necessary contributor to nation building and progress. Social justice requires educational constructs in order for social justice to become not only a valid theory, but also a lived reality. The very *necessity* for a social justice theory is education. If that is the case, then as educators, we are justified, based on logic and actual world events, in making our voices heard with respect to *new leadership* and *new theories* for social justice.

framework: counters Rawls and his conception of
justice to advance the argument that education
and its potential for proliferating justice
have been ignored by thinkers concerned with
justice

11

EXAMINING THE EVIDENCE: A DEFENSE OF EDUCATION

Why is it that most theoretical accounts of social justice artificially begin with fully developed human beings, adults, ready to engage in every aspect of adult life with their worldly values, cultural, national, and religious, already in place and accounted for? This pre-supposition of individuals in adulthood as the embodiment of evolved reason is without empirically grounded *educational facts*. How strange since childhood and the various activities of teaching and learning have been present inside every society throughout history. Erickson (1963) remarked: "One may scan work after work on history, society, and morality and find little reference to the fact that all people start as children…" (p. 17). Even Rawls (1999) admits that beginning with rational adults is *not* how the actual processes of justice happen (p. 176).

Philosophers and social theorists take their views of education second hand, admittedly ignoring the complexities and details of education (Rawls, p. 411). Rawls states that "a consideration of…the learning of concepts and principles would also be necessary" (p. 433) and that the simplistic "causal sequence intended to bring about as an end result the appropriate moral sentiments" (p. 452) has been ignored. An educator's reading of Rawls would note that while he may view education as necessary, it is not sufficiently significant for *his* theory of justice. Thus, Rawls' own words seem factually empty when he proclaims the connectedness among education, freedom and reason (p. 452).

The specific arguments of Rawls (1971, 1999) illustrate his deliberate omission. For Rawls, adults come to the *original position* to establish the principles of social justice. In coming together, they must know the following:

> … the general facts about human society. They understand political affairs and the principles of economic theory; they know the basis of social organization and the laws of human psychology. Indeed, the parties are presumed to know whatever general facts affect the choice of the principles of justice. There are no limitations on general information, that is, on general laws and theories, since conceptions of justice must be adjusted to the characteristics of the systems of social cooperation which they are to regulate, and there is no reason to rule out these facts…. This kind of information is admissible in the original position" (p. 119).

It is evident from this central passage that Rawls has presupposed a broad range of knowledge for individuals who come together in his original position. The question is how did these citizens, *at any age,* obtain this range of prior and sophisticated knowledge? In his *Theory of justice*, Rawls does not ignore education altogether, but rather he discussed and accepted the psychological stages of learning development. But as an historical and *educational* fact, he did not address education as it happens as a necessary aspect of life- throughout life- as a basic right. Rawls and others are more concerned with establishing the concepts of *rationality* and the *autonomy* of individuals than of describing the purposes and processes of education which make these concepts possible and meaningful.

It is ironic, sad really, that Rawls relies on a metaphor called a *veil of ignorance* to justify the universality of his theory which ensures that decisions being made benefit all in society, both for today and for future generations. The *veil* prevents citizens from focusing on self or group member interests and, therefore, being prejudiced. The *ignorance* prevents citizens from favoring one generation over another. For Rawls, social and economic benefits are to be distributed fairly in that they are guaranteed [up to a social minimum] and proportional for everyone in society. That is, everyone benefits, but the least advantaged benefit most. One can see and even support Rawls' logic, but his choice of language belies his stated respect for education as a moral human process.

As an educator I wonder why education [that is, the knowledge of the general facts about human society as well as how that knowledge is taught, learned, and used] has been ignored as a pre-requisite for nation-building. This question hardly comes up in scholarly debates. Instead, philosophers and theorists, such as Rawls, debate whether the resources being distributed will be adequate to provide a social minimum for all or whether the present generation will ensure a viable future for coming generations. To which I respond by asking *why has all prior and on-going education been omitted from philosophical discussions of social justice?* What is the role of education and specifically educational leadership in social justice?

It seems as if education as lifelong processes of teaching and learning, whether of children or adults, has been relegated to instrumental, pre-rational, pre-moral, pre-legal, and a non-historical status. Discussions of the human condition and social contract theories have ignored the complex, interactional, educational processes by which children *and* adults develop socially, mentally, politically, economically, and spiritually throughout one's life. It is through education that we learn how to interact and negotiate for mutually beneficial ends (Deutsch, 1985), including our knowledge of the fairness principles articulated by Rawls himself. For a theory of justice to assert the need for equity without understanding how it is to be mutually accepted by all participants is to fail to see the power and necessity of education theoretically and practically in societies around the world. It also, according to Roberts (2005), privileges those who are already most advantaged by society, that is, educated adults. If so, what of minority rights and minority voices who are not assumed to be at the *original position*?

My voice, throughout this text, is that of an educator, not the voice of either a philosopher or social theorist. In that sense, it must be heard as a minority voice that has been missing in serious social justice debates. According to Shklar (1990), "[The putative victim] is the privileged voice because hers is the one voice without which it is impossible to decide whether she suffered injustice or a misfortune" (p. 90). This minority voice comes from not only the omission of educators' voices in philosophical and social theory debates, but also from political and social structures that do not understand the nature of educational theory and educators' work.

With respect to theory, the educator "sees" the world of theory [i.e., concepts, ideas] and practice [i.e., actions and consequences] differently from other social scientists and philosophers as well as from other citizens. Education begins with interpersonal interactions, of people and texts. It is social at its core. It is also universal in that education begins naturally at birth. Humans, by necessity, learn.

Therefore, a valid theory of social justice would have to emerge inside educative social relationships [i.e., teaching, learning, and leading], and advanced through critiques, reflections, and experimentation. These dynamics are not limited to only children or to schooling.

With respect to educators' work, the minority status encompasses others including students – those eager to learn, those resistant to learn, those able and disabled, those literate and illiterate. These interactions give educators different and unique perspectives in terms of different generations [i.e., K-12, postsecondary, and adult learning]. In these contexts, I hear the educators' voice as that of an oppressed minority. Yet, even if one were to deny minority status to educators [and to those whom we teach], there is no denying the educational fact that the primary role of educators is to extend privileges and develop voice in *others*. Thus, it is by extending privileges through education to others that education is, in fact, the *true* original position for any society, not just in the present, but also for the future.

Nevertheless, I understand the many reasons for education's omission. Competing necessities such as food, housing, and health, various social and cultural conceptions of children, notions of state-sponsored schooling and teaching, and the necessity to transmit culture are all valid arguments for minimizing the role of education. That said, I trust that my claim that *education has been ignored* is a defensible one. The question becomes, following the pragmatist William James, whether education is necessary to the validity of a theory of social justice? What are the consequences in the real world for ignoring education with respect to social justice? To answer these questions, we must understand the *problems* inherent with education which philosophers, social theorists, as well as educators have not successfully overcome. Our leadership and research voices have not been sufficiently powerful constitutionally, institutionally, organizationally, or even in our own practices and theories of education to overcome the limitations of education.

History, of course, is not on the side of educators or education. Educationists have made strong pro-educational arguments before (see Foster, 1986; Giroux, 1988; Noguera, 2003; etc.); yet, education continues to be viewed as less urgent with respect to serious and immediate worldwide problems. Why should this introduction or even this volume on educational leadership and social justice be any more convincing? We are not so naïve to believe that education alone holds the answers to the world's problems. That is, the very same complexities and contradictions that have limited every other disciplinary path from achieving more successes theoretically and practically [i.e., peace, health care, literacy, the end of poverty, etc.] are in play inside education as well, especially when education is viewed institutionally (Illich, 1971) and/or ideologically (Apple, 1979). Thus, my objective will be to make plain the inherent problems of validity in education as theory and practice while at the same time address the solutions, possibilities, and leadership powers of education.

Central to these arguments is the fact that by rethinking social justice as an educational construct, it becomes valid under any and all human conditions, however harsh and inhumane. According to Freedom House (2005), a pro-democracy group in the US, 89 countries were classified as "free," which equates to around 46 percent of the world's population that live in "a climate of respect for civil liberties". It is a mistake as well as a conceit to equate social justice with any one system of government, laws, economy, religion, race, etc. As long as individuals can think and act for themselves *and* for others, there are possibilities for social justice, including just decisions to be silent, to flee, to resist, or to revolt. In fact, when individual choices are most limited, if not also dangerous, then the need for social justice as an educational construct will be the greatest. That will be the lesson that Americans learn from what happened in New Orleans prior to and during Hurricane Katrina in 2005. Those who stayed did not have choices. Even in settings below economic subsistence, social justice cannot be deferred. Social justice is accessible to all peoples of the world regardless of ideology or culture. "The virtue of social justice allows for *people* of good will to reach different—even opposing—practical judgments about the material content of the common good (ends) and how to get there (means). Such differences are the stuff of politics" (emphasis added) (Novak, 2000), n.p.). Yet, what makes difference contingent and in process is education and educational leadership. The challenge throughout is to insert educational processes – as leadership toward social action – as relevant politically and morally into world events (Miron, 2006).

JACKIE BLOUNT

HISTORY AS A WAY OF UNDERSTANDING AND MOTIVATING

Social Justice Work in Education

One important strand that has stretched through much of the history of education in the United States has been the impulse to provide social, political, and economic opportunities to persons who might otherwise languish in oppression or relative poverty. This is evident in the stories of newly-freed slaves who fought in the Civil War and then brought their battle-earned literacy skills back to their communities. It is plain in narratives of the enterprising women who founded female seminaries and academies so that girls might demonstrate the academic capabilities expected of their male peers – and perhaps eventually enjoy expanded political and economic opportunities beyond those females had enjoyed in years past. It is clear in accounts of the LGBTQ [Lesbian, gay, bisexual, transgender/transsexual/two-spirited, queer/questioning] rights movement as activist educators have insisted on the right to exist, be visible, and support those same fundamental rights for their students. This strand – to provide social, political, and economic opportunities for those who have been denied on account of status – essentially represents the heart of social justice work, broadly-conceived, not only in the United States, but around the world. There is a rich legacy, then, of educators – formal as well as informal, in the classroom as well as in administrative offices – who have worked for social justice.

Strangely, however, the field of educational leadership and administration generally lacks an overarching historical self-awareness, much less one concerned more specifically with such social justice projects. Certainly some scholars in the field refer to essential work by the venerable David Tyack, such as *The One Best System* (1974), the classic tale of educationists in search a singularly perfect mode of operation, or *Managers of Virtue*, co-written with Elisabeth Hansot (1982), an exploration of the tightly constrained expectations of individuals deemed acceptable for the work of school administration. Alongside these scattered references may be found citations of Callahan's classic statement on the mechanization of school administration, *Education and the Cult of Efficiency* (1962). Few other historical works are noted.

Indeed, when scholars of educational administration have attempted to render a history of the field, they have tended to step chronologically through an insular body of preeminent educational administration scholarship rather than focusing on

Ira Bogotch et al. (eds.), Radicalizing Educational Leadership: Dimensions of Social Justice, 17–37.

the scholars producing the work, the school administrators described by that work, or especially the larger social contexts in which the field has unfolded. Furthermore, this kind of historical work typically has grouped developments in educational administration scholarship into self-referential theoretical periods, rather than those that are more external and broadly socially/culturally-situated. This work, in essence, is neatly isolated from the messiness of school affairs or the rich contexts in which they are embedded. Finally, much existent historical work produced by scholars of educational administration generally has conveyed an ever-improving, evolving arc to the field's development, an inevitable and progressive march into the future. In this regard, Ellwood Cubberley's enthusiastic grounding texts in the field, published a century ago, still reach like a ghost from the past into the thinking of the present, even though the influence is seldom acknowledged (1919, for example). Indeed, contemporary analyses of educational administration rarely stretch back more than a few decades; consequently, they suffer from a somewhat narrow historical perspective-a phenomenon not limited by national boundaries.

The lack of a well-developed historical consciousness is not just a characteristic of the field of educational administration, however. Arguably, it is pervasive in our society, which privileges the future, rather than the past. Our capitalist economy demands attention to earnings in the days ahead; we live in a technology-rich environment that pulls our attention toward new advances while dampening our relationships with older technologies; our media push freshly-minted stories, news, and other entertainments – each with relatively short shelf-lives; our work environments pulsate with demands that we keep up, prepare for and lead change; and we continually search for new solutions to emerging problems, all with the expectation that we are continuing the long, steady march toward a greater society.

Though we maintain some collective awareness of this steady gait into the future, its corollary is much less evident: as we look to the future, we tend to devalue or ignore what has come before. By this implicit logic, the earlier or lower stages of the journey must be inferior. During the early decades of the twentieth century, for example, progressive reformers searched for scientifically sound ways to address a host of new social problems as a way of moving our society forward. While colleges and universities also raced to implement practical, progressive curricular reforms, they simultaneously lost to a corresponding degree a reverence for our cultural past. Kathleen Mahoney carefully details this phenomenon in her award-winning book, *Catholic Education in Protestant America* (2004), which explores how turn-of-the-twentieth-century skirmishes between Catholics and Protestants in higher education played out in many dimensions, but certainly in regard to the study of the past. Catholic educators emphasized cultural antecedents and the rich study of history while Protestant educators tended toward practical curricula that prepared students for future careers and/or leadership. Though the religious undertones of this Progressive-era clash are no longer so evident in our recognizable curricula of today, they were unmistakably formative.

Although I argue it is unfortunate that our historical consciousness has diminished greatly over the past century, I do not wish to say that knowledge of history is, in and of itself, necessarily good or useful. Many kinds of historical work exist that fail to trigger a larger, deeper understanding of our social relations

– or that otherwise fail to inspire us as humans. Without doubt, some histories are hardly more compelling than a dramatic rendition of a phonebook, especially if they simply emphasize the entrances and exits of persons across the historical stage or step through a finely-graded, though poorly interpreted chronology. Some histories document the lineage of those privileged with power, while ignoring the important mechanisms by which those persons obtained and preserved their dominance. Historical accounts incorporated into our school curricula often have been stripped of some of the most important aspects of our cultural past. Some are steeped in fallacies inserted either for ideological reasons or through negligence and shoddiness in historical craft (Zimmerman, 2002; and Loewen, 1996).

Historians can avoid these pitfalls, however. Thoughtfully interpreted histories can show us with unparalleled depth and fullness how our social relations have come to exist as they do, to understand more deeply our social conditions, and to enhance our ability to ask the kinds of questions that might provoke social justice work in the future. Though historical analysis cannot offer specific answers regarding how conditions will play out, it can assist us in moving into the future with thoughtfulness and awareness. And it can inspire us to action.

Not surprisingly, social justice movements have unfolded in the context of historical understanding. The extended project of racial equality in the U.S. has been punctuated and enhanced with historical accounts that have illuminated the complex, multi-dimensional ways that dominant racial groups have maintained their privilege at the expense of those they oppress. Contemporary queer rights activism has been bolstered by studying the ways that categories of sexuality, gender, and sex have been created over time to perpetuate privileged and oppressed classes of persons and relationships. The women's suffrage and modern women's liberation movements leapt into existence in part as activists came to understand far-reaching historical patterns of sex and gender inequity. In short, historical understanding can motivate social justice work by making clear larger patterns of cumulative privilege and oppression along status lines. This understanding may stir persons to social justice work as they recognize that current conditions of oppression have grown from unique prior circumstances and human actions. As such, our current circumstances are open to question; they certainly are not part of an inevitable, predetermined path toward continued oppression. Historical insight, then, contributes to the sense of agency that any social justice work requires. For this reason, many social justice movements have stressed the importance of "reclaiming history," "telling our stories," or "showing the face of our oppressor."

THREE KINDS OF HISTORICAL PROJECTS

At least three different kinds of historical projects can aid social justice work. First, historical accounts that reveal how individuals and groups have acted with intentionality – in the midst of great resistance and perhaps complexity – can help us ask powerful questions about our future directions. Second, histories can allow us to see the full temporal sweep of how social forces have interacted in varying conditions and thus make clearer the deeper principles at work. Third, histories specifically can illuminate the origins and directions of our social relations so that we can more fully understand why we interact as we do, how collectively we have come to value some things and not others, and how we might be able to direct our future social relations with greater consciousness. And as Dewey insisted, such understanding is a necessary underpinning for the practice of true democratic decision-making, an important goal of social justice work.

ASKING BETTER QUESTIONS

In his critically acclaimed work, *More than One Struggle* (2004), Jack Dougherty spins the remarkable story of how activists in Milwaukee have fought for equitable schooling for black and white students throughout the twentieth century. This nuanced account describes how community members have worked in ever-mutating alliances for a variety of school-based programs, sometimes at cross-purposes, in the quest to eliminate entrenched racial discrimination in education. Dougherty argues against the notion that struggles for equal opportunities in schools all have revolved around monolithic, mid-century Civil Rights era campaigns for integration, or school desegregation. Instead, he contends that the larger story is far more complex, interesting, and filled with timeless human dramas that each can help us understand this larger social justice project.

Dougherty ends the volume with the observation that in many ways, racially inequitable conditions continue to plague Milwaukee schools, perhaps to a degree as powerful as in past eras. The reader might be left to ponder the point of such a book, then, if the story remains so disturbingly unresolved. Policy-makers might drum their fingers on the table as they wait for concrete answers to the seemingly intractable problems described in the volume. There is in his book, as he concedes, no "specific list of useful prescriptions for 'what works' regarding race and education" (200). For others who wish to see in such an account a celebration of the remarkable achievement of the Brown decision, *More than One Struggle* will prove disappointing.

What Dougherty accomplishes in this book, though, is far more powerful than any of the just-mentioned possibilities. It stimulates the historical imagination. He quotes from Richard Neustadt and Ernest Maypose's book, *Thinking in Time*, as he explains that "Seeing the past can help one envision alternative futures." Furthermore, Dougherty argues, "While history cannot tell policy-makers what to do, studying the past can teach us how to ask probing questions, especially about our presumptions about contemporary policies" (201). *More than One Struggle* succeeds remarkably well in triggering fresh and potentially powerful questions about the quest for equal opportunities in schooling. It is a prime example of historical research that suggests better questions. Rather than "why hasn't the battle for integration been won?" the larger, deeper story compels us to ask instead: "How have the privileged endeavored to preserve their social and economic advantages in the face of active demands for equality?" In this case, the battle for integration is not the issue of deepest interest, although it has been quite important in certain phases of civil rights campaigns. Instead, the focus is on seeking equality.

What is so important about asking questions, though? Do we not have a more pressing need for answers? At the most elemental level, questions provide the process by which we sort through all that we experience, perceive, or know. They cut through our individual and social understandings to allow us to find ideas that pertain to our purposes. They separate background noise from what we deem most important. Most significantly, though, they compel conscious movement. Lacking questions, we may drift in whatever wash of environmental messages happens to bombard us at any given time, just moving with the prevailing current. Another statistical probability. However, when we ask questions, we create a mental space that our thinking can fill. We define the space. We fill it. We ask more questions. In this process, we consciously open new possibilities. We move with awareness. And with historical accounts of the ilk of *More than One Struggle*, the questions we might ask could be ones that allow us to reframe this whole social justice struggle in ways that address the deepest issues, rather than the ones that happen to drift in our paths first.

Of course, quality historical work is not the only way we might be stimulated to ask powerful, compelling questions. No doubt, a wide range of other disciplines or pursuits can lead us into such fruitful questioning. Qualitative studies can help us to better understand the lived experiences of persons for whom we have dedicated our professional and/or personal efforts, for example. Philosophical inquiry can awaken and stimulate us to conjure important questions at the greatest levels of abstraction. A well-executed quantitative study can show us the fallacy of some taken-for-granted notions while opening up areas for future questioning or inquiry. The arts and other humanities also can provoke us to ask some of the most profound questions about our human conditions.

If so many other avenues of exploration can lead us to ask compelling questions about our social justice projects, is there anything uniquely important about historical analysis? In a simple sense, historians take static three-dimensional social phenomena and then put them in motion. Time, then, essentially animates. It is, as physicists describe, the temporal, or fourth dimension. Aspects of three-dimensional reality that may seem random or part of the background noise miraculously may become centrally important organizing concepts when seen in motion. Suddenly, trajectories and apparent magnitudes of force operating on them become evident. Lacking this awareness of movement, though, we miss fundamental understandings about our social conditions. Just as the proverbial flatlander, confined forever to existence in two dimensions, never can comprehend existence above and below her plane, an analysis of our social conditions is equally limited if it is constrained to one moment in time, usually the present or near future. Intricacies of movement into and out of our current contexts are lost. The interplay of forces that operate in short and especially in long cycles of time becomes invisible. Historical analysis, at root, is concerned with revealing the motion and forces at work in our social reality. It fully embraces the temporal dimension. Although many disciplines and pursuits can provoke us to ask important questions, historical analysis specifically attempts to stimulate understandings that unfold through time or that exist as a consequence of time.

DEEPER PRINCIPLES

Aside from historical projects that provoke us to ask powerful questions about our social justice projects, questions that require the animation of time, a second kind of historical work helps us to see the full temporal sweep of how social forces have interacted in varying conditions and thus makes clearer the deeper principles at work. Immediately, however, the question springs to mind: Even if we could see deeper principles at work through our study of history, how does this help us? Does it simply help us maintain vigilance so that, as Santayana suggested, we can understand history as a way to avoid repeating it? This seems an unlikely or unreasonable goal in the sense that history never repeats itself precisely. Patterns may be recognizable in retrospect, but each historical circumstance is unique with its own peculiar contextual factors (Dougherty, 2004).

From our study of history, should we be able deduce theories that will allow us to know what will happen in the future? Theory is a way of reducing a complex reality to essential components that can be translated across contexts. If theory can be deduced from historical study, it is difficult to determine the precise level of analysis that theory should describe or govern. Does theory operate at the microscopic level of social interaction, at the level of individual relationships, at group levels, or all the way through to pan-social analysis? Do the forces or ideas described by theory operate within the inanimate environment, in individuals, in clusters of persons, or do they instead play out in a realm external to all of these possible components? Certainly many social theorists in the past have endeavored to identify the largest level of analysis in an attempt to create the most universally applicable theory. A key drawback to such an approach is that detail necessarily must drop from the analysis, and in such detail, significant information may be lurking. Scholarship from the past few decades, though, has mined more extensively local realms, or those of small scales. While meaningful relationships can be determined from studies with such tightly drawn boundaries, the drawback here is that resulting theory does not reliably translate to other contexts. Can meaningful theory possibly exist both in the realms of the large and small? And if it can, could it possibly cohere in any sort of self-consistent or comprehensible manner?

One way that these seemingly disjointed theoretical realms might join is if we consider applying the metaphor of complexity theory. Complexity theory considers how complex phenomena or entities can produce simple behavior. When some systems exhibit apparently infinitely complex behaviors, occasionally order emerges of its own accord. This can occur when component parts individually behave within the confines of a relatively small set of behavior-guiding rules. Then, in the environment of a richly interacting system, those rules gradually play out by producing discernable order, though not order that can be predicted. Essentially, complexity theory is at work when large numbers of entities operate together and create self-organizing systems. An outside force or prime cause is unnecessary for such complex systems. A simple and often-cited example is that of the flying formations of migratory geese. The familiar "V" patterns of geese, it turns out, results from each goose operating by the same set of rules that maximize visibility, maximize drafting from other birds, ensure proximity so calls can be heard, and other factors. Computer models can generate flight patterns like those of geese with a similar rule set.

It is unlikely that social science research will ever produce rule sets that reliably lead to computer-generated models exactly mimicking our complex social systems. The number of possible interacting variables is so great that it is beyond our current capabilities for defining or calculating. Furthermore, it is improbable that sufficient sample size for analyzing any individual variable could be identified with enough clarity to be useful. To this date, social science scholars have been hard pressed to test complexity theory directly in the manner that physical and computational science scholars have. For this reason, complexity theory cannot be argued as a basis for understanding the social sciences. Instead, it only can offer a metaphor by which we can organize ideas on a highly contingent basis.

With the understanding of this important limitation clearly in mind, I will now explore how the metaphor of complexity theory might enhance our understanding of the role of historical research in social justice projects. First, to address the question of where theory operates, from the infinite to the infinitesimal, the metaphor of complexity theory suggests that it can exist at all levels simultaneously. The small set of rules that governs the behavior of any isolated part of a system interacts with those of all other components until (or if) order emerges. The rules at any one place/time are not any more or less important than any others. They just operate in a different local context while at the same time playing an essential role in the emergence of larger recognizable order. Emerging order then becomes a boundary condition for any subsequent interaction. The entire system is dynamic in the sense that it plays out over time, which, of course, means that it generates a history.

Second, the metaphor of complexity theory might suggest that patterns never repeat themselves precisely from one context to the next, from one time to the next, yet they are unmistakably recognizable. Certainly, any analysis of history shows that, despite Santayana's admonition, events do not repeat themselves because there are always notable changes in conditions and interacting historical players from one era to another. However, there are similarities between historical moments. There even are recognizable similarities from small levels of historical analysis to large ones. These similarities are the result of the self-organization of the whole system. The delicate balance between all interacting components of the system plays out throughout. Essentially, in complex systems, what happens in small local contexts is completely connected with what happens in larger contexts – and vice-versa. The ways in which components interact are governed by the same rules, but the permutations visible at each level are endless, though clearly recognizable as of the same system.

In some ways, these complex systems resemble how societies interact over time. Consider, for example, the remarkable work of Jared Diamond, author of the Pulitzer Prize-winning *Guns, Germs, and Steel: The Fates of Human Societies* (1997) as well as *Collapse: How Societies Choose to Fail or Succeed* (2005). In the groundbreaking book, *Guns, Germs, and Steel*, Diamond set out to answer his Papua New Guinean friend's question about why westerners have so much "cargo," or material wealth when New Guineans have so little. The answer, which Diamond initially surmised might be simple, turned out to be anything but and required years of dedicated work to piece together. He found that everywhere on Earth, humans have carved out their existence in remarkably varied environments, each with a range of benefits and disadvantages. These benefits and disadvantages have shown up in stark relief when societies have interacted: through war, coexistence, trade, or separation. In interactions such as these, the cumulative advantages that certain humans have enjoyed on account of climate, the availability of domesticable plant and animal species, local geography, natural resources, and other factors, show up clearly. Advantaged peoples trade more successfully, wage and win wars, and acquire wealth that accumulates in small and large ways across generations. Diamond traces these varied interactions, showing how, on almost every continent, social privilege and wealth has been distributed over time. He concludes that westerners have been remarkably lucky to have originated in lands that afforded them geographic advantages, the benefit of naturally occurring animals and plants that could be domesticated, and a full range of other favorable factors. The differences are not intrinsic to the peoples themselves.

Diamond's epic analysis reveals that although precious resources have been distributed unevenly around the planet, the interactions of peoples have been governed to some degree by the cumulative advantages that each brings to the point of contact with others. These kinds of interactions are recognizable from small levels of analysis to the largest. They are, however, never exactly the same. The patterns, the stories, the sorts of rules he deduces only become clear when societies are examined over broad stretches of time and compared across spatial expanses. What Diamond has revealed is how local patterns of dominance clearly are connected to larger patterns of global economic dominance – phenomena that are created and rendered more evident over time as privilege accumulates. In this case, is there an external condition of economic dominance or social hierarchy? Without question. Is this disconnected from the smaller stories, the cases of individuals negotiating within their own unique contexts? No! They absolutely are connected, one building on and influencing the other.

Although we have few such epic works in the history of education as Diamond's *Guns, Germs, and Steel* (in fact, there may not yet be a comparable work in *any* field), Cremin's *American Education* trilogy comes immediately to mind (1972, 1982, and 1990). In this landmark series, Cremin set out to show the history of education in the U.S., defined in its broadest cultural sense. Lacking in this work, however, is any attempt to provide an explanation of how all component parts of the story have interacted with each other, in orders of magnitude large and small. To his credit, that was not Cremin's goal. Of a less epic nature, the works of Tyack (1974), Tyack and Hansot (1982), and Callahan (1962) together have told us much about how persons in the field of public school administration slowly labored to create places of esteem within their communities and places of dominance over other school workers and students. Not unlike what happens in Diamond's study, these histories of educational administration show the steady accumulation of advantage as well as the reification of larger social structures that bound future developments. Similarly, in work that is more overtly intended as part of social justice struggle, Dougherty's *More than One Struggle* shows the long, complex battles waged in one city for racial equality in schooling. In this book, there is no sense that the battle has been won, but rather that there have been ever-shifting actors and skirmishes, continually changing strategies, and an overall trajectory showing some whites laboring to maintain their cumulative privilege while persons of color have employed novel counter-strategies.

DEWEY: UNDERSTANDING SOCIAL RELATIONS

Beyond histories that provoke us to ask better questions about our social conditions, and those that provide us with insights into deeper organizing principles, a third kind simply helps us develop better social understanding. Such work enables us to see more clearly how we have come to our current conditions. John Dewey argued that historical work of this sort prepares us to interact more richly, mindfully, and ultimately more democratically in the sense that he elaborated throughout his career, but certainly in *The School and Society* (1990) and *Democracy and Education* (1916).

In *The School and Society*, Dewey commented extensively about the role of history instruction in elementary schools, the incubator for future democratically prepared members of our society. His remarks are worth quoting in full here:

> If history be regarded as just the record of the past, it is hard to see any grounds for claiming that it should play any large role in the curriculum of elementary education. The past is the past, and the dead may be safely left to bury its dead. There are too many urgent demands in the present, too many calls over the threshold of the future, to permit the child to become deeply immersed in what is forever gone. Not so when history is considered as an account of the forces and forms of social life. Social life we have always with us; the distinction of past and present is indifferent to it. Whether it was lived just here or just there is a matter of slight moment. It is life for all that; it shows the motives which draw men together and push them apart, and depicts what is desirable and what is hurtful. Whatever history may be for the scientific historian, for the educator it must be an indirect sociology – a study of society which lays bare its process of becoming and its modes of organization. Existing society is both too complex and too close to the child to be studied. He finds no clues into its labyrinth of detail and can mount no eminence whence to get a perspective of arrangement.

> If the aim of historical instruction is to enable the child to appreciate the values of social life, to see in imagination the forces which favor and allow men's effective co-operation with one another, to understand the sorts of character that help on and that hold back, the essential thing in its presentation is to make it moving, dynamic. History must be presented, not as an accumulation of results or effects, a mere statement of what happened, but as a forceful, acting thing. *The motives – that is, the motors – must stand out. To study history is not to amass information, but to use information in*

> *constructing a vivid picture of how and why [women and] men did thus and
> so; achieved their successes and came to their failures* (pp. 150-151). [emphasis
> added]

In the end, Dewey's concern was for our growth as a truly democratic society.
Such a society, as he construed it, concerns itself essentially with social justice in
that we strive to understand one another, endeavor to think together and without
coercion, and seek to make decisions for our mutually agreed-upon good. This
process, he argued, is not simple, but requires well-sharpened social understanding
that is developed continually. Implicitly, it requires concern for the welfare of
others, for the larger good – and it also requires the recognition that the oppression
of one is the oppression of all. Because schools play such a vital role in the
development of this understanding, as Dewey elaborated it, the work of teaching
and leadership in education is, by definition, fundamentally concerned with social
justice work.

On the other hand, lacking this awareness and pursuit of a truly democratic
society, we are left with our own present circumstances –in which self-interest
frequently trumps the common good, in which accumulated privilege goes
unchecked in its encounter with accumulated disadvantage. At root, many
interactions become ones about winning or losing. Someone advances at the
expense of another. Such interactions, played out across a larger society, result in a
social system that similarly advantages some and oppresses others, until a fully
fleshed out system of social stratification results. In turn, this emergent order
serves as a boundary condition for future interactions.

It is necessary, then, for schools to play a primary role in creating a truly
democratic society in which individuals think about and consciously make
decisions for the welfare of all, rather than exclusively for self-interest. To do this,
schools must be places where students and school workers alike strive to
understand fully their social circumstances. In time, we must interact respectfully
with each other and understand how our interactions at a personal level resemble,
but never precisely match, those at larger levels of social analysis, and furthermore,
that both are fundamentally connected.

An important way to develop this understanding is through studying the
historical sweep of our social conditions, small and large, with an eye toward how
persons in the past have made decisions regarding the collective good. To this end,
biographical works, among other historical genres, can be remarkably powerful in
assisting with developing this understanding. Here, Dewey was quite specific:

> … [H]istorical material appeals to the child most completely and vividly
> when presented in individual form, when summed up in the lives and deeds
> of some heroic character…. If biography is presented as a dramatic summary
> of social needs and achievements, if the child's imagination pictures the
> social defects and problems that clamored for the [wo]man and the ways in
> which the individual met the emergency, then the biography is an organ of
> social study (1900, p. 154).

Kate Rousmaniere's book, *Citizen Teacher: The Life and Leadership of Margaret Haley* (2005), offers an impressive example of how a biography of an educational leader can help us think about our decisions. In this vivid account, Rousmaniere shows us how Haley, the organizer of the Chicago Teachers Federation (which eventually became the first teachers union in the country), came to understand the deep economic and social constraints within which elementary teachers operated a century ago. The book recounts how Haley forged alliances; developed political strategies; reacted, regrouped, and charged forward when confronted with the inevitable obstacles that materialized throughout her entire career; and yet still managed to articulate a clear and compelling vision around which thousands of teachers organized and agitated. *Citizen Teacher* tells us much about Haley's social conditions and furthermore, much about how Haley negotiated her way through them. Though Haley may not have achieved the lasting changes she sought, this book makes plain the importance of the central issues about which Haley tried so mightily to educate the citizens of Chicago, issues that remain as relevant to today's educators as they were a hundred years ago even though particular historical circumstances are not quite the same. This book offers no blueprint for activism. It provides no step-by-step guide for changing the working conditions of teachers. However, it does show the reader how Haley thought about her work, the questions she asked, and the kinds of historical contingencies that she had to consider. It shows us how one person became fully aware of the social conditions of her life and endeavored to reshape them for a larger social good. In this way, the book offers an inspiring example of what one highly thoughtful individual with a commitment to social justice can achieve in schools.

Historical understanding plays a critical role in social justice work, then. Thoughtfully interpreted historical accounts can compel us to ask better questions about our social conditions, questions that might direct more fruitful efforts to engage in social justice activism. Histories also can help us to see the deeper patterns at work in our society, from the microscopic to the macroscopic levels. Although such understanding does not then allow us to predict future events, it provides a better mental framework for our actions. Finally, as Dewey has suggested, histories simply allow us to see more clearly our social conditions, which tend to be muddled and confused in our minds the closer we move toward the present. Historical perspective can elucidate our circumstances and show how they have come to be as they are. With this understanding, we then can learn to interact better with one another in the pursuit of a truly democratic society, as Dewey envisioned it. Such a society is implicitly concerned with social justice work.

A PERSONAL ACCOUNT

I have not always valued historical understanding. In fact, history may have been my least favorite subject from grade school through my undergraduate years. One pivotal experience changed this for me, though. When I taught high school physics in a small urban school district in central North Carolina, we noticed that our African American teachers were leaving in notable numbers and white teachers taking their places. One teacher expressed exhaustion after having worked with disproportionately large numbers of students. Another found himself squeezed out of the coaching position he had long enjoyed. Another, the beloved elderly dean of male students, retired – and quickly found that the sense of community he had build with students around the school and his deep commitment to fair treatment for all students created a vacuum that new administrators did not fill. Although about half of the student body was white and half black, a system that once could boast a somewhat congenial and nicely integrated faculty had reached the point were the number of black teachers was vanishingly small.

A few teachers in the system met to discuss this shift. We decided to ask our central administration for data describing the numbers of black teachers over the previous decade. After repeated requests that obviously and clearly were ignored, we reached out to teachers in every school to help us piece this data together for ourselves. We asked retirees. We canvassed friends. And then we put it all together. The numbers we generated verified our worst fears. The drop had, in fact, been precipitous. Furthermore, we collected stories of what had compelled individual black teachers to leave the district and how their replacements had been hired. In the end, we had created a history of very damaging developments – that energized us to launch into a series of actions aimed explicitly at reversing them. We called the central administration and school board on their varied tactics for subjecting black teachers to inadequate or otherwise unsupportive working conditions. We demanded that policies be instated specifically requiring that outstanding black teachers be recruited and hired. And we held the administration to account for its actions in this regard. By learning about the history of how our school district had been desegregated, how teachers had been assigned to schools by race, and how working conditions had varied by race as well, we came to know explicitly and powerfully what we all had suspected or known implicitly. And for the first time, I respected the power and possibility of historical understanding.

I had hoped to become a school administrator at least in part because of an earnest desire to work with young people closest to the social friction points where privilege and oppression grind together – in schools, in local communities, on the doorsteps of poverty and opportunity. After my activism in my school district, however, my chances for an administrative career diminished. It did not help that school board members told our Associate Superintendent, whom everyone adored and respected, that she would not be considered for the superintendency because the district was not ready for a woman. Women bore administrative responsibilities in that and many other districts in the region against all odds and usually at great cost. They typically held the most challenging principalships as well as the most time-intensive and critical, yet underappreciated central office positions. Clearly, I as a woman would face resistance should I work toward an administrative position. Any shred of hope I may have harbored for such work, though, disappeared when I began to live with my female partner. The district had purged or punished employees across ranks who were rumored to be lesbian or gay. The galvanizing event seemed to occur during my final year of teaching when a series of letters written by local religious leaders to school board members pleaded for the removal of any perceived homosexual influences from the schools. In rapid succession, personnel changes dotted the system. One teacher was singled-out and told never to wear khaki pants again – at the same time that she was removed from coaching the girls' volleyball team. Two high school teachers were moved against their will to elementary teaching positions. Another was sent a letter of reprimand for an offense she verifiably had not committed. The list went on.... Although persons in the district did not yet know that I was a lesbian, I knew that it was just a matter of time. North Carolina offered no employment or any other protections for LGBT persons – and furthermore, same-sex sexual behaviors were legally punishable offenses.

I was fortunate enough to enter graduate school at this point where I found a warm, welcoming community in which I could begin to figure out why my career plans had gone so terribly wrong. A single course on the history of western education ignited my imagination by revealing broad, sweeping patterns in which some classes of persons have systematically enjoyed enriching educational opportunities while others have been denied. At each point that I felt as though I could almost grasp the clear pattern at work, however, I would read more books, talk with professors and fellow grad students, and squeeze every relevant resource out of our vast library that I could. And I came to understand that there was simply so much more for me know.... What I learned in my studies changed everything for me.

The most overwhelmingly powerful thing that I learned is that a personal history such as my own was far from unique. I encountered numerous accounts of figures who had endeavored to address social inequities by working in schools – and also who had met with bracing resistance. I discovered incontrovertible evidence that school administrative work had been configured to align well with social expectations for men, but poorly for women. Consequently, I found exceedingly few women in school superintendencies, something, of course, that everyone knew, but that had not been clearly tracked historically before. And I learned that there had always been educators who desired persons of the same-sex. During some historical eras, this was not considered problematic. By the mid-twentieth century, however, visibly homosexual educators had disappeared from the classroom and administrator's office. Some had been purged; a few committed suicide; many left out of fear; substantial numbers went into hiding, straining to appear as gender-conforming and heterosexual as possible; and a few convinced themselves that their same-sex desires did not exist. Even as the modern gay/lesbian/bisexual/transgender/queer rights movements had secured significant social gains, I learned countless ways that schoolwork had remained remarkable impervious to these advances, essentially constituting a last bastion of enforced gender-conformity and heterosexuality.

In short, I learned that across these dimensions, I was not alone. I was simply one person in a long history filled with individuals struggling against social inequities in and through schools. I was only one of many women to face insurmountable obstacles – or nearly so – in attempting to lead a profession numerically dominated by women. Also, I was just one of the countless persons throughout the past with same-sex desire who had found a calling and commitment to excellence in the work of the classroom.

In light of this realization, I decided that I would piece together historical accounts that might help others similarly understand that their experiences were part of much larger, though little recounted narratives. I wanted others to know as well that they were not alone, but joined by sisters and brothers from earlier eras who had understood similar struggles. My scholarship, then, became part of my own social justice work. In the following sections, I will discuss three strands of this work.

WOMEN SCHOOL LEADERS

As I recounted in *Destined to Rule the Schools* (1998), schoolwork historically has been structured so that it is gender-segregated and stratified. Tyack and Hansot's collective work on this subject inspired me to understand in detail how this happened. Through my research, I discovered several clear patterns. First, women have moved into particular realms of schoolwork when men have chosen to leave them for better opportunities elsewhere. Second, when women have begun to dominate a particular kind of schoolwork numerically (i.e., teaching positions, elementary principalships, and county superintendencies), other gender-associated changes have followed such as lower pay, reduced authority, and lowered respect. These shifted gender associations have further exacerbated men's exodus from that realm. Third – and conversely, men who have remained in schoolwork have endeavored to carve out acceptably safe niches in which male gender identity, social status, and economic status are preserved. School administration, especially high school principalships and coaching positions as well as superintendencies of large districts have become such niches. The preservation of these niches has entailed a range of subtle and overt mechanisms on the part of school administrators as well as of their local communities to enhance positional status while simultaneously keeping women out. Fourth, despite these efforts to deny women opportunities for school leadership, some women, individually and collectively, have made inroads, demonstrating impressive agency in the process.

My work on this topic focused on three key areas: 1) determining the extent to which women had attained school superintendencies (the formal position for which I could obtain the clearest and most complete data); 2) bringing to light the mechanisms by which some men sought to elevate their own status while denying women access; and 3) telling the stories of women who had resisted and somehow become school superintendents, effectively helping to clear paths for others who might follow. To piece this story together, I compiled a complete database of superintendents who served over the twentieth century. I pored through volumes of published material in which male scholars and school administrators steadfastly refused to speak publicly about efforts to limit women's participation in school leadership positions. And I strained to find women superintendents in the pages of school reports or newspapers or speeches....

Nonetheless, I found some powerful stories. For example, though some male school leaders publicly questioned the value of women's suffrage during the state-by-state campaigns, they learned to utter such thoughts only behind closed doors once women won the vote. Newly enfranchised women voters had the disturbing tendency of driving unresponsive male superintendents out of office, often electing promising women instead. Some former male superintendents organized closed conferences to discuss counter-strategies. Usually in short order, those same forces launched campaigns to "take the politics out of schools" by making superintendencies appointed rather than elected. The explicitly stated rationale was to ensure that the best educated and most capable person might be chosen rather than one prone to corruption or ineptitude. The net effect of this sweeping reform is that women who had been elected to superintendencies by eager and newly enfranchised women voters lost their positions to men who were appointed.

I also found that the mid-twentieth century push for the professionalization of school administration similarly limited women's inclusion. Widely instituted reforms in the professional training and certification of school administrators increasingly required graduate study – usually in institutions that severely limited or precluded women's participation. Perhaps one of the most pervasive and long-standing patterns in the gendered history of school leadership, though, is silence. Women's participation, or lack of it, simply has not been discussed in the professional talk of the field until relatively recently. Without such discussion, women's marginal opportunity for school leadership was not problematized.

In recounting these stories in *Destined to Rule the Schools*, I began to ask myself better questions about gender and school leadership. Initially, I simply had wanted to know if there had been meaningful representation of women in superintendencies, and if so, where. When I learned that women made notable progress in attaining superintendencies in some regions, some states, during some years – but then their numbers dropped sharply at other times, I not only wanted to know the specifics of what had happened, but I also wanted to understand the deeper intent behind women's low or declining numbers. The mechanisms for keeping women out of school leadership have shifted considerably over the past century and a half, but deeper, unresolved social discomfort about women's roles in our society may not have shifted anywhere nearly as much. My own historical analysis has allowed me to ask better questions in the sense that they have brought my thinking closer to the deeper "stuff" that needs to shift before true gender equity may be possible throughout every aspect of schooling. Just as in Jack Dougherty's book, *More than One Struggle*, where he recounts how a century of civil rights activism in the Milwaukee schools has left us with schools just as racially segregated as ever, the story I have told in *Destined to Rule the Schools* is one where the school superintendency currently is as gender-stratified as it was one hundred years ago. Though neither book outlines a set of prescriptions for change, they both (hopefully) provoke better questioning that might lead to more meaningful and fruitful approaches to these seemingly intractable social justice issues.

SAME-SEX DESIRE, GENDER, AND SCHOOLWORK

In my book, *Fit to Teach: Same-Sex Desire, Gender, and Schoolwork in the Twentieth Century*, I sought to tell the complex story of how intertwined and changing notions of sexuality and gender have shaped schoolwork in the United

States over the past century. I started by recounting the conditions that compelled me to leave the teaching career I loved. Then I traced how it is that local communities and administrators shifted school hiring patterns in response to social unease about women's changing roles as well as awareness of a range of sexualities, some of which might be fluid, rather than immutable. Essentially, even though in the 1980s I could not retain my teaching position as a lesbian, such a state of affairs had not always existed. On a personal level, this was a powerful insight because I had grown up with the understanding that lesbians and gay men could not work in schools. I had tacitly assumed that this had always been the case.

I encountered difficulty in gathering sources and putting this narrative together, however. To start, broad social anxieties about same-sex desire have run so deep that profound taboos have kept most discussion of it out of the historical record. This has been particularly true in the realm of schoolwork. Then I faced the very practical decision about whether or not such research would hinder my quest for tenure. This was quite a difficult choice because the only other faculty member at my university who acknowledged being and generally was known as either gay or lesbian had lost a high-profile discrimination lawsuit and subsequently departed. I decided to take the risk.

In piecing the story together, I found several significant patterns. First, communities and schools have hired schoolworkers who are available at a modest cost – and usually secondarily who might possess excellent preparation and skill. This has been true unless a compelling reason has emerged to mitigate this tendency. For example, from the mid-1800s through mid-1900s, school officials strongly preferred hiring single women to teach because they were cheap, plentiful, well-prepared for the money, and not prone to trouble-making. However, by the mid-1900s, the growing association of spinster teachers with lesbianism overpowered otherwise practical concerns. Consequently, the proportion of single women teachers plummeted as married women filled the classroom – to a far greater extent than their representation in the general workforce.

A second noteworthy arrangement that I encountered is that social anxieties about gender generally have been intertwined or even conflated with those concerning sexuality. As women fought for and then won suffrage, they were accused of losing their sexual attractiveness, their marriageability, and even their maternal capacities. Instead, they often were taunted as representing some third sex, of deviance, or possibly as being lesbian. Conversely, men who pursued teaching, particularly at lower grade levels, ran the risk of being labeled effeminate, seeming emasculated, or generally considered homosexual.

A third and powerful thread that has run throughout this history has been the notion that during times of greatest social unease about gender and sexuality, teachers have been pressed into service to provide supposedly correct gender-role modeling as well as to enforce rigid rules about physical displays of affection among youth. When male boarding schools were accused of fostering deviance or overly close relationships among students, faculty reconfigured physical spaces to minimize chances for hidden encounters. They restructured daily routines so that youth engaged full-bore in a range of exhausting activities that might leave them too tired to think of much else. And they penalized previously acceptable behaviors such as hugs. At the same time faculty were held to account for such enforcement, they also were scrutinized intensely to ensure that their own sexuality/gender identities seemed either wholesome or pleasantly nonexistent.

Fourth, mid-twentieth century fears about otherness in the form of homosexuality proved so formidable that one could face career and social ruin merely with the accusation, founded or unfounded, of same-sex desire. Teachers routinely lost their jobs based only on rumors. Their legal recourse was practically nonexistent. To avoid the possibility of being thought homosexual, schoolworkers learned that they needed to maintain gender-conforming personas. Because of links in the popular imagination between same-sex desire and gender non-conformity, any cross-gender trait or behavior could translate to questions about one's sexuality, a severe career risk. Schools, then, became sites of extreme gender conformity, enforced strictly, and modeled relentlessly through the hypermasculinized realm of the superintendency (almost exclusively held by men who had been coaches and veterans and who were married with children) to the elementary classroom teacher (nearly always a married woman recruited in part for feminine appearance and manner).

Finally, LGBTQ schoolworkers have in recent decades mounted resistance to this state of affairs. After the Stonewall riots in 1969, lesbian and gay teachers who were fired on account of their sexual orientation began fighting to keep their jobs. The ACLU, and then eventually the NEA and AFT offered legal support for such challenges. Though individual teachers who challenged their dismissals ultimately were unsuccessful in returning to the classroom, their lawsuits gradually chipped away at restrictive legal doctrine, thereby improving the rights of other gay and lesbian school workers. In urban areas around the country, associations of lesbian and gay school workers formed coalitions. They endeavored to support each other, lobby for the inclusion of sexual orientation in their schools' nondiscrimination policies, and join in the festivities of annual lesbian and gay pride parades. The participation of lesbian and gay school worker associations in pride parades particularly caught the attention of conservative Christians who feared that "homosexual" teachers either would a) influence their children to become "homosexual," or b) molest them. In a fearsome backlash movement initially led by Anita Bryant, openly lesbian and gay teachers became the focus of a national campaign to drive them back into the closet or out of schools altogether. These battles raged through the 1990s and even beyond.

Though school workers rarely have won decisive victories for their employment rights, they have managed to avoid further restrictions. And during the mid-1980s, attention regarding LGBTQ persons in schools shifted from school workers to students. Many reasons account for this shift, but an important one is that young people increasingly have demanded the right to choose their sexual and gender identities in a manner free of coercion, to be protected from discrimination in schools on account of sexual/gender identity, and to enjoy a supportive school atmosphere. Because of student activism around these matters, especially in coalition with gay/straight alliances, some schools, districts, and states have changed their policies decisively to eliminate discrimination against LGBTQ persons in schools.

In telling the stories in *Fit to Teach*, I saw clearly that patterns at small levels of analysis resembled those at larger levels, though they never precisely matched. An individual teacher might be feared because her/his same-sex desire was considered contagious and dangerous. At the state level, government officials might institute personnel sweeps to clear the ranks of anyone suspected of homosexuality – even if no evidence existed that same-sex sexual behaviors had ever occurred or that homosexuality in and of itself adversely affect professional competence. As explained earlier, I noted that patterns also span expanses of time, such as the time-honored practice of regulating school personnel heavily during periods of social uneasiness about gender and sexuality. Perhaps most important, battles regarding sexuality and gender in schools have represented deeper transactions in which power is established and maintained. Each passing generation sees the transmission of some cumulative privilege as well as disadvantage. Though *Fit to Teach* does not address a question as all-encompassing as the one posed by Jared Diamond's Papua New Guinean friend about why westerners have so much cargo, it does in a modest and limited manner attempt to lay out some of the historical mechanisms by which power and privilege have accumulated in schoolwork along the lines of sexuality and gender.

ELLA FLAGG YOUNG

As I worked on these two previous historical projects, I repeatedly encountered Ella Flagg Young, who served as superintendent of the Chicago schools nearly one hundred years ago and also who became the first female president of the NEA. She inspired suffrage-era activists around the world to envision the good that women in public positions might accomplish. She seemingly held the door open for thousands of women who would follow her into school superintendencies as well as a variety of other school leadership positions. In addition to these noteworthy accomplishments, she was a scholar, University of Chicago professor, national leader in teacher preparation, active suffragist, and philanthropist. She enjoyed such a degree of fame that she routinely was listed among the ten most important women of her time. That she essentially could revolutionize schooling and national thought in so many ways has captivated me. That she did so while sharing her life with her female companion, Laura Brayton, has left me dazed – and yet fiercely determined to understand her life, thought, and work. I am now fully immersed in the project of writing her biography.

Just as Dewey suggested a century ago in *The School and Society*, biographical accounts can be particularly helpful in enriching our understanding of our social contexts. They allow us to see how heroic individuals faced challenges and attempted to address them. Through their experiences, we can understand the very real human struggles that shape the lives of persons we admire. And so we might then feel emboldened, yet chastened as we attempt to navigate our own experiences.

Strangely enough, since beginning this biographical project, I have become an administrator. I am not the principal or superintendent that I envisioned some twenty-five years ago, but rather an associate dean of a college in a Midwestern university. I inescapably find that as I weave Ella Flagg Young's story together, I must consider my own unfolding story as well. As seemingly impossible challenges arise at work, I think about how Young tackled those that confronted her. She is in some ways heroic to me, but not as a model of simple, unerring perfection. Instead, I regard her as a person who stood toe-to-toe with immense, almost unfathomable obstacles, yet she felt fear, worried about finding the best possible outcomes for vulnerable persons or those who needed it most, and still managed to summon the strength to bear the pain and do the right thing. She made what I would consider mistakes. However, I have come to understand many of the complexities that factored into her decisions. These understandings do not preclude my appreciation for her efforts, but only enhance it.

I need to see the face of someone who has felt the restrictions of gender in her desire to provide educational leadership. I want to comprehend how someone from an impoverished and improbable background might draw from it the inspiration to minimize the chances that the same would be perpetuated on others. I want to know the details of how a person with a desire to engage in social justice work wholly confronts the inevitable pain that accompanies the work and yet keeps moving ahead powerfully. And, of course, I personally want to comprehend how someone like Young negotiated her closest sustaining relationship in the context of her larger work, especially because she could so easily have been stigmatized on account of that relationship – or on account of her committed connection to networks of strong women. The answers I find are not simply helpful in drafting Young's biography, but they also figure mightily into how I think about my own life and work. They inspire my sense of possibility for engaging in social justice projects in my administrative work. In a very real sense, Dewey's advice about the importance of biographical accounts has become a central consideration in my own life right now. I am writing Young's biography in part out of a desire to bring research to bear on social justice work. I also am inspired by her story in ways that deepen my ideas of what social justice projects I may be able to accomplish in other parts of my professional and personal life.

CLOSING THOUGHTS

As I look back on my three major historical research projects to date, one thing that is overwhelmingly clear is that I have written (or am writing) each from the perspective of a class of person(s) somehow denied access or power. I obviously wrote *Destined to Rule the Schools* from the vantage of a woman who at one point had aspired to school leadership. Without question, I told the story of *Fit to Teach* from the perspective of a lesbian who, on account of status, felt compelled to leave teaching. Should my work consequently be dismissed because I seem to have an axe to grind, so to speak?

Prior to my writing *Destined*, scholars of school administration somehow had not found the topic of women school superintendents to be sufficient interesting to merit research. Expressed differently, the lack of women school leaders did not seem to be a matter that required change. I reasoned that this lack of interest or willingness to change drove much of the silence that historically had surrounded the topic. I, however, adamantly wanted the situation to change. Similarly, before I wrote *Fit to Teach,* education scholars generally had not regarded equity for LGBTQ persons in schoolwork as an issue necessitating investigation – with the significant exception of Karen Harbeck, who wrote a dissertation on the history of LGBT teachers, but then left the field to become an attorney and social justice activist in the broader social realm. (Harbeck's groundbreaking dissertation later was published in 1997 as *Gay and Lesbian Educators: Personal Freedoms, Public Constraints.*) Policies and practices that effectively marginalized LGBTQ schoolworkers seemed acceptable to the public at-large as well as to school officials and education scholars. Once again, though, I wanted this status quo to change.

Quite simply, it is persons who feel the brunt of oppression who typically first take up the charge to change things, to engage in social justice work in the sense of assuring fair access and opportunities for all persons regardless of individual or group status. Individuals with some degree of privilege in a given social dimension are less likely to want to see things shift, especially if such shifts might entail loss of taken-for-granted privilege. Not surprisingly, African, Asian, and Latino Americans have led these respective civil rights movements that have revolved in large part around access and educational opportunity for children of color. Allies of other races/ethnicities have joined these movements, but mainly they have been led by persons of the affected status. The women's liberation movement of the 1960s and 1970s was fomented by women who demanded that they enjoy equal economic, social, and political rights on account of sex/gender. Male allies helped tremendously in the movement, but in the end, it needed to be led by women. Similarly, the LGBTQ rights movement has been directed by self-identified LGBTQ persons.

The end result here is that a person from the affected status group is the most likely one to take up the charge to lead, to conduct extensive research on the experiences of that group, and who probably possesses the greatest motivation to change things. If such efforts are simply written off as having an axe to grind, then by implication, members of any oppressed group will be dismissed in this manner for bringing their plight to wider attention. I argue instead that this is social justice activism in that it is leadership, action, and/or research explicitly intended to bring about equitable opportunities regardless of individual or group status. It is social justice work just as surely as the teacher who grew up in abject poverty might strive to teach young people living in similar poverty so that they might enjoy real opportunities to discover their own powers.

Allies often play vitally important roles in social justice work. Though they may not have experienced first-hand the tang of oppression along one specific dimension, they probably have experienced it along another. It is their willingness to translate their knowledge of this experience to another status group. For example, former Los Angeles mayor Tom Bradley, who had been a stunning civil rights leader, brought his experiences as an African American to bear in the battle for LGBTQ rights. He proved to be a powerful ally of LGBTQ persons during the 1978 California Briggs' Initiative that, if passed, would have compelled the dismissal of LGBTQ persons – and those who supported them – from schoolwork.

Allies, though not centered in the particular status group at issue, remember the ways they have been oppressed themselves. They then choose to leverage their relative privilege to help achieve social justice for members of another status group. Social justice work and movements, then, require the leadership of persons in the status group and also the active support of strong allies.

As I have argued directly and implicitly throughout this essay, historical research is one important way that individuals can heighten their awareness of their own conditions. It can inspire understanding that compels social justice leadership on account of one's status. It can assist potential allies in learning how their own lived experiences of oppression might translate to persons experiencing subjugation along other social dimensions. It can accomplish these ends by provoking us to ask better questions, to understand larger patterns more deeply, and to find inspiration in the infinitely varied stories of human frailty and courage. And it can motivate us to join together in working for true social, political, and economic fairness for all persons.

FLOYD BEACHUM

TOWARD A TRANSFORMATIONAL THEORY
OF SOCIAL JUSTICE

INTRODUCTION

Many colors were present in this multicultural stew of suffering, but the
dominant color was black. From the sight of it, this was the third world – a
misnomer, to be sure since people of color are two-thirds of the world's
population. The suffering on screen caused cognitive dissonance; it suggested
that this must be somewhere in India, or the outskirts of Biafra. This surely
couldn't be the United States of America – and how cruelly that term seemed
to mock those poor citizens who felt disunited and disconnected and just
plain dissed by their government. This couldn't be the richest and most
powerful nation on the globe, leaving behind some of its poorest citizens to
fend for themselves (Dyson, 2006, p. 2).

This quote comes from the book *Come Hell or High Water: Hurricane Katrina and
the Color of Disaster* by Michael Eric Dyson. Back in 2005, as I watched the
limited initial response, I was struck by feelings of helplessness and hopelessness. I
remember thinking about a much-touted term called "social justice," and asked
where did it fit in the Hurricane Katrina aftermath? Is social justice simply a "just"
society or is it couched in abstraction and only accessible to scholars and
philosophers who can decipher its complex meanings for the mediocre masses
(much like cracking the *The Da Vinci Code*). Whatever the case I knew that it was
something I was interested in exploring for myself.

I had the opportunity to participate in a series of important sessions on the topic
of social justice in educational leadership at the 2005 and 2006 Annual Conventions
of the University Council for Educational Administration and the 2006 Annual
Meeting of the American Educational Research Association with my enlightened
and insightful colleagues who co-authored this book. On these panels, we accepted
the gargantuan task of addressing, defining, exploring, and debating social justice.
Each time the panel presented, we updated, revised, and amended our papers. I am
also grateful to the audiences who came to our sessions and provided feedback,
posed questions, and challenged our thinking. Discussants like Charles J. Russo
and Judy A. Alston synthesized our work highlighting similar theoretical threads
and elucidating divergence. This process was long, painstaking, and necessary. The
subject is too critical for short-sighted soliloquy, pompous pontificating, or
rhetorical rhapsody. This project is an ongoing discourse aimed at expanding

Ira Bogotch et al. (eds.), Radicalizing Educational Leadership: Dimensions of Social Justice, 39–60.
© *2008 Sense Publishers. All rights reserved.*

philosophical, ideological, and theoretical boundaries into meanings, interpretations, and praxis of social justice. Therefore, this essay is part scholarly endeavor and part personal quest.

First, I begin by tracing the history of the term social justice, comparing and contrasting its original meaning with today's conceptions. Second I describe a pedagogy of injustice, what Myers (1988) would describe as a sub-optimal conceptual system. This forms the basis for oppression as evident in the outward manifestations of racism, sexism, and classism, which are discussed. Third, I interject the experiences of African Americans in order to glean insight into complexity, contradiction, and controversy when addressing social justice. Fourth is a theoretical analysis of contested notions within social justice. Here, I highlight seemingly dualistic notions of social justice as recognition and/or redistribution. I supplement this discussion with a similar explanation of social justice that emphasizes the individual and/or the community. Fifth is the discussion of social justice as transcendence, translation, or transformation along with a new framework for enhanced understanding (Dyson, 1997). Within each frame strengths and weaknesses are addressed in relation to aforementioned concepts. Finally, practical aspects of social justice in educational leadership are discussed along with a deeper discussion of social justice and emergent virtues which coincide. As mentioned earlier, this is part personal quest as I struggle with making sense of how I view social justice in the face of so many social issues (e.g., the response to Hurricane Katrina, the plight of urban schools, the continuance of oppression, etc.). As you read on, I invite you to equip yourself with the armor of intellect, put on the helm of humanistic thought, and unsheathe the sword of the scholarly mind. The battlefield of social justice awaits us.

EDUCATIONAL LEADERSHIP AT THE CROSSROAD

A society which makes provisions for participation in its good of all members on equal terms and which secures flexible readjustment of its institutions through interaction of the different forms of associated life is insofar democratic. Such a society must have a type of education which gives individuals a personal interest in social relationships and control, and the habits of the mind which secure social changes. – John Dewey

The field of educational leadership has reached a crucial crossroads. Educational leaders have the great potential to actualize the kind of society and educational system John Dewey alludes to in the above statement. The new millennium manifestation (at least with regard to semantics) is a term called "social justice." Opposed to this is an ideology in education characterized by being ahistorical, acontextual, with an overemphasis on technical efficiency which ultimately maintains the status quo. Such an ideological clash is by no means rare. However, the social justice perspective (at least in this analysis) is not being threatened overtly. Social justice is in danger of being covertly undermined, co-opted, and/or re-directed. At the same time, social justice remains critical to the preparation and success of educational leaders (Brown, 2004).

TRANSFORMATIONAL THEORY OF SOCIAL JUSTICE

For all of us, but particularly for people of color, social justice represents a double-edged sword. On the one hand it is time for educators to make fairness, equity, and liberty a priority. On the other hand, within the possibilities of social justice lie the same oppressive thoughts and actions that it seeks to eliminate. In other words, social justice can be adopted by individuals who consciously or unconsciously continue to exclude the voices of people of color. For this reason, Dyson's conceptions of transcendence, translation, and transformation/transpersonal are relevant to social justice theory. Specifically, the three "t's" combat what Myers (1988) referred to as a sub-optimal conceptual system. Thus, people of color and their allies seek to find socially just strategies to overcome oppression. Here, the thoughts and writings of influential African Americans become a critical and constructive historical lesson that teach all people that social justice requires sacrifice, suffering, tireless struggles, and the passionate concern of dedicated individuals. The double-edged sword is that without social justice theory as an ally, insurgent and primitive forces of irrationalism and social destruction may overtake social justice actions.

THE ORIGIN OF THE TERM "SOCIAL JUSTICE"

The term "social justice" was originally coined by Luigi Taparelli, "an Italian Catholic priest and philosopher, around 1840 in his formidably titled book, the Theoretical Treatise on Natural Law Based on Fact…Writing during a generation of dramatic economic and social change and political violence, Taparelli was looking to find a way for the Catholic Church as a whole to understand and to respond to these changes in a way that went beyond pious platitudes" (Behr, 2005, p. 3). This gives insight to the idea that social justice for us today should similarly surpass piousness and redundant rhetoric. "The revolutionary tide had left traditional religious discourse about poverty and social order, both Protestant and Catholic, in an untenable middle ground between radical laissez-faire liberals and socialists of various sorts. Advocating patience and the virtue of work to the proletariat left such religious critics open to the charge, familiar to Marxists,of being the 'opiate of the masses,' while condemning capitalist greed was viewed by the propertied classes as fanning the flames of revolution" (Behr, 2005, p. 3). This contentious middle ground is also where social justice advocates find themselves today. Contemporary social justice discussions are not necessarily easy, fluid, or concrete. This middle ground is an intersection of competing ideologies such as redistribution/recognition, macro/micro, and sameness/difference (North, 2006). In fact, social justice remains largely undertheorized in education (Gewirtz, 1998). To get a clearer picture of the possible meaning of social justice, we must address the conflict of these aforementioned competing ideologies as well as examine notions of injustice.

THE PEDAGOGY OF INJUSTICE

An epistemology explores the nature, structure, and limits of knowledge. It creates theoretical space for the cultivation of ideas and determines the parameters for

41

behavior and action. The dominant epistemology in American society supports a broader ontology which can be described as Eurocentrism or a Western world view. This view is characterized by the following: external knowledge; either/or reasoning; technology as highly valued; power as defined by money, influence, and power; ownership and possession; primary values such as materialism, competition, and individualism and control as a primary goal (Ginwright, 2004; Kunjufu, 1993; Myers, 1988). This ontological paradigm forms the basis for a pedagogy of injustice.

What I am calling a pedagogy of injustice emanates from the broader aforementioned conceptual system or worldview. Table 1 describes this worldview as ultimately sub-optimal. The sub-optimal worldview is juxtaposed with an optimal worldview (closer to social justice).

Table 1 World Views/Conceptual Systems

Optimal	Sub-Optimal
Self knowledge – the basis of all knowledge	External knowledge – the basis of all knowledge
Both/And reasoning	Either/Or reasoning
Dependency on spirituality	Dependency on technology
Primacy of faith	Primacy of control
Logic – union of opposites (both/and conclusions)	Logic – emphasize duality (either/or conclusions)
Values – spiritualism, oneness with nature, communalism	Values – materialism, competition, individualism

Adapted from L. J. Myers, 1988

The persistent problem here is that the sub-optimal conception of reality dominates in America. Thus, it affects epistemology, axiology, and consequently reality. Simply put, it impacts not only how we see the world and others, but controls knowledge bases, pedagogies, and behaviors. Commenting on ideology and the Academy, Na'im Akbar (2002) asserted:

The European American academic ideology assumes "materiality" to be the essence of reality. Those things that are not observable by the senses and ultimately measurable are not considered real. Conclusions that cannot be validated by reference to such observable reality are rejected. This certainly precludes the possibility that the essence of things that may be in fact unobservable and of a spiritual form. Such speculation is inadmissible in the Academy because of its fundamentally materialistic perspective. However, most of the civilized world, while not invalidating materiality as real, would not conclude that the essence of all things is seen in the material form. Nor would they conclude that causation can only be attributed to logical positivism that sees any material effect must only be caused by something that is temporally and spatially connected to that effect. (p. 35)

Dr. Akbar's remarks illustrate how a sub-optimal conceptual system can be the root of misjudgments, misconceptions, falsehoods, and oppression. If this way of thinking is characterized by external (not internal) knowledge, either/or reasoning, dependency on technology (including weapons), emphasis on control, and values materialism, competition, and individualism (Ginwright, 2004), then such a conceptual system could easily spawn racism, sexism, classism, and all kinds of hegemonic policies and practices which promulgate oppression (Freire, 2000; Kunjufu, 1993; West, 2004). Myers (1988) concurred:

> Careful examination and analysis of dominant cultural beliefs in this society led me to the fuller realization that the depth and pervasiveness of the racism/ sexism problem went to the very core of the world view and subsequent conceptual system that characterizes Western thought and European American culture. To the extent we internalize and materialize word view, racism, sexism, or some other societal "isms" are guaranteed based on the principle of limitation or scarcity. (p. 10)

Therefore, the exclusively sub-optimal conceptual system is highly problematic for society in general and education specifically. Thus, the manifestations of a sub-optimal conceptual system appear in the forms of injustice characterized by racism, sexism, and classism.

RACISM

In the early 20th century the noted African American scholar, DuBois, made a haunting prediction as he insightfully predicted that race would be the nation's most daunting barrier. As the United States begins to traverse the new landscapes of the 21st century, it unfortunately carries the "baggage" of the preceding century: the "problem of the color line" (DuBois, 2003). DuBois eloquently identified the problem of race which still blinds, holds, and binds us in the new millennium. Du Bois described this as an American problem; it soon became known as the "Negro problem." "Shortly after World War II, a French reporter asked expatriate Richard Wright for his views about the 'Negro problem' in America. 'There isn't any Negro problem; there is only a white problem.'" (Tardon as cited in Lipsitz, 2002, p. 61). The genius of Wright's response was that it illuminated the automatic assumption that the problem is with African Americans as opposed to the beliefs and behaviors of whites. Furthermore, it positions African Americans as burdens, problems if you will, as opposed to equal citizens and deserving of equal levels of justice. Interestingly, this is the essence of racism; it is in the problematic existence of the racialized "Other." "Historically, the idea of race emerged in Europe in the 17th and 18th centuries, coinciding with the growth of colonialism and the transatlantic slave trade. Attempts were made to classify humans into 'natural,' geographically distinct 'races,' hierarchically ordered by their closeness to God's original forms. Europeans were, not surprisingly, at the top, with the most perfect form represented by a female skull from the Caucasus Mountains, near the purported location of Noah's ark and the origin of humans" (Mukhopadhyay &

Henze, 2003, p. 670). For the purposes of this discussion, racism can be understood as individual, institutional, and cultural.

On an individual level, racism is evidenced by overt person to person acts of violence, discrimination, exclusion, and/or oppression (Delgado, 1990; Schmidt, 2005). The history of the United States is ripe with examples of lynching, mob violence, physical threats, rape, and intimidation based on one's race. Once upon a time in America, the physical/psychological boundaries were clearly marked by signs which read "whites" only or "colored only." In addition, laws and practices segregated people into separate neighborhoods, schools, and ultimately separate lives. If one tried to counter this dominant ideology of the day, they would be subjected to racism (as described above) in a very personal way. In this era, a person of color clearly knew when someone from the dominant group (i.e., whites) did not like them or did not approve of the person of color's behavior. Even in the 21st century, we still see evidence of racism on an individual level when people of color are called derogatory names (e.g., the "N" word). Tatum (1997) defined this form of racism as active racism, "blatant, intentional acts of racial bigotry and discrimination" (p. 10). In modern times (post-American Civil Rights Movement and subsequent laws and policies), much of this individual racism seems to have dissipated; however, many people of color experience smaller encounters where they may feel disrespected (Perry, 2003; Tatum, 1997). Schmidt (2005) opined:

> There are many readily available examples of racism at the individual level, ranging from the daily occurrence of racial epithets and jokes directed at people of color by white individuals or groups of individuals, to the senseless brutal murder of a person of color by white people. It includes the actions of any white person who refuses to hire, serve, or provide equal and appropriate treatment for any person of color because of his or her race. This form of racism is clear-cut, tangible, and very few people could contend that this does not exist. (p. 113)

Although the walls of legalized segregation which solidified separate social systems are long gone, the legacy of racism and its core of marginalization of people of color is still alive. The legacy is maintained through institutional racism.

Institutionalized racism deals with the idea that racism not only exists on an individual level, but also in the very institutions upon which this nation is built. This includes, but is not limited to, businesses, schools, courts, etc. According to Scheurich and Young (1997) "institutional racism exists when institutions or organizations, including educational ones, have standard operating procedures (intended or unintended) that hurt members of one or more races in relation to the dominant race" (p. 5). It can also be understood as "the network of institutional structures, policies, and practices that create advantages and benefits for whites, and discrimination, oppression, and disadvantage for people from targeted groups" (Wijeyesinghe, Griffin, & Love, 1997).

Institutional racism is hidden behind an invisible veil. This veil goes by several names: meritocracy, individualism, boot-strap theory, and old-fashion hard work. The cultural ethos of the United States is steeped in idealistic concepts such as the

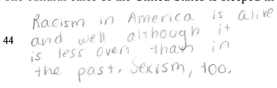

Racism in America is alive and well although it is less overt than in the past. Sexism, too.

Protestant work ethic, and the Horatio Alger myth (belief in the idea of going from rags to riches as applied to everyone equally). Such ideas are systematically ingrained into the psyches of nearly all Americans through sophisticated socialization (Harro, 2000). Commenting on this subject with regard to educators, Villegas and Lucas (2002) asserted:

> They lack an understanding of institutional discrimination, including how routine practices in schools benefit young people from dominant groups while disadvantaging those from oppressed groups; and they have an unshakable faith that American society operates according to meritocratic principles and that existing inequalities in social outcomes are thereby justified. (p. 32)

Lipsitz (2002) explained how institutional racism worked in a concept he called "The Possessive Investment in Whiteness." He wrote:

> The increased possessive investment in whiteness generated by disinvestment in U.S. cities, factories, and schools since the 1970s disguises as *racial* problems the general social problems posed by deindustrialization, economic restructuring…It fuels a discourse that demonizes people of color for being victimized by these changes, while hiding the privileges of whiteness by attributing the economic advantages enjoyed by whites to their family values, faith in fatherhood, and foresight – rather than to the favoritism they enjoy through their possessive investment in whiteness. (p. 75)

Interrogating and investigating institutional discrimination is a critical aspect of properly reading our society and addressing society's impact on schools. The aforementioned quotes unearth the fact that schools are built upon and promote similar idealistic concepts such as merit, hard work, and individualism, which is somewhat true, but only part of a broader picture. In reality, privilege, unearned benefits, and collectivism are very influential factors in schools (Schmidt, 2005; Tatum, 1997).

Institutional racism was actualized in the formation and proliferation of suburban communities and suburban schools. According to Lipsitz (2002), "By channeling loans away from older inner-city neighborhoods and toward white home buyers moving into segregated suburbs, the FHA and private lenders after World War II aided and abetted segregation in U.S. residential neighborhoods" (p. 64). He goes on to assert:

> As increasing numbers of racial minorities moved into the cities [often migrating from the South], increasing numbers of European American ethnics moved out. Consequently, ethnic differences among whites became a less important dividing line in U.S. culture, while race became more important. The suburbs helped turn Euro-Americans into 'whites' who could live near each other and intermarry with relatively little difficulty. (p. 65)

The result is the evolution of today's suburban schools and the plight of many urban schools. Both are products of a social history which is more intentioned than episodic. This geographic isolation/segregation leads to different lives, experiences, and worldviews of residents, educators, and leaders. "This spatial segregation provides most white teacher candidates [and leadership preparation candidates] with little opportunity for contact with people from oppressed groups, thus depriving them of a window into the day-to-day realities, concerns, interests, dreams, and struggles of these groups" (Villegas & Lucas, 2002, p. 31). In this situation it is easy to believe (if born into the right community) that success in life is totally dependent upon the amount of work one is willing to do to attain success. It also breeds a kind of "social blindness" to the plight of others in impoverished communities.

Cultural racism can be defined as "cultural images and messages that affirm the assumed superiority of Whites and the assumed inferiority of people of color" (Tatum, 1997, p. 6). Tatum elaborates, exclaiming that this cultural racism is like "smog" in the air which we all breathe on a daily basis. This smog is actually the messages found in stereotypical media images, racial/ethnic jokes, and our daily interactions upon which we develop negative attitudes, assumptions, and categorizations of others largely based on prejudice (Beachum & McCray, 2004; Kailin, 2002; Tatum, 1997). Harro (2000) describes a similar cycle of socialization which is pervasive, consistent, circular (self-supporting), self-perpetuating, and invisible (unconscious and unnamed). Our thinking and beliefs are shaped by unquestioned and stereotypical messages which ultimately impact what we believe about others and ourselves (Harro, 2000). Commenting on cultural racism, Perry (2003) wrote:

> Today the ideology of Black intellectual inferiority is expressed...vividly and constantly and with considerable force in the media, which inserts itself into all aspects of our lives. The ideology of African-American inferiority is perhaps more robust today, in terms of its impact on students, than it was in the pre-Civil Rights era...Few respectable people will publicly assert that Black people are intellectually inferior. The visible manifestations of oppression have been mostly eliminated. But you can scarcely find a Black student who cannot recall or give you a litany of instances when he or she was automatically assumed to be intellectually incompetent. (pp. 96-97)

Unfortunately, the concept of cultural racism is up against a powerful form of cultural denial. The prevalent message in mainstream media is that society is open, we have overcome our discriminatory past, and all have an equal opportunity to succeed if one tries hard enough. Once again the meritocracy myth clouds the vision of the people. In addition, those who differ ideologically have reframed the "race" issue. Today, if one even brings up the idea of cultural racism, one is immediately cast as a radical, a whiner, or an individual who is out of touch with mainstream American values (Gorski, 2006; McLaren, 1994). Furthermore, "many students [and Americans in general] hold so tightly to a view of racism as an 'incident' in history and to beliefs in meritocracy that it is very hard for them to see that racism can be anything more than random acts of thoughtlessness and hatred" (Schmidt, 2005, p. 110). Even in the face of this denial, cultural racism not only exists, it many times pre-dominates.

SEXISM

The notion of a sub-optimal conceptual system not only exudes racism, but also sexism. Sexism, which can be defined as discrimination based on gender, in most cases works to disadvantage women. Sexism can be accompanied by corollary negative beliefs such as limited notions of gender and misogyny. Sexism can promote false notions of gender which usually privilege overt or benevolent forms of patriarchy (hooks, 2004). The aforementioned socialization we all receive, similar to race, also reinforces gender roles. For instance, television many times promotes gender stereotypes and negative images of women. A study conducted by Mamay and Simpson (as cited in Bush, 1999) concluded that "women in commercials were typecast according to three stereotypical roles: mother, housekeeper, and sexual objects" (pp. 35-36). Some research indicates that television has the ability to affect the way people view gender roles. Katz (1995) wrote stressing gender differences in this context means defining masculinity in opposition to femininity. This requires constantly reasserting what is masculine and what is feminine. One of the ways this is accomplished, in the image system, is to equate masculinity with violence (and femininity with passivity)" (p. 135). A response to these notions is feminism. According to Marshall and Gerstl-Pepin, feminism (2005):

> acknowledges the existence of patriarchy, which privileges male norms such as objectivity and marginalizes feminine concerns such as emotions and caring. These perspectives demonstrate how arrangements of political structures, legal systems, and hierarchies and curricula in schools exclude the realities of gendered existences and the legitimacy of subjective needs. (p. 79)

Misogyny can be defined as the distrust or hatred of women. It is also an unfortunate characteristic of American masculine culture. Contemporary male culture is impacted by this theme. This attitude is spawned from the same cultural crucible which births racism and prejudice (Harro, 2000; hooks, 2004). In fact, they can operate together, feeding off one another in a process of collusion. The outcomes of this misogynistic mind frame are a false sense of gender-based superiority over women, the objectification of women as sex objects, and the active belief that gender is a determinant of mental/emotional capability and life trajectory.

Misogynistic and sexist attitudes and behaviors are part of the American landscape. Many of such attitudes can be attributed to learned behaviors, but also the media. The culture of misogyny is also confirmed by Patton's research (1998), who observed that the culture of male gang members was one that was "patriarchal and women were not considered the equal of males" (p. 62). Although television influence and male gang culture do not reflect the totality and diversity of youth culture, both provide cultural cues and highlight very real circumstances and situations.

In the end, misogyny is harmful for everyone. For men it engenders a false reality and undermines genuine mutually beneficial relationships (Powell,

2003). For women, it subjects them to emotional and physical harm, lessens their quality of life, and forces them into myopic male-determined roles. Katz (2000) contextualizes the problems of a culture of misogyny when he opined:

> The level of male violence against women in this society is out of control. Despite decades of feminist activism, boys and men are still sexually abusing, battering, raping, and murdering girls and women at an alarming rate. While this violence has no single cause, the dehumanization and objectification of women in the media is surely one of the contributing factors. Consider the pervasiveness of sexual harassment that women suffer from men in school, the workplace, on the street. Men aren't biologically programmed to harass women. We learn it. (p. 250)

Therefore, men learn sexism and promote the same cultural values they learn from others and institutions. In response to the criticism heaped upon Black youth Dyson (1996) retorted: "While these young black males become whipping boys for sexism and misogyny, the places in our culture where these ancient traditions are nurtured and rationalized – including religious and educational institutions and the nuclear family – remain immune to forceful and just criticism" (p. 186). This problem is indeed pervasive, persistent, and powerful. It is not just about the hyper-macho posturing of males but the moral mirrors that we all must face with regard to how we see gender in American society.

CLASSISM

America not only espouses values of equality, meritocracy, and individualism, but also free-market and competition. The U.S. has its own caste system, not as rigid as other countries (according to rhetoric), but just as real. Class, much like race, is seldom talked about or up for discussion or critique. According to hooks (2003), "Class is rarely talked about in the United States; nowhere is there more intense silence about the reality of class differences than in educational settings" (p. 142). The great irony here is that because the subject is little acknowledged, it is even more damaging in its functions and results. Simply put, those with power and influence get to make the rules; they can name others. With this, they frequently categorize people at lower classes as "Others." Middle class norms, values, and behaviors are solidified as American to the benefit of upper classes and to the detriment of lower classes (Brantlinger, 2001; Kailin, 2002). From this it is understood that hierarchies create ranking systems, which lead to situations of subordination and domination (Brantlinger, 2001). Domination was equated with oppression by Eagleton (1990). Young (1990) noted components of oppression which included exploitation, marginalization, powerlessness, cultural imperialism, and violence. These are normal experiences for those at lower ends of the social class spectrum. While addressing the issues of political economy, class, and schools, Darder, Baltodano, and Torres (2003) asserted:

> Contrary to the traditional view, schools actually work against the class interests of those students who are most politically and economically

vulnerable within society. The role of competing economic interests of the marketplace in the production of knowledge and in the structural relationship and policies that shape public schools are recognized as significant factors, particularly in the education of disenfranchised students. From the standpoint of economics, public schools serve to position select groups within asymmetrical power relations that serve to replicate the existing values and privileges of the culture of the dominant class. (p. 11)

It seems commonsensical to state that there is a relationship between quality of education and wealth, but this point cannot be overstated. Epps (2005) asserted, "The quality of education available to children is based on the relative power, prestige, and wealth of their families. Schools, as institutional agents of society, are not designed to eliminate established patterns of domination and subordination among competing groups" (pp. 220-221). Therefore, schools play a catalytic role in exacerbating class-based distinctions instead of the common belief that schools are actively eliminating such distinctions. Epps (2005) summarized the connection of poverty to academic achievement when he wrote, "Wealth affects achievement in several ways; through its effect on the amount of cultural capital to which a child is exposed, the ability of families to live in communities with good public schools or to choose private schools, and the provision of an ethos of high academic and career expectations, students' achievements are maximized" (p. 222).

Not surprisingly, the major tenets of this same sub-optimal conception are similar to the major tenets which influence traditional educational leadership.

THE DOMINANT PARADIGM, INJUSTICE, AND EDUCATIONAL LEADERSHIP

Within educational leadership or educational administration, the sub-optimal conceptual system is masked in the convenient covert cloak of positivism, scientific management, and/or structuralism. Progressive scholars have provided scathing critiques of these ideologies in recent years (Dantley, 2002; English, 2003; Giroux, 1997). Dantley (2005) opined, "The scientific management paradigm that emphasizes quantifiable measures of success, rationality, predictability, and routinization has historically grounded educational leadership practice" (p. 652). Dantley (2002) further noted, "Educational leadership has sought legitimacy through immersing itself into larger more trenchant discourses such as the sciences, scientific management, and even literary criticism. It has borrowed idioms and syntax from economics and the business world all in an effort to legitimate itself as a valid field" (p. 336). This quest for legitimacy is a doubled-edged sword. Seeking intellectual/academic legitimacy is a laudable goal; however, seeking it through solely appropriating and mimicking aforementioned fields is problematic. Furthermore, the idolization of an ideology that rests on positivistic notions as explanation, prediction, and technical control once again mirrors a grander narrative of sub-optimal supremacy (Dantley, 2002; Ginwright, 2004; Giroux, 1997).

The supremacy of a sub-optimal conceptual system and its resulting positivistic paradigm is further undermined by accusations based in context and history. "The penchant for rationality, order, and empiricism that inspires these positivist abstractions is hardly crafted in a frictionless social or ideological environment, although their maxims would lead one to believe that they have been birthed from an ahistorical and apolitical context" (p. 336). Dantley poignantly points out that the advantage of injustice is its invisibility. Without the examination of political/historical context, the status quo remains intact (i.e., people stay oppressed and marginalized). Educational leaders are uniquely positioned to challenge, critique, and transform these social arrangements. The history of injustice (i.e., sub-optimal conceptions) is rooted in slavery, colonialism, imperialism, segregation, and other forms of oppression. The status quo has had to be altered, changed, or eradicated for humanity to progress. English (2004) denoted the importance of history and observed that in its absence, the subject (positivism in this case) is left "floating in a kind of 'contextualless' vacuum" (p. 6). According to Dantley (2002), "Obfuscated in the fiber of positivist thinking is the social and political agenda it engenders. One can only see this plan manifest when one takes the opportunity to deconstruct positivism" (p. 337). This social and political agenda serves the greater purpose of a sub-optimal conceptual system which is synonymous with a pedagogy of injustice.

This injustice in educational leadership is damaging to the field and schools they serve. With regard to the field, over-emphasis on the sub-optimal invalidates other philosophies, epistemologies, and realities. For instance, scholars who might do research on spirituality or ethical leadership might be shunned, patronized, or negated. The same could be true for researchers interested in Afrocentricity, feminism, or queer theory. In K-12 schools, the sub-optimal pushes the experiences of people of color to the margins and validates a single canon or regime of truth (Akbar, 2002; Dantley, 2005; Shields, 2004). Conversely, insight into effective social justice can be obtained through a more optimal conceptual system.

TOWARDS SOCIAL JUSTICE: AFRICAN AMERICANS AND AN OPTIMAL CONCEPTUAL SYSTEM

To truly reflect a greater level of humanity in society and in schools, we must resist the cyclic reinforcement and rationalization of institutionalized injustice and delve deep into more emancipative discourses that counter "sub-optimalism." Steps toward social justice begin with realizing the existence and value of a more optimal conceptual system (see Table 1). The perspective, struggles, and experiences of African Americans are particularly relevant to this discussion.

THE CASE OF AFRICAN AMERICANS – A BRIEF HISTORY

We black folk, our history and our present being, are a mirror of all the manifold experiences of America. What we want, what we represent, what we endure is what America is. If we black folk perish, America will perish. If America has forgotten her past, then let her look into the mirror of our consciousness and she will see the living past living in the present, for our memories go back, through our black folk of today, through the recollections of our black parents, and through the tales of slavery told to us by our black grandparents, to the time when none of us, black or white, lived in this fertile land. The differences between black folk and white folk are not blood or color, and the ties that bind us are deeper than those that separate us. The common road of hope which we all traveled has brought us into a stronger kinship than any words, laws, or legal claims. (Wright as cited in West, 1994, p. 17)

The struggle of African Americans in the United States in trying to attain educational parity is a testament to the challenge of equity and fight against trenchant forms of injustice. Africans arrived on American shores in 1619, first as indentured servants (Bennett, 1984). Later, millions more were kidnapped and brought to this country to participate in the peculiar institution known as slavery. Apparently, slavery "uprooted their culture and was designed to rob memory, create dependency upon the Euro-American world, and create a self-hatred complex that would last for generations" (Rogers, 2000, p. 124). To uphold this insidious system, an array of customs, traditions, and laws were developed; one of such laws strictly forbade teaching a slave to read or write. Furthermore, if a slave was caught reading or writing, there were harsh penalties (Blassingame 1979; Wade, 1964). Even though the law and society were not on their side, slaves still valued education and fought to gain it amid incredible odds. According to Perry (2003), "for the slaves, literacy was more than a symbol of freedom; it was freedom. It affirmed their humanity, their personhood. To be able to read and write was an intrinsic good, as well as a mighty weapon in the slave's struggle for freedom" (p. 13). This educational odyssey would take the slaves (later to become African Americans) to the 20th century still guided by the struggle for equity.

As the battle for human rights continued, the fight against injustice remained constant. The Civil War would eventually bring an end to slavery, followed by a brief period of progress called Reconstruction. During this time period, African Americans made significant gains in many areas including politics and education (Bennett, 1984). Unfortunately, White southern backlash and northern apathy would set the stage for an era of segregation in which "separate but equal" was the rule of the day (Rothstein, 1996). Yeo and Kanpol (1999) confirmed that:

During the latter part of the 19th century and the first half of the 20th, education for minorities in this country varied, not so much in quality, but in its response to geographic, demographic, and legal contexts. Two major developments shaped the nature of schooling for Black Americans during this time period; the evolution of segregated education, both de jure in the south and de facto in the north, which was given the force of law by the Supreme Court decision of *Plessy v. Ferguson* in the 1880s, and the dramatic demographics of Black relocation to urban areas of the north to escape rural poverty in the South....Both of these trends, socially and economically derived and generated, gave rise to the distinct educational institutions intended and actualized to segregate the majority of Black Americans from the mainstream of U.S. society. (p. 2)

51

From the story of African Americans, it is apparent that there was a deliberate creation of inequity within education settings, which is a microcosm of the grander sub-optimal conceptions that gave rise to, invigorated, and institutionalized oppression.

LESSONS FOR SOCIAL JUSTICE FROM AFRICAN AMERICANS

To be an Afro-American, or an American black is to be in the situation, intolerably exaggerated, of all those who have ever found themselves part of a civilization which they could no wise honorably defend – which they were compelled, indeed, endlessly to attack and condemn – and who spoke out of the most passionate love, hoping to make the kingdom new, to make it honorable and worthy of life. (Baldwin as cited in West, 2004, p. 1)

Concurrently, as African Americans struggled for a modicum of humanity they developed a piercing perspective, characterized by unique critique and moral magnitude. W.E.B. DuBois (2003) wrote:

The Negro is sort of a seventh son, born with a veil, and gifted with second-sight in this world, - a world which yields him no true self-consciousness, but only lets him see himself through the revelation of the other world. It is a peculiar sensation, this double-consciousness, this sense of always looking at oneself though the eyes of others, of measuring one's soul by the tape of a world that looks on in amused contempt and pity. One ever feels his two-ness, - an American, a Negro; two souls, two thoughts, two unreconciled strivings; two warring ideas in one dark body, whose dogged strength alone keeps it form being torn asunder. (p. 9)

DuBois' keen commentary is insightful in many different ways. First, it highlights the context and conflict within African Americans, in terms of how they view themselves. Secondly, he makes an interesting assessment on America's viewpoint with the words "pity" and "contempt." Finally, by emphasizing "dogged strength" he characterizes the continuing struggle of African Americans and encourages hope in the midst of hopelessness, joy in a world of pain, and faith in times of frustration. Interestingly, these are also lessons for an optimal conception of social justice. One, we should recognize the social and political context and the conflict within ourselves. Two, we should acknowledge deeply entrenched biases in others and within systems. Three, we should imbue our efforts with hope and heart.

Nearly 100 years later, Cornel West (1994) would also provide impressive racial analysis in the book *Race Matters*. In reference to the plight of Black America and the dichotomous debate which ensued, he wrote:

We must acknowledge that structures and behaviors are inseparable, that institutions and values go hand in hand. How people act and live are shaped – though in no way dictated or determined – by the larger circumstances in which they find themselves. These circumstances can be changed, their limits attenuated, by positive actions to elevate living conditions...Culture is as much a structure as the economy or politics; it is rooted in institutions such as families, schools, churches, synagogues, mosques, and communication industries (television, radio, video, music). Similarly, the economy and politics are not only influenced by values but also promote particular cultural ideas of the good life and society. (pp. 18 - 19)

From these comments we actually can extract the remnants of an optimal conceptual system. We see evidence of self-knowledge, both/and reasoning, the union of opposites, and values of oneness and communalism. Once again, moving towards effective social justice means learning lessons from such analyses and and the histories of diverse and sometimes disparate communities. As we learn the lessons, we run into ideological conflicts, which must be negotiated.

NEGOTIATING CONTESTED SPACES IN SOCIAL JUSTICE

Discussions around social justice frequently involve issues such as race, class, and gender (to name a few). Part of the problem pertains to the way in which justice should be addressed. The contested space here is between the politics of redistribution and recognition. Social justice that emphasizes redistribution highlights economically defined "classes" struggling for their "interests," ending "exploitation," and achieving fair access to resources for equality (Fraser, 1997). The politics of recognition entails the struggle for basic recognition and affirmation of humanity amongst "feminist, communitarian, cultural studies, queer, (dis)ability, postcolonial, psychoanalytical, and poststructuralist theories," individuals, as well as groups represented within these theories (North, 2006, p. 513). Social justice struggles have witnessed a shift from redistributive measures and strategies to recognition and/or cultural politics (Fraser, 1997). North (2006) explained the complex relationship between the two when she wrote,

> "The relationship between redistribution and recognition, then, is complicated. On the one hand, a focus on recognition can distract from the ongoing exploitation of workers and the marginalization and powerlessness of impoverished people. On the other hand, an emphasis on redistribution does not necessarily challenge the underlying social structures" (pp. 510-511).

Drawing from our lessons from African Americans, we see that what is needed here is a form of insight (similar to double-consciousness) which allows us to recognize the merit and meaning of a politics of redistribution and recognition. In addition, we must utilize both/and reasoning, an aspect of an optimal conceptual system. Thus, what is needed is a politics of redistribution and recognition that acknowledges how both "economic disadvantage impedes equal participation in the making of culture, in public spheres and in everyday life" and "cultural norms that are unfairly biased against some are institutionalized in the state and the economy" (Fraser, 1997, p. 15). In schools, the tension between the two has implications for school funding, curricular issues, pedagogical approaches, hiring practices, etc.

A similar contested space is the area between notions of the individual and the community. With regard to the individual, Young (1990) wrote:

In the United States, the idea of individual effort and merit is highly prized. Similarly, this supports what can be termed a "liberal notion of individual autonomy" (North, 2006; Young, 1990). According to Starratt (1991), "Individuals are driven by their passions and interests especially by fear of harm and desire for comfort" (p. 192). The individual is the source of moral judgment according to this nonconsequential assertion. This position coincides with the concept of equal respect. The principal of equal respect involves three subsidiary principles: (a) people must be treated as ends rather than means; (b) people must be regarded as free and rational moral agents; (3) as moral agents, people must have equal value (Strike, Haller, & Soltis, 1998).

At the same time there are problems with such a perspective. First, people are not always treated fairly and are many times used in order to maintain power and privilege (Darder, Baltodano, & Torres, 2003; Dyson, 2004; Kailin, 2002; Freire, 2000) thus undermining their equal value. Lynch and Baker (2005) argued, "Equal respect and recognition is not just about the liberal idea that every individual is entitled to equal rights and the privileges of citizenship in the country in which they live...It is also about appreciating or accepting differences rather than merely tolerating them" (pp. 132-133). Furthermore, formalized procedures, laws, and policies all in the name of equality can serve to "legitimize the unequal distribution of material resources among groups and individuals," (North, 2006) not to mention the fact that individual emphases negate the impact and influence of history, wealth, privilege, and power (Gewirtz, 1998; Schmidt, 2005). The competing notion is one that places the community (or society) at the forefront.

The second notion signifies the community as the primary source of human reality. "Participation in the life of the community teaches individuals how to think about their own behavior in terms of the larger common good of the community" (Starratt, 1991, p. 193). This school of thought is realized in practice by the concept of benefit maximization. According to Strike et al. (1998), "The principle of benefit maximization holds that, whenever we are faced with a choice, the best and most just decision is the one that results in the most good or the greatest benefit for the most people" (p. 16). This consequentialist theory is motivated by the maximization of societal benefit. Here too, are several problems. First, if a decision is made for the greatest benefit for the most people, what if that same decision significantly disregards, disparages, or disempowers the few left? In schools, this has been actualized in the form of segregated schools, tracking, and misidentification, misassessment, miscategorization, and misplacement in special education (Obiakor, Obiakor, Garza-Nelson, & Randall, 2005; Obiakor & Ford, 2002). Young (1990) also identifies the problem associated with an overemphasis on community, especially to the point of homogeneity when she stated that it puts "unassimilated persons and groups at a severe disadvantage in the competition for scarce positions and resources" and it "requires that persons transform their sense of identity in order to assimilate" (p. 179). As we reflect on social justice, we learn the value of both the individual and the community. The ideology of individualism could lead to actions which overemphasize difference over commonality. Similarly, the ideology of community could encourage practices that overemphasize unity at the expense of individuality. Social justice must acknowledge the uniqueness of individuals and difference and at the same time utilize commonality and unity in the creation of a better community. When these claims conflict, decisions must be made with regard to context as leaders weigh individual/individual's interest versus benefit maximization (Starratt, 1991).

SITUATING SOCIAL JUSTICE: TRANSCENDENCE, TRANSLATION, AND TRANSFORMATION

The discussion thus far has shed light on the pedagogy of injustice (sub-optimal conceptions), outlined a more optimal conceptual system, examined the example and experiences of African Americans as a guide to the promised land of a more socially just society, and recognized ideological areas of contestation within social justice. Dyson (1997) details a framework for exploring the state of race relations in America. Utilizing aspects of this framework I will pose a new framework for understanding the plight of social justice in educational leadership. The three broad categories are: transcendence, translation, and transformation (see Figure 1).

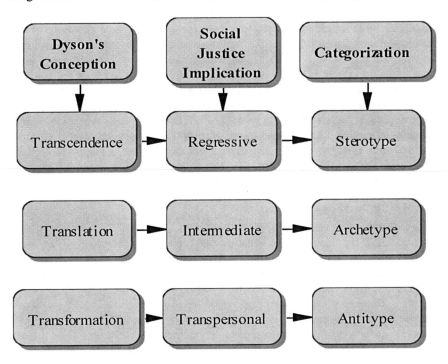

Figure 1 An Optimal Social Justice Framework

There is a certain difficulty when trying to define terms like social justice. Part of the problem is the propensity to personalize our conceptions, thus situating the definition closer to our own experiences and ideologies. Young (1990) posited a more nuanced elucidation of social justice:

> This provides us with at least a better understanding of the ideology of social justice.

TRANSCENDENCE

Based on this understanding and the new millennium popular rhetoric, some will surely try to transcend social justice. By this I mean that the difficult discussions that it encourages and liberation-language it promotes will make some uncomfortable. Then the reaction will be to soften the language and impact of the concept. The term can exist, but it must be systematically watered down – applying to everything, and yet applying to nothing. The transcendence of social justice lets the discussion proceed but only in terms of how far we have come, how good we are doing, while immersing the discourse in a kind of historical amnesia and a willful disregard for socio-political context (Dyson, 1997). The transcendence tactic is buttressed by the unseen forces of positivism and ultimately sub-optimal thinking. As previously noted, we make a serious ideological error when we ignore history and negate political and social context. According to Figure 1, this approach is regressive as it ultimately seeks to undermine the progressive intentions of social justice-minded leaders. Much like the aforementioned discussion of institutional racism, transcendence is a way to veil substantive issues and subsequently support the status quo. West (2004) warned that "to remain satisfied with the status quo may well lead to disaster" (p. 11). As a result of its dim vision, covert intentions, naivety, and/or attempts to reframe our understandings, social justice as transcendence is categorized as stereotype. Dyson (2005) opined, "stereotypes may contain strands of truth wrapped around knots of willful ignorance and deadly distortion. At its heart, a stereotype is a lazy assessment of the other, a sloppy projection of bias onto a vulnerable target" (p. 31). Not to mention this perspective gives tacit recognition and is devoid of redistribution.

TRANSLATION

Advocates of the translation of social justice are almost obsessed with the concept (which could be a good thing); they fall short because their analysis extends only as far as their frame of reference permits. Thus, the scholar who investigates racial inequity hops on the social justice bandwagon but only promotes her own racial agenda (for example). The same could be true for feminists and other academic interests; many of these interests were previously explained. It is not that they do not care about a diverse range of injustices, but they are relatively low on the list of educational problems as compared to their own. Dyson (1997) highlighted the same problem when discussing race and black leadership when he wrote, "A race translation model of black leadership fails to express the broad array of interests contained in the grammar of black liberation and resistance" (p. 188). The same is true for social justice scholars; such individuals must address the broad array of interrelated interests and find ways to construct a grammar of liberation and resistance known and respected by all who subscribe. Social justice as translation has aspects of both sub-optimal and optimal conceptualization because it seeks overall human improvement, but is consciously or unconsciously self-limiting due to personal agendas. Social justice as translation is an intermediate perspective better than transcendence, yet not fully developed. Translation is categorized as archetype because it embodies efforts to define oneself and situation (individual and recognition), yet it still lacks the perspective of the collective and underestimates or negates unified efforts (redistribution).

TRANSFORMATION  *important point*

What I am advocating here is a transformational form of social justice. This form of social justice should do three things: first, counter the oppression of injustice. Second, navigate dichotomous approaches with multiplicity (informed by notions of double-consciousness). Finally, it should unite various forms of resistance in a relationship of respect and equal recognition with the intent of redistribution (Dyson, 1997; North, 2006). Transformational social justice is the antithesis of the "pedagogy of injustice" explained earlier in this essay. It eschews the sub-optimal premises of control, rampant materialism, hyper-competition, and aggrandized individualism. This must be the heart of any approach to define or enact social justice. At the same time, transformational social justice is not confined or stagnant. In other words, it cannot be reduced to simply to either/or, them/us, or good/bad. It rejects the reductionism of transcendence, which seeks simplicity at the expense of complexity and a deeper understanding. Gorski (2006) explains this process in writing about the undermining of multicultural education:

> Transformational social justice, in a similar way, eludes the sly traps of transcendence (i.e., reframing and comfort instead of change). It is transpersonal in the way it regards the individual (or individual interests) within the context of the community (broader interests) (North, 2006). In Figure 1, transformational social justice is categorized as an antitype, because it transgresses "against received beliefs or accepted norms" in the interest of greater equity (Dyson, 2005, p. 32). At this point, transformation goes beyond translation. While the latter emphasizes one group's struggle (individual interest), the former highlights their collective struggle. Writing with regard to the state of Black leadership in America, Dyson (1997) insightfully stated:

The antitypical inclination here links the causes of those oppressed by injustice (a sub-optimal conceptual system) and also reifies the parity of recognition and redistribution as important components of social justice. In other words, not only should oppressed groups be recognized as human beings, with respect to their particular struggle; at the same time collective insight helps to also seek redistribution in order to address the problem of unequal access to power (Fraser, 1997; North, 2006).

TRANSFORMATIONAL SOCIAL JUSTICE IN PRACTICE

Social justice for transformation should address three things: relationships, flexibility, and morality. Relationships are important to human interactions and organizations. "Relationships with others affect our own sense of self." (Shields, 2004, p. 116). In reference to education, Sidorkin (2002) argued that "relationships ontologically precede the intrinsic motivation for learning and should therefore be placed at the center of educational theory" (p. 116). Social justice for transformation is deeply woven into human relationships and in schools; it means open lines of communication among administrators, teachers, staff, and communities. It means confronting our own biased-based assumptions, presumptions, and actions. As Shields (2004) opined, "Relationships make up the basic fabric of human life and must not be pushed to the periphery of educational considerations" (p. 116).

Social justice as transformation needs flexibility. By this I mean that it cannot be necessarily confined to a uni-historical/uni-contextual existence. At the same time, it cannot be viewed as ahistorical or acontextual. That means that the struggles we see in education today are part of a long series of social, political, and historical events that shape, influence, and impact educational reality. Educational leaders do themselves a great service when they understand the interplay of context, social history, and politics (Blanchette, Beachum, & Mumford, 2005; Cunningham & Cordeiro, 2003). At the same time, transformative leaders for social justice are able to acknowledge the centrality of issues like race while denying the exclusivity of the same issue (Dyson, 1997). From this perspective our personal ideological crusades (race, class, and gender) become two-way streets whereby scholars and practitioners inform and enhance each other instead of deploying rhetorical weapons against each other in the "great ideological battles of diminishing returns."

Finally, social justice as transformation needs morality. This is a moral and ethical force that supports the struggle against oppression. "Race transforming black leadership [educational leadership] must highlight the role of moral and spiritual values in the social reconstruction of American life" (Dyson, 1997, p. 190). (The common denominator for making these kinds of connections across diverse interests is the investment and belief in a set of values at the moral core of those who long for true social justice. Bolman and Deal (2001) stated that "the heart of leadership lives in the hearts of leaders" (p. 17). Similarly, Sergiovanni (1992) asserted that moral leadership fuses the head, the hand, and the heart. As Starratt (2004) observed:

> Social justice as transformation is a moral activity uniquely integrated into the hearts and minds of leaders who see schools as places that teach the whole child (mentally, emotionally, and physically). They define success in broader terms than only standardized test scores and understand that school is about personal and professional preparation for a global society of diverse

peoples (Dantley, 2005; Obiakor & Beachum, 2005). This moral force behind social justice as transformation might best be summarized as follows: "Moral purpose is about both ends and means. In education, an important end is to make a difference in the lives of students. But the means of getting to that end are also crucial. If you don't treat others fairly, you will be a leader without followers" (Fullan, 2001, p. 13).

CONCLUSION

"Justice means liberating others from injustice and orientating oneself away from biases and partial passions and toward universal ethical principles" (Walker & Snarey, 2004, p. 4).

With the above quote in mind, I conclude this essay with an ethical direction for transformational social justice. In the previous section, I noted the importance of a moral and ethical intent within transformational social justice. In the work of Walker and Snarey (2004), they discuss notions of dual values and emergent virtues. For instance, race + gender = liberation, resistance + accommodation = pluralism, religion + ethics = hope, agency + legacy = empowerment, and community + individual = uplift (p. 132). Adapting the applicable concepts according to the discussion posited here, the resulting product appears in Table 1. Elaborating on the African American perspective in moral education, Walker and Snarey (2004) asserted:

Understanding this "two-ness" is important as we address the idea of a transformational social justice. On the left side of Table 1 there are values listed. For example, race or gender certainly represents the center of reality for many individuals. In a way, it represents a value. What is being proposed here is the idea that a broader virtue of liberation should be of importance to those who struggle against racism or sexism (or whatever mechanism of oppression applies). "Just as when one evenhandedly blends the color blue and yellow and creates a new color, when one optimally balances the dual tones of a primary value, a new virtue emerges. By virtue, we mean an ethical attitude that becomes a new strength at the center of an individual's personality or character" (Walker & Snarey, 2004, p. 132). Transformational social justice should be founded with the emergent virtues of liberation, empowerment, and uplift.

Liberation, empowerment, and uplift are the pillars of transformational social justice.

This analysis has identified an overarching pedagogy of injustice and further named it as a sub-optimal conceptual system (Myers, 1988). An outcome of this in educational leadership is the overemphasis and over-reliance on positivism. Next, additional insight was gleaned from the African American experience as a guidepost towards social justice (an optimal conceptual system). Finally, social justice was addressed according to three categories: transcendence, translation, and transformation. Furthermore, this framework was buttressed with the assertion of social justice virtues (i.e., liberation, empowerment, and uplift. The situation within educational leadership is crucial because leadership in schools ultimately impacts the lives of numerous children. Students cannot afford to be the victims of sub-optimal thinking, especially when so many of us know better. The question is: Will we do better?

Table 2 Transformational Social Justice as Emergent Virtues

VALUES	EMERGENT VIRTUES
Race, Gender, Class	Liberation
Recognition and Redistribution	Empowerment
Community-and-Individual	Uplift

Here at the end, the reader might still be at a loss with regard to how social justice is being defined here. It is my intention not to oversimplify, overstate, or essentialize the topic, but for the sake of clarity I will attempt to posit a social justice definition that is more like a direction, a guidepost rather than a guide.

Social justice can be defined as an optimal belief system that emphasizes equal recognition of all groups and individuals along with redistribution to address social inequity, while emphasizing virtues such as liberation, empowerment, and uplift.

The caveat here is that we all must continue to explore the multiple meanings of social justice for educational leadership and for our society. Earlier, I extended an invitation to the battlefield for social justice; the battle does not end here. The battle rages wherever there is injustice and it requires all of us to fight in one way, shape, or form.

The situation reminds me of the words of Dr. Martin Luther King, Jr. when he wrote:

Human progress is neither automatic nor inevitable. Even a superficial look at history reveals that no social advance rolls in on the wheels of inevitability. Every step toward the goal of justice requires sacrifice, suffering, and struggle; the tireless exertions and passionate concern of dedicated individuals. Without persistent effort, time itself becomes an ally of the insurgent and primitive forces of irrational emotionalism and social destruction. This is no time for apathy or complacency. This is a time for vigorous and positive action (1987, p. 44).

JEFFREY BROOKS

FREEDOM AND JUSTICE

Conceptual and Empirical Possibilities for the Study and Practice of Educational Leadership

INTRODUCTION

In 2002, I attended an education conference. The sponsor was a consortium of research universities and the theme was educational leadership. Amidst sessions devoted to logistics of school administration and management was a smattering of other topics: the work and lives of teachers, recruitment and retention of women and people of color into a profession traditionally dominated by white males, critical approaches to conducting research, and novel strategies toward creating better environments for student learning. Discussions of multicultural issues, democratic schooling, and gender politics echoed through the hotel halls. Certainly, there was irony in that the majority of sessions were delivered by and to white males—myself included. I suppose that the fact such topics were being broached at all was in the broadest sense some kind of step forward, but more often relegated what could have been pluralistic dialogue to pedagogical monologue. I went about the business of conferencing: attending and delivering presentations, listening to the presidential address on the state and direction of the consortium, and I sat attentively as a keynote speaker exhorted those in the room to place their work in relation to the only imperative that all Americans must reconcile: freedom.

On September 11, 2001, the keynote speaker watched a plane explode into the side of the Pentagon from his nearby office. According to my notes from his presentation, he said: "the attacks of 9-11 have forever changed our lives, society, and work as educators…terror is laying siege to freedom…the great and successful American experiment in democracy is threatened by a new and evil force." In the broadest sense, and in the shadow of 9-11, this seemed a meaningful assertion—but hardly a novel insight; anyone in the United States who has tuned in the evening news or read a newspaper since that fateful day has heard similar rhetoric. It seemed to me then, as it does now, that what educators needed was someone to elucidate the manner of change, to plot a course of action rather than idly suggest change was needed. The Keynote's concluding assertion raised my eyebrow and my suspicion:

"The foundation of American freedom was set by the hard work of great men such as Mr. Adams and Mr. Jefferson. Their collective legacy, the United States Constitution and the Bill of Rights, are the very pillars of society in

Ira Bogotch et al. (eds.), Radicalizing Educational Leadership: Dimensions of Social Justice, 61–78.

this country. Yet, this 'foundation' is only something to build upon; it is not a guarantee and is not realized without sacrifice and great effort." He pounded the podium: "As educators, we must erect a scaffold of liberty on this foundation and build around it walls of justice and equality!"

As the people around me rose to their feet and applauded, I wondered: Whose sacrifice, liberty, justice, and equality was he envisioning?

Later that day, I attended an interactive session devoted to "honoring and advancing multicultural perspectives in education." A self-described panel of two African-American women, an African-American man, a Latino, a White woman, and an out-lesbian, all successful professors of educational leadership, delivered speeches describing various aspects of their American experience in society-at-large and more specifically in higher education. The four speakers delivered distinctly different addresses, yet evoked a similar language. Words like strange, wrong, sensitive, inequality, oppression, inequity, liberty, representation, assimilation, justice, them-and-us, and…freedom, filled space between attendees in the half-full lecture hall. Freedom was again the topic, but the freedom described was not built on the Bill of Rights or the Constitution of the United States. This was freedom with different lineage: Sojurner Truth, Paulo Freire, Martin Luther King, Jr., bell hooks, W.E.B. Du Bois, Maya Angelou, Cornel West, Nel Noddings, Henry Giroux, and Michel Foucault. The massacres that motivated these speakers did not only occur in New York and were of a wholly different ilk; certainly measured in lives lost, but also assessed as cumulative psychological, social, economic, physical, and emotional tolls exacted from disadvantaged and oppressed peoples for centuries: ideological, racial, sexual, and gender persecution; physical and mental slavery; segregation and re-segregation; discrimination; ethnocentrism and anglocentrism, and; cultural and achievement gaps, both perceived and actual. As educators, one speaker implored, we must "forcibly free ourselves from the tyranny of education's violent institutions and establish a new tradition that embraces all folk—not just those who have enjoyed privilege by being born a certain gender or race." This was a legacy of a different sort: different America, different Americans.

I couldn't help but connect the two presentations. I imagined the keynote speaker as a fifth member of the panel—their discussion seemed an extension of themes he had raised earlier. All used the same words, but to different effect, with different meaning. One's liberty was another's tyranny. One's founding fathers were another's brutal step-parents. One's freedom was another's bondage.

In this essay, I invite you to join me on a journey of personal exploration that began in many ways at that conference I attended many years ago. In an effort to make sense of the concepts described above, I began this exploration by reading about the concept of freedom. On these pages I will discuss three distinct perspectives of freedom and ask you—as an aspiring or practicing educational leader, or person who trains, prepares, and/or works with educational leaders, to consider your pedagogy, practice, and philosophy in relation to these concepts and traditions. However, like so many journeys, the path takes twists and turns and this one doesn't end where I thought it might. After discussing freedom, I turn to the concept of justice, looking particularly at the way the concept has been conceived in several social sciences, and then ultimately consider what these interrelated concepts might mean for the study, preparation and practice of educational leadership. While written text is not an ideal means of *discussing* ideas, per se, I entreat you to accept what follows as the beginning of a conversation. I am also inviting you and your peers to the discussion. It is my hope that in working to bring issues of freedom and justice to the forefront of consciousness and scrutiny, a dialogue might ensue that would bring educational leaders together as they debate and reflect on discrepancies and commonalities in their perspectives on how best to serve students.

FREEDOM₁ IS NOT FREEDOM₂

Freedom means many things to many people, often realized as freedom *to*: to wear hair and clothes the way they like, to speak their mind to whomever they choose, to have the license to travel, to participate in government, to have an equal opportunity to attain, hold, and be fairly promoted in the profession of their choice, to have an education, to practice a religion, to have access to medical supplies and care, to eat, to stay alive. To others freedom is flight, a freedom *from*: from entrenched tyranny and oppression, from institutions that engender racism, sexism, classicism, ageism, or bias against a certain sexual orientation, from hatred, from jealousy, from evil. While these aspects of freedom are useful on a broad and abstract level, neither the ideas of "freedom to" and "freedom from" nor these lists can hope to adequately define the complex, ever-changing, and context-bound experience of either individual or social freedom (Fromm, 1965). The processes and products of individual freedom, as both ideological concepts and lived reality, are consistent and central components of each person's ongoing operational definition of the human condition.

At the very least, freedom entails the reconciliation of individual, social, political, ethical, and moral dilemmas with racial, ethnic, cultural, sexual orientation, gender, and class-related dimensions; and a plethora of interrelated issues broadly related to epistemology, ontology, and psychology. These dimensions of freedom continue to inspire and inform contested areas of research, public policy, individual thought, philosophy, popular opinion, and visions of "adequate" and "excellent" education. From these complex and multifaceted roots spring forth more specific questions: What is freedom as a human experience—both to the individual, and to society? Is freedom only the *absence* of external pressures or is it also the *presence* of something? In an increasingly pluralistic society, what opportunities are you, and others, differentially afforded in order to realize our potentially competing visions of freedom? What opportunities are we each provided and denied? What, if any, are individuals' duties and responsibilities to self and to society? What, if any, are society's duties and responsibilities to the individual? Are you free? Can you be free (Fromm, 1965, p. 4)?

As the nature and meaning of freedom is interpreted in different ways, so are responses to each of the above questions. Some will answer in light of global relationships grounded in inter-nationalistic political ideology: "As a citizen of Country X, I am more (or less) free than citizens of Country Y. Therefore, I am free (or not)." Others will define freedom more immediately, in formal and/or informal relation to their intracultural peers and/or fellow country-people: "We have a democracy, and therefore all have the opportunity to participate in the crafting of our freedom." Alternately, "I am a member of Ethnic/Gender/Socioeconomic/ (Sub)cultural Group A, a historically oppressed and underrepresented people in this country; I am less free than members of Ethnic Group B, who enjoy privilege through pervasive and institutionalized inequality." There are also those who define freedom solely as an existential experience; looking inward to answer freedom's questions: "I am an individual, autonomously responsible for my decisions and actions. My freedom is experienced only through the degree to which I am true to myself and allow others to influence me." Of course, in many instances freedom is better defined by characteristics not heretofore mentioned: power, law, economics, justice, family, church, tribe, agency, hegemony, liberty, oppression, discrimination, spirituality, a glass (or actual) ceiling, bigotry, poverty, literacy, and so on. This list, if not endless, is at least infinitely complex (Giroux, 1983a; Freire, 1973; McLaren, 1989). Certainly, interpretation of these issues and formulation of theoretical and/or actionable solutions to them are spread over a broad range of ideology and pedagogy—vigorously debated at many levels, from barbershop to street-corner, from coffeehouse to congress and beyond.

CONCEPTUAL AND EMPIRICAL FREEDOM

Implicit in this discussion of freedom is the idea that individual and social freedoms are not only *conceptual*, but also *empirical* phenomena—experienced and perceived in various ways by various people at various times. This may seem obvious but is important to keep in mind as it suggests that we can engage freedom not only as a philosophical construct, but also through dynamic action. Put differently, freedom evolves; it is not a static or monolithic "thing" that looks any one way. While the protean nature of this phenomenon may make it elusive as an object of study, it is observable nonetheless. We should be able to identify freedom as experienced by individuals in a particular setting and conduct our work in light of our observations about the nature of freedom. Still, two central questions remain—why and how? How can these seemingly abstract ideas inform the thinking and work of educational leaders and why should they approach their work informed by these perspectives?

My own perspective is that educational leaders stand to gain insight into their paradoxically demanding and rewarding vocation by examining their work in relation to these concepts. Understanding freedom, and justice, can help educational leaders identify inequity and can inform their courses of action. Further, to study and reflect on freedom is to accept a challenge; the challenge of looking critically into ourselves and at the institutions that frame our lives. As Schmitt (2003) suggested:

"one can make an effort to try and understand one's life, one's person, and one's condition, and try to lead a life that makes some sense under the conditions in which one finds themself, or one can evade the ambiguities and perplexities and live from day to day, more or less oblivious to how one's life unfolds" (p. 52).

The following anecdotes illustrate how recognizing and then reflecting on the concept of freedom can inspire a leader to action.

STRIDE TOWARD FREEDOM

Every parent at some time faces the problem of explaining the facts of life to his child. Just as inevitably, for the Negro parent, the moment comes when he must explain to his offspring the facts of segregation. My mother took me on her lap and began by telling me about slavery and how it ended with the Civil War. She tried to explain the divided system of the South—the segregated schools, restaurants, theatres, housing; the white and colored signs on drinking fountains, waiting rooms, lavatories—as a social condition rather than a natural order. Then she said the words that almost every Negro hears before he can yet understand the injustice that makes them necessary: "You are as good as anyone."

"All right, boy, pull over and let me see your license."

My father replied indignantly, "I'm no boy." Then, pointing to me, "This is a boy. I'm a man, and until you call me one, I will not listen to you."

The policeman was so shocked that he wrote the ticket up nervously, and left the scene as quickly as possible.

So wrote Martin Luther King, Jr., recalling formative events from his childhood in *Stride Toward Freedom* (1958), "the chronicle of 50,000 Negroes who took to heart the principles of nonviolence, who learned to fight for their rights with the weapons of love, and who, in the process, acquired a new estimate of their own human worth" (p. 9). This is the story of King's involvement with the civil rights movement in Montgomery, Alabama in the mid 1950's. *Stride Toward Freedom* records a dual awakening, one personal, the other social; it is at once about King, the learned preacher who grows into a world leader and at the same time the book is about a community that rose collectively to demand liberty in a land of compromised freedoms and outright oppression. As King explains, members of this community were not joined in bonds that defined traditional Southerners, or even "Negro" folk; they came from all social classes and professed diverse religious denominational (although decidedly Christian) affiliation. Instead, they "came together in the bond of a cause they knew was right" (p. 9). For King as an individual, the experience was nothing less than epiphany—he was profoundly influenced by Mahatma Gandhi, whose philosophy of Satyagraha, literally translated as love-force (Gandhi, 1951), provided him with a method for implementing Christ's doctrine (King, 1958, pp. 96-97). As King strode toward the challenge of confronting the deep-rooted institution of enculturated (and acculturated) and legal and social bigotry, he was his lord's instrument of love—of freedom. For others the experience was undoubtedly less cathartic, but was nonetheless an intensely felt and personally meaningful fight for personal and social liberation.

When King pointed out that the movement's solidarity crossed social delineations such as class and religious affiliation, he apprehended and articulated an important point: Action borne of an innate sense of personal and social justice has compelled people throughout history to rise up against unjust forces of institutionalized oppression (Spring, 1995). The spirit of 1950's Birmingham is transcendent—reaching through time and across borders. We saw it in the Gandhi-led nonviolent overthrow of Colonial Britain in India; in the hand of King's namesake Martin Luther, who in moral outrage nailed protestations to the door of a Catholic church; in the words of Sitting Bull, whose famous speech to the United States Congress detailed the injustices and treachery suffered by his own Native American peoples, and by extension countless other Indigenous peoples; in the gifted and defiant Sojurner Truth, who proudly proclaimed her black womanhood at a time when it might have brought her death; in the violent upheaval of the French, Russian, and so many other revolutions, and also; in the bloody birth of the United States of America.

King, and others such as Rosa Parks, who on December 1, 1955 refused to move from a "white" front seat of a segregated Birmingham bus to a rear "black" seat, garnered worldwide admiration for their moxie, commitment to ideology, and personal fortitude; and, as King would later proclaim to posterity, for the "content of their character" (King, 1958, pp. 43-45). Likewise, each of the movements mentioned above (and to be sure, many others) facilitated the rise to public prominence of a few remarkable individuals; we remember these surges to freedom largely through their stories. Yet, while movements have pillars of strength and inspiration upon which they rest, such as King, Parks, Truth, and Sitting Bull, they are not solely the work or experience of any *one* person. To draw on the previous illustration, subtracting Parks and King from the 50,000 strong Birmingham protest still leaves 49, 998 stories of freedom of which we are largely unaware; much less the stories of those who subsequently reaped the benefits of their collective legacy and continue the unfinished fight for civil liberties. Freedom is most visible in revolution and through the tales preserved in history's annals—in battles won and lost, in poetic and passionate oratory, in political manifestoes, and through legal and legislative landmarks. However, as these struggles for freedom and their outcomes are remembered through institutional change or as zeitgeist, they are likewise an individual experience; remembered as moments sitting next to a proud father in a car or on the knee of a strong and wise mother.

As freedom is both personal and social, it is also a pluralistic concept. Consider that the King-led civil rights movement ripped asunder another freedom: a freedom enjoyed by Montgomery's White, privileged majority. To understand freedom in the context of contemporary United States society is to engage many traditions at once—and to understand that the freedoms of the oppressor are in direct juxtaposition to those of the oppressed. With every pull, there is a push.

For purposes of the work at hand, I am particularly interested in those conceptions of freedom that contribute most directly to a greater understanding of the way they are realized in the milieu of public education just past the turn of the millennium. In an effort to understand freedom in the context of public schooling in general, and the work of educational leaders in particular, I examine theoretical underpinnings of three prevailing conceptualizations of freedom in the United States. The first form I attend to is formal freedom. I begin this section with a brief discussion of freedom as conceptualized in the European Enlightenment, an intellectual predecessor to several 18th century American writers and politicians that molded the United States in its infancy. Chief among Enlightenment figures are philosophers Wilhelm von Humboldt, John Milton, David Hume, and economist Adam Smith. This segues into an examination of the work of some "founding fathers" of the young United States. Here, I focus on Thomas Jefferson and Benjamin Franklin, but also include James Madison, John Adams, and Alexander Hamilton. After this modest historical survey I turn to another kind of freedom: critical freedom. Critical freedom challenges the codified, ratified, and institutionalized freedom of the founding fathers, and addresses inequity and oppression that escapes a strictly formal depiction. In this section I focus primarily on key ideas in the works of Martin Luther King, Jr., and Paulo Freire. Finally, I consider two other thinkers who clearly attend to relationships between freedom and education: John Dewey and Maxine Greene. As these thinkers focused so much attention on education, this section is entitled educational freedom.

FORMAL FREEDOM: ENLIGHTENMENT SPIRIT AND THE "FOUNDING FATHERS"

Merrill, Gade, and Blevins (2001) characterized the European Enlightenment as an intellectual dawn:

> "During the 17th and early 18th centuries, this early-Enlightenment sunlight was bearing down on Britain and shining on the Italian city-states and Germany. Even more strongly it shone down on France...Italy felt the intellectual warmth, but to a much less degree. It was actually England that the Enlightenment was most prevalent. The fundamental and characteristic ideas originated there" (p. 2).

These fundamental and characteristic ideas included a renewed interest in reason, mathematics, and empiricism; also a concern with personal, political, economic, and social progress (Karier, 1986; Merrill et al., 2001). Enlightenment thinkers vigorously debated the relationship of individual to society and to government. Some of the loudest voices belonged to a trio of social contract theorists: Locke, Hobbes, and Rousseau.

In Germany, the Enlightenment was called Aufklaerung. The Aufklaerung included the likes of Nietzsche, Hegel, and Kant. Kant was interested in freedom, but is mainly remembered for his deontological ethical construct, the categorical imperative and numerous contributions to the philosophy of science (Durant, 1961). Kant's contemporary, Willhelm von Humboldt, was not only more focused on the concept of freedom, but was chiefly interested in education. As Merrill et al (2001) observed, "Humboldt...believed...that the only justification for governmental interference is to prevent harm to others" (p. 4).

In England, the Enlightenment also shone brightly, and included poet John Milton and economist Adam Smith. In 1644, Milton "wrote *Areopagitica*, a powerful tract against official licensing of the press and for freedom of religion" (Merrill, et al, 2001, p. 6). In Milton we find a powerful liberal stance: "People must hear all sides of questions and issues and not be exposed to a single side. Only then can they understand goodness and decency, or as he put it, human virtue" (Merrill, et al, 2001, p. 6). Milton believed that through twin freedoms—those of the press and of religion, citizens would not only be informed, but also be capable and willing practitioners of logical and rationally motivated action. Hume, on the other hand,

> "was an influential proponent of libertarianism—the constriction of state control and the maximization of individual freedom. He was not only a skeptic, questioning everything and believing in no absolutes, but he was a supreme relativist in ethics, believing that moral action depends on individual cases rather than general principles" (Merrill, et al, 2001, p. 9).

Hume was an empiricist, believing that we could learn what we needed to know by observation; he had little time for abstract ideas. Adam Smith was not only skeptical of governments, but in human nature as well. Smith believed that people act largely on their own interests, and would prey on their fellows if given the chance for personal gain. Predictably, Smith suggested that the main function of government was to promote and ensure justice. In *The Wealth of Nations*, Smith's most famous work, we also find two interesting ideas related to the present topic of freedom: (1) Smith believed that human progress was intimately connected to the economic conditions of nations. That is, he believed that humans as a race would flourish in all respects in direct relation to the amount of wealth accrued and generated by the aggregate citizenry, and; (2) He believed that the most efficacious way to promote prosperity was by means of "laissez faire" governance, a hands-off approach that would result in a spontaneous and natural socio-economic order (Smith, 1991).

The French Enlightenment saw the emergence of the philosophes, who "were bound by a few common beliefs—in rational and intentional progress, in tolerating various sects and non-Christian religions, in systematizing intellectual disciplines, and in overcoming human cruelty and violence through social improvements and government structures" (Merrill, et al, 2001, p. 11). Importantly, for the philosophes, freedom was the property of the elite. "They were, in spite of their changing social philosophy, still essentially aristocrats. Freedom of expression, for them, was mainly *their* freedom of expression and, as John Stuart Mill reiterated in the next century, did not extend to those segments of society not prepared for it" (Merrill, et al, 2001, p. 10). We will read criticisms of this idea in the section devoted to critical freedom, but now we turn to some key political thinkers who embraced these ideas.

ENLIGHTENMENT INFLUENCES ON 18TH CENTURY AMERICAN THINKERS

The European Enlightenment had a profound impact on the "Founding Fathers" of the United States of America. Although lagging some half-century behind their European counterparts, an affinity to Enlightenment thinking was evident in the new nation's constitution, Bill of Rights, Declaration of Independence, and other writings of their leaders. As Karier (1986) explained,

> "the leaders of the Revolutionary and constitutional eras, from Benjamin Franklin to James Madison, consistently reflected Enlightenment ideas and values in much of their thought and action. This leadership not only guided a political revolution but also inspired an ideological revolution which was to have profound consequences on the way future generations of Americans would view human nature, the good society, and the purposes of education" (pp. 20-21).

Among leaders of the "American Enlightenment," the influence of Thomas Jefferson is arguably second to none. Jefferson's ideas of freedom related directly to his great faith in freedom of inquiry and reason. Jefferson believed that "all" the young country's citizens should be afforded a modest education at the public expense. This education would allow people basic skills such as reading and writing and would last three years. Equipped with these rudimentary intellectual tools, the average citizen would be able to understand enough to participate in a democratic society, recognize oppression, and should the need arise, rise up against it. To Jefferson, the correct action would always become apparent through rational discourse; he encouraged dissent, but only so long as reason prevailed. To this end, he encouraged all to speak their mind and engage each other's ideas dialogically and politically. Jefferson was understandably a major proponent of freedom of speech and also became a champion for freedom of religion in his native Virginia (Karier, 1986).

However, while Jefferson is to this day admired by many for his vision of a free society populated by an educated citizenry, certain legitimate criticisms have been leveled at this legacy. First, for all his lofty talk of freedom and democracy, Jefferson owned slaves; an obvious and troubling paradox. Second, he seemed to believe at various times in a natural aristocracy of learned landowners. Third, there are those who question Jefferson's ideal place of the individual in a democratic society. Karier (1986) cites Babbitt (1924) who noted that Jefferson "emphasized men's rights over their responsibilities and thus 'corrupted' the American mind" (Karier, 1986, p. 28), and thereby promoting a society that existed for the individual rather than the other way around. Fourth, some decry the methods by which Jefferson "helped" the young country's growth. Spring (2001) in particular took umbrage with Jefferson's role as intellectual and political instigator of a policy of insidious cultural violence directed at Native American peoples. Citing passages from some of the 50,000 letters Jefferson wrote during his lifetime, Spring made a powerful and well-supported argument that Jefferson actively pursued a policy of cultural indoctrination and encouraged Native Americans to abandon their traditions in favor of an Anglo consumer culture. This cultural war averted the need in many instances for an actual war and allowed the government to "purchase" and "acquire" land through dubious and unethical means.

Several of Jefferson's contemporaries also played a major role in the development of the United States of America. Benjamin Franklin was a key figure who

> "converted the religiously sanctioned Puritan values of hard work, frugality, and investment into values justified by the secular notion that 'they pay off'. He thus encouraged the emerging merchant and industrial classes in a vigorous and unembarrassed pursuit of capital for its own sake or for the sake of national 'progress'" (Karier, 1986, p. 27).

Other powerful thinkers made major contributions to the nascent country. Alexander Hamilton supported a vision of freedom that countered Jefferson's. Hamilton "was a kind of economic 'nationalist,' a position alien to Jefferson's mindset. It was Hamilton who pushed for internal and external taxes, the creation of a national bank, and the development of a manufacturing infrastructure" (Tucker & Hendrickson, 1990). James Madison put a great deal of faith in the formal documents upon which the United States was built. Madison "was convinced that a bill of rights would limit governmental powers, preventing legislative and executive abuse of power, and would thwart the majority from taking advantage of the minority" (Merrill, et al, 2001, p. 15). Another founding father, John Adams,

> "desired a government that was carefully engineered so that human passions could be controlled. Always an advocate of law and order, he wanted a well-balanced and law-bound social system that would serve the public by producing what he called 'social happiness'...The state, according to Adams, must maintain the balance of power between the aristocratic and democratic elements of society—between 'the few and the many'...Not a democrat like Jefferson or Madison, Adams believed that man's ambition, lust for power, and passions must be controlled by government. This involves setting up instruments of 'order and subordination' that would inculcate feelings of esteem, sympathy, and admiration in the public. Adams saw rank, status, nobility as natural and necessary parts of an orderly society" (Meyer, 1976).

These men's views of freedom have had a profound impact on the U.S. citizenry and continue to exert a great deal of influence today. The Bill of Rights and the United States Constitution frame local and national discourses about the phenomenon in political and legal domains. For all their ambiguity, these documents have helped form a kind of monolithic, legalistic, and formal freedom—one that shapes many important discussions and manifestations of the phenomenon. However, not all thinkers agreed with the ways freedom was shaped by these "great men."

CRITICAL PERSPECTIVES: FREEDOM OF THE ELITE, BY THE ELITE, AND FOR THE ELITE

"Schools are a microcosm of society." This statement has been evoked so many times and in so many contexts that it has nearly become a truism, unquestioned and beyond critique. Yet what might such a statement suggest about the public schools that shape the educative experiences of so many lives in the United States? Are we to understand this metaphor by comparing the formal doctrines of society to those of school? If so, we can believe that the public school system is borne of ideology embodied in documents such as the Bill of Rights and the Constitution; a fair and legal foundation of equality, liberty, respect, democracy, and opportunity—a place where hard work and talent are rewarded. That is, we can understand the institution of schooling to be based on "life, liberty, and the pursuit of happiness" (Urban & Wagoner, 1996). Students graduating from these schools would issue forth into a merit-based democratic and capitalistic system, wherein the realization of personal freedom and prosperity was guaranteed by meaningful and willful participation in a social contract (Pulliam & Van Patten, 1995). Admirable ideas; yet for a rising chorus of educational pundits, practitioners, and researchers this is far from an accurate portrait of the nation's schools or the experience of freedom for those employed by it.

Jonathon Kozol's (1992) heartbreaking descriptions of impoverished children's lives and the everyday horrors of a public educational system indifferent to their hopeless plights is rightly characterized as "savage inequality"; a far cry from the aforementioned constitutional equality. Kozol portrays communities and individual administrators, teachers, and students that toil in sewage, despair, and bureaucracy to little positive effect (Kozol, 1992; 1967). Others have added conceptual depth and empirical support to Kozol's affective appeals: critical theorists such as McLaren (1989; 1997), Giroux (1983a, 1983b; 1997), West (1997), and Aronowitz and De Fazio (1997) have adapted ideas from Marx and other social theorists to articulate powerful perspectives that challenge the status quo; Marshall (1997) has expanded the critique, drawing powerfully from feminist pedagogy; Kohn (1999) has taken on the Enlightenment borne one-true-answer-through-empirical-certitude tradition, extant in today's school culture as an emphasis on standardized testing as an exclusive method for ascertaining academic successes and failures; Ayers, along with Hunt, Quinn, Klonsky, and Lyons (Ayers, 1993; Ayers, Hunt, & Quinn, 1998; Ayers, Klonsky, & Lyon, 2000) and Darling-Hammond, French, and Garcia-Lopez, (2002) implore educators to take the advocate's stance in their work and actively seek social justice for themselves and oppressed peoples in school and community. These writers have drawn inspiration from Kozol (and others) to build not only on the work of Marx, but also Michel Foucault, Pierre Bourdieu, Max Weber, John Rawls, Hannah Arendt and a host of other thinkers who question institutionalized injustice in society and school. No concise statement could hope to collectively describe the views of these individuals, but let us say that one theme is central: by virtue of an institutionalized hegemony, the formal scales of social justice are informally tipped in favor of the "haves," leaving the "have-nots" at a distinct disadvantage, and often powerless and defenseless to effect change for themselves or others. How do these critical perspectives change our vision of public schools and of educational leadership? We can now understand schools and school systems as arenas of conflict and unevenly distributed power—of individuals and groups with competing interests. Suddenly, new dynamics emerge: race matters, gender matters, sexual orientation matters, ethnicity matters, class matters, power matters, money matters, agency matters, etc. In this conception of society and school, individuals and their interests have shifted from abstract components of an idyllic political plenum to flesh and bone. "We the people" is no longer solely a statement of *unum*, but also of *pluribus*. Several thinkers present powerfully articulated critical perspectives on freedom—the list in the previous paragraph is more beginning than end. I have chosen to highlight two perspectives: Martin Luther King, and Paulo Freire.

MARTIN LUTHER KING, JR. AND SATYAGRAHA

On September 1, 1954 Dr. Martin Luther King, Jr. assumed the pastorate of the Dexter Avenue Baptist Church in Montgomery, Alabama. The decision to accept that post, made in close consultation with wife Coretta, was more than a turning point in a promising professional career; it was a turning point in United States history. King, an accomplished student of both philosophy and theology, was also a charismatic leader and gifted orator. He played a key role in galvanizing a complacent Negro (sic) community and uniting them in a nonviolent civil rights protest against formal and informal institutionalized racism. Although the initial impetus for the protest was desegregation of Montgomery's whites-in-the-front, blacks-in-the-back public buses, the stakes were much higher; Justice and liberty hung in the balance (King, 1958; Spring, 1995).

Historical and cultural context are especially important to an understanding of King's freedom. Despite court-ordered racial desegregation of public institutions such as transportation and schools, many white-controlled Southern cities ignored legal mandates and instead enforced time-worn norms through violence, economic monopoly, and intimidation in an effective and systematic perpetuation of gross inequities between black and white (Urban & Wagoner, 1996). The South of King's day was a perilous place for African Americans. Infinitely more so for any who dared stand up to the might of the white establishment, which included not only local government, but also many powerful informal unions and the Ku Klux Clan. Yet with all of the entrenched power wielded by white militants, there came a breaking point for King and his associates.

Miss Rosa Parks was a respected member of Montgomery's Negro community. Like so many of Montgomery's poor, she worked long hours and rode the city's public buses to and from work. On a December afternoon in 1955, Parks road the bus home as she had so many times before. However, rather than walking to the back of the bus, where *Negroes* were required to sit, she wearily sat in a seat toward the front. For this she was arrested. Word of the arrest spread quickly through the community, eventually prompting Negro community leaders to meet and organize a boycott of the buses. This boycott was exceptionally successful; Negroes constituted approximately 75% of Montgomery's bus riders and within a few days nearly all had joined the cause (King, 1958).

King's personal conceptualization of freedom rested on a well-considered and comprehensive religious and philosophical foundation. Drawing from Christian theology, King believed that healthy communities are bound together by agapeic love, that is, a caring and considerate benevolence for one's neighbor. Importantly,

King suggested that the only way a person might know their love was truly agape was by offering it to one's enemy; love free of the expectation of reciprocation was a morally just expression. King's (1958) studies in philosophy took him from Thoreau's (1993) *Essay on Civil Disobedience*, and also "Bentham and Mill, the revolutionary methods of Marx and Lenin, the social contracts theory of Hobbes, the 'back to nature' optimism of Rousseau, and the superman philosophy of Nietzsche," (King, 1958, p. 97). King was intrigued with Thoreau's suggestion that if a citizen found themselves in "an evil system," (1993) they could simply refuse to participate in it, thereby challenging and undermining the system without resorting to violence. King found Marx and Lenin too focused on materialism and felt that their concepts of morality and spirituality were both underdeveloped and misguided, but found their critiques of capitalism insightful. Hobbes and Rousseau stimulated King's interest in political philosophy but were likewise ultimately unsatisfying. Nietzsche's glorification of power and characterization of religion and morality as weakness disgusted King, as it denied humans their spiritual potential. Finally, King found an intellectual muse who would also provide him a method through which to practice and promote his Christian-inspired vision of agapeic freedom: Mahatma Gandhi. Through Gandhi's life and works, King learned about satyagraha—nonviolent resistance. Importantly, satyagraha "excludes the use of violence," but "is not conceived as a weapon of the weak"—it is not inaction or pacifism but nonetheless demands noncompliance (Gandhi, 1951, p. 3). Instead, satyagraha is a method of resistance akin to Thoreau's civil disobedience; a technique of crippling an evil system by refusing to partake in it.

Adopting the code of the *satyagrahi*, King was convinced that he and his associates stood firmly on moral high ground; so equipped, he led a massive display of nonviolent civil disobedience in the form of an organized and extremely effective boycott of Montgomery's segregated buses. The protest lasted over a year, ended finally by a Supreme Court decision in favor of King and the protestors. However, as Spring (1997) points out, this federal judicial action presaged a slew of legislation, including the Civil Rights Act of 1964, which

> "Under eleven different titles, the power of federal regulations was extended in the areas of voting rights, public accommodations, and employment. Titles IV and VI of the legislation were intended to end school segregation and provide authority for implementing the Brown decision" (p. 363).

In King we find the essence of critical freedom: a refusal to accept the wolf of injustice though it is clothed as the sheep of tradition. People are not free because a government tells them they are free. Freedom for King meant challenging that which insulted his soul and inspiring solidarity of action and purpose in the name of equality: "Men and women who had been separated from each other by false standards of class were now singing and praying together in a common struggle for freedom and human dignity" (King, 1958, p. 86). But how might educational leaders assume this stance? What does it mean to inspire resistance from positions of positional power in educational systems?

In 1971, Neil Postman and Charles Weingartner co wrote a book titled *The Soft Revolution*. The book, and its companion, *Teaching as a Subversive Activity* (2000) could stand to be dusted off and re-read by a new generation of educational leadership students and professional educators. Considered in tandem, the two books are a blueprint for engaging, and disengaging, an evil or inflexible educational system with social and interpersonal dexterity. The book sustains a coherent thesis through a collection of discontinuous ideas and vignettes designed to encourage students, teachers, parents, and administrators—and anyone who recognizes a need for institutional change toward greater social justice and individual authenticity—to oppose inflexible and insensitive public school systems by starting their own after-school programs, classes, and even schools. *The Soft Revolution* suggests that students and teachers become active members in the school system and local political community by seeking to understand and then using their extant powers and rights, rather than exist as Nietzsche's Last Men—passive and disaffected subjects floating through an alien realm.

Postman makes judo the metaphor for student-facilitated educational change. When using judo, one uses an opponent's strength against them; proactive and thoughtful defense is the only possible form of offense. He transposes this notion to schools by suggesting that working within the system is a more effective solution for instigating change than striking at the system as an outsider. The implication for educational leaders is clear, and in keeping with King's approach—the most effective *revolution* is achieved by guiding *evolution*. Rather than seek revolution, Postman and King would have educational leaders dismantle evil systems in education by using their power and influence to change policy and practice *within the system* at the grassroots level, building support and peer solidarity until the force of change is a new social, and eventually legal, norm. In doing so, educational leaders willing to facilitate change must also understand many things they may have previously taken for granted, and identify what they can change and what they cannot change: in their professional contracts; building, district, and state policies; in their rights as citizens, and; the informal subtleties and legal precedents that pertain to social action they wish to undertake.

The judo metaphor also acknowledges an orientation toward non-violent and creative engagement of a system that affords educators. Essentially, Postman's assertion was that true change will not happen in schools until those educational leaders who recognize injustice instigate a systematic, sustained, and well-considered challenge of formal and informal school norms which disconnect people and groups from their freedom and limit the learning opportunities of students and school professionals. *The Soft Revolution* is a cry for freedom to replace inequity as the dominant social norm and legalistic policy dictum of public schooling.

PAULO FREIRE AND THE PEDAGOGY OF FREEDOM

Freire saw society as marked by severe oppression and poverty, and in education found both the root of the problem and a solution. He called the predominant educational paradigm of his time the "banking concept of education." This banking concept entailed

"...an act of depositing, in which the students are the depositories and the teacher is the depositor. Instead of communicating, the teacher issues communiqués and makes deposits which the students patiently receive, memorize, and repeat...the scope of action allowed to the students extends only as far as receiving, filing, and sorting the deposits" (Freire, 1970).

People educated in such a system lose their humanity. They become unthinking automatons that accept whatever those above them in the institutionalized hierarchy present as valid or truthful. Freire believed that the way forward for oppressed peoples of the world was through the development of critical consciousness, or "the state of seeing one's position in life and the conditions in which one lives as neither unalterable nor inevitable" (Freire, 1973; DeMarrais & LeCompte, 1999). Critical consciousness is developed through a process of dialogics—an iterative process of discovery and learning between people. The result of educating students in a dialogical tradition is the development of conscientizacão, a form of critical consciousness characterized by "learning to perceive social, political, and economic contradictions, and to take action against the oppressive elements of reality" (Freire, 1970). Freire's ideas, which articulate an educational "pedagogy of the oppressed" have inspired oppressed people around the world and helped educators understand the machinations of power in educational systems. In Freire, as in King, we find not only recognition that the dominant freedom was unjust, but also a method for facilitating change through learning and unlearning. A lesson we learn from both King and Freire is that freedom is as much a process toward attainment as it is a quality denied or an outcome denied.

TWO EDUCATIONAL FREEDOMS: DEWEY AND GREENE

For many, discussions of freedom begin and end with the work of philosopher John Dewey. The sheer volume and breadth of Dewey's work is awe-inspiring, representing perhaps the most complete philosophy of education since Plato. Dewey believed that learning occurred progressively, and he "recognized that the child is an active, exploring, inquisitive creature, so the task of education is to foster experience infused by skills and knowledge" (Blackburn, 1996, p. 103). While this assertion may seem a common position among modern educators, it was revolutionary at the beginning of the twentieth century.

Beyond Dewey's interest in learning, he was also fascinated by political philosophy. Specifically, Dewey advocated democracy; but democracy for Dewey was "more than a form of government; it [was] primarily a mode of associated living, of conjoint communicated experience" (Cahn, 1997, p. 292). That is, Dewey believed that a democratic society was "one which makes provision for participation in the good of all its members on equal terms and which secures flexible readjustment of its institutions through interaction of the different forms of associated life" (p. 274). Through this social organization, a conjoined and respectful pursuit of knowledge and freedom would ensue.

As Dewey was concerned with democracy, he was by extension interested in the place and experience of the individual in school and society. Importantly, Dewey wrote a great deal about freedom—as both philosophical and social psychological construct. To Dewey,

"Freedom means essentially the part played by thinking—which is personal—in learning;—it means intellectual initiative, independence in observation, judicious invention, foresight of consequences, and integrity of adaptation to them. But because these are the mental phase of behavior, the needed play of individuality—or freedom—cannot be separated from opportunity for free play of physical movements. Enforced physical quietude may be unfavorable to realization of the problem, to undertaking the observations needed to define it, and to performance of the experiments which test the ideas suggested...But the whole cycle of self-activity demands an opportunity for investigation and experimentation, for trying out one's ideas upon things, discovering what can be done with materials and appliances" (Dewey, 1916/1944, p. 302).

Moreover,

"Regarding freedom, the important thing to bear in mind is that it designates a mental attitude rather than external unconstraint of movements, but that this quality of mind cannot develop without a fair leeway of movements in exploration, experimentation, application, etc. A society based on custom will utilize individual variations only up to a limit of conformity with usage; uniformity is the chief ideal within each class. A progressive society counts individual variations as precious since it finds in them the means of its own growth. Hence a democratic society must, in consistency with its ideal, allow for intellectual freedom and the play of diverse gifts and interests in its educational measures" (p. 305).

So to Dewey, there was an external, social freedom and an internal, personal freedom. While stimulating in students the internal freedoms associated with free inquiry should be the focus of the educator, educational leaders cannot ignore the powerful sway that external freedom has on an individual; nor can they ignore their responsibility to influence formal and informal policy toward the end of protecting and facilitating exploration of various forms of freedom.

Dewey was highly critical of public schools in the United States. Like Freire, he believed that society was doing a great disservice, even malevolence, to its children, handicapping the potential of its youth and compromising the future with drill-and-kill instructional methods and sit-down-and-shut-up authoritarianism. He characterized proponents of his own progressive methods and democratic orientation as being on the side of freedom, the side of "new" education, alternately labeling detractors as adherents to the "old" way. Throughout his work he placed these two perspectives in antagonistic opposition:

"There is a tendency on the part of both the upholders and the opponents of freedom in the school to identify it with absence of social direction, or sometimes, with merely physical unconstraint of movement. But the essence of the demand for freedom is the need of conditions which will enable an individual to make his own special contribution to a group interest, and to partake of its activities in such ways that social guidance shall be a matter of his own mental attitude, and not a mere authoritative diction of his acts" (p. 301).

In what ways are you an upholder and opponent of freedom?

Dewey saw schools of his era as undesirable and unwelcoming institutions "which internally and externally [set] up barriers to free intercourse and communication of experience" (Cahn, 1997, p. 301). Where there should be efficacy there was powerlessness, where there was potential for inclusion, engagement, and meaningfulness, there was isolation, estrangement, and a lack of value. For Dewey, the anodyne for the country's ailing schools was authentic democratic thought and organization. To Dewey, schools should not only protect, but should also *nurture* and facilitate the exploration of internal and external freedoms.

MAXINE GREENE AND THE DIALECTIC OF FREEDOM

In *The Dialectic of Freedom*, Maxine Greene (1988) lamented that few members of society and fewer educators had seized onto Dewey's notion of freedom. Rather, "freedom is still taken to be a given in this country: to be an American is to be endowed with freedom, whether or not one acts on it or fights for it or does anything with it" (p. 26). What is potentially a responsibility to action is viewed as a right, a birthright even. To Greene, much talk of freedom is vapid platitude. She found it maddening that educators refused to walk the path Dewey had blazed before them: Freedom could be used to connect people meaningfully in dialectic processes of authentic learning. Moreover, education—freedom's instrument—was still falling short of realizing its potential.

Greene built on Dewey's ideas of meaningfully connected communities by drawing heavily on Sartre. Greene explained that the existential imperative of action was used by too many as an escape from freedom; that is, people used their freedom of choice to disconnect, to become egocentric, to estrange themselves from meaningful communal relations rather than realize their existential potential for self-emancipation through community (Davies, 1998, p. 43). She argued that people should go forth from their self-constructed enclaves of isolation and (re)join their peers in a caring milieu wherein each became an engaged participant in others' search for freedom.

To Greene, the claiming and protection of personal and communal spaces for the purpose of exploring and realizing freedom is of paramount importance. Indeed, "to find such openings is to discover new possibilities—often new ways of achieving freedom in the world" (Greene, 1988, p. 2). Importantly, when she speaks of space she uses the concept in both a physical and metaphysical sense, and stresses the importance of acting: "We might think of freedom as an opening of spaces as well as perspectives, with everything depending on the actions we undertake in the course of our quest, the *praxis* we learn to devise" (p. 5). For

Greene, the pursuit of an authentically connected community and an authentic personal experience are intimately conjoined:

> "The aim is to find (or create) an authentic public space, that is, one in which diverse human beings can appear before one another as, to quote Hannah Arendt, 'the best they know how to be.' Such a space requires the provision of opportunities for the articulation of multiple perspectives in multiple idioms, out of which something common can be brought into being. It requires, as well, a consciousness of the normative as well as the possible: of what ought to be, from a moral and ethical point of view, and what is in the making, what might be in an always open world. In contexts of this kind, open contexts where persons attend to one another with interest, regard and care, there is a place for the appearance of freedom, the achievement of freedom by people in search of themselves" (Greene, 1988, p. xi).

Greene's voice is distinct among educational scholars. She writes beautifully, if at times a bit abstract, and it is possible to become intoxicated by her stylistic flourishes. In addition to Sartre, Dewey and a host of philosophical and educational sources, Greene repeatedly evokes her muse: literature. In her work we find the words of Woolf, Eliot, Twain, hooks, and Melville. However, her purpose is far from ornamental, Greene (1988) offers a compelling case for aesthetic study and appreciation as a bridge between people where previously we have mostly seen an emphasis on reason (a la Enlightenment influence) or scientific method (a la Dewey or Francis Bacon). Yet, as an old maxim asserts, teaching is both science *and* art. Using aesthetic expression as communication and exploratory tool can be yet another form of dialectical engagement, one that allows a reader/thinker/ educational leader to see the world through another's eyes, heart, and mind—thus engaging their thinking and passion in a powerful perspective (Barone, 1998).

A FINAL THOUGHT ABOUT FREEDOM

The three visions of freedom discussed in this essay—formal freedom, critical freedom, educational freedom(s)—are intended to act as catalyst for both individual reflection and dialogic conversation among educational leaders. As educators increasingly engage concepts such as social justice, equity, and equality and seek to enact them (or ignore them) in thought and practice, there can be no more important discussion than one centered on freedom. The authors reviewed here, and my fellow authors in this book, are by no means the only ones to engage these concepts, but their words and thoughts may serve as a point of departure for many personal and collective journeys toward the exploration and creation of freedom. Ultimately, it is important for educational leaders to position these activities in relation to the freedoms students entrusted to their charge either enjoy or are denied. Again, catalysts for thought are only intended here to be the precursor for action, the beginning of a personal journey that like King and Gandhi's leads to personal and collective liberation for and by just means.

IRA BOGOTCH

SOCIAL JUSTICE AS AN EDUCATIONAL CONSTRUCT

Problems and Possibilities

In this essay, I extend my introductory argument that neither philosophy nor social theories have adequately guided world leaders in how to bring about social justice. The time is now to hear from new voices – particularly those of educators.

In world affairs, educators speak with a minority voice, if they speak at all. We may hold a privileged status in certain parts of the world and receive rhetorical support, but educators often slide into default positions where education is counted among the world's pressing problems. Our power, in both theory and practice, has yet to be heard. Yet, we possess great strength constitutionally, institutionally, politically, and intellectually. The question is how can we unleash our power?

The thesis of this entire book is that *theories of social justice matter*. For this reason alone, I must question existing theories. I do so because I believe that education brings new dynamics to the meaning of theory (e.g., Kemmis, 1996), namely the power of pedagogy, leadership, and educational research methods. It is a power that is meant to improve the world. Thus, my objective here is to re-center social justice debates around new theories and practices of education.

In prior research studies, I relied primarily upon Dewey's dynamic concepts of experience (Bogotch & Taylor, 1993), morality (Bogotch & Roy, 1997), temporality (Bogotch & Roy, 1994), and laboratory learning (Bogotch, 2002) to reveal the paths toward social justice – always, however, as contingent possibilities. Both individuals and communities have deliberately, yet under contingent circumstances, extended learning/education beyond schooling to include the possibilities of social justice, however the term has been defined within international contexts.

Now, in this essay, I offer other theories aligned with Dewey in order to broaden what Britzman (2007) calls our educational imaginations. While the examples used here demonstrate both the problems and possibilities for *social justice as an educational construct*, the arguments are grounded in the premise that neither education nor social justice can ever be guaranteed, not by philosophers, social theorists, constitutions/laws or by ourselves as educators. Real world outcomes result as much from demography, geography (Diamond, 1997), genetics, or any of the social circumstances of life (Hayek, 1976) as they do from being educated. If we can at least make it evident that non-educative definitions of justice and social justice come without guarantees, then hopefully we can open up new spaces for bringing new theories of social justice and education closer together. This will

Ira Bogotch et al. (eds.), Radicalizing Educational Leadership: Dimensions of Social Justice, 79–112.

involve making changes in how we think and act. Specifically, it calls for educators to become *more political* internationally, nationally and locally, *more active* socially in their communities and organizations, and *more critical* of existing educational theories and practices.

I have divided the discussion into two broad categories: the problems of social justice and the possibilities for social justice (see Table 1 below). The latter category extends social justice arguments into pedagogy, leadership, and research as both theories and actions. Under the heading of problems, I describe how and why there can be no guarantees of a better future in this world. Schooling itself is capable of producing suicide bombers, trained killers – e.g., God's Army, child laborers, Nazi youth, spelling bee winners, chess champions, class clowns, as well as adult physicists, mathematicians, economists, soldiers, mechanics, journalists, philosophers, artists, etc. (see Bush & Saltarelli, 2000). All of these outcomes have come to pass and will likely continue into the future. Thus, as both children and adults, we are all connected by our indeterminate futures – some more advantaged than others.

How has education responded to these contingent problems? On the one hand, there are theories and practices that embody critique, reflection, and uncertainty, most recently, the work of Britzman (2007). On the other hand, the dominant mindsets of schooling have been framed by a narrow set of theories, mostly derived from psychology, organizational theory and behaviors, and from externally driven institutional forces, such as markets. The above bodies of knowledge and their resulting practices have served the day-to-day necessities of management and administration of classrooms and schools. They have collectively inscribed strong beliefs in the efficacy of rational planning, best practices, discipline, and problem solving as the aims and ends of education. As a result, the dominant educational practices and theories we hold to be effective, whether from psychology, organizations, or institutionalism have prevented us from actively engaging in politics [e.g., nation-building, community-development] as part of our pedagogy, leadership, and educational research. These limited mindsets hold education and societies captive in terms of future possibilities.

In contrast, there has been a spirit of discovering or, more accurately, re-discovering educational possibilities. Within this sphere of possibilities, education becomes a basic right, has an extra-institutional status beyond schooling, and offers alternative educational theories for pedagogy, leadership, and research.

That said, even if we were to maintain our current ways of thinking or do nothing differently tomorrow – in terms of educational practice or theory, there would still be individuals who are fervently committed to improving the world as they find it. This fact, however, is not a persuasive argument against theorizing, for the test of any social justice theory must be measured against the *status quo*, against the evidence of current educational and worldwide facts. In this light, I urge readers not to think of theory as an abstract discussion; for, the enemies of education already have a clearer understanding of education's political power, and, thus, have increasingly terrorized educators in the 21st century. Witness Taliban Rule No. 25: teachers who ignore Taliban warnings will be killed (multiple sources from The Associated Press and CNN). I do not want to minimize the countless heroic efforts of individual educators, past and present, who make a material difference in peoples' lives every minute of every day in both safe and dangerous settings around the world. Social justice theory explains, critiques, and intervenes in *all* circumstances of life, not just in privileged or western democratic societies. Social justice as an educational construct, therefore, must apply to the material conditions found around the world.

Table 1: Problems and Possibilities of Social Justice as an Educational Construct

The Problems of Social Justice as an Educational Construct	The Possibilities of Social Justice as an Educational Construct
Philosophy and Social Theory have provided no valid predictions or guarantees of a better future.	Education as a basic right.
Organizational thinking: When education is perceived as synonymous with schools and schooling	Beyond schooling: Connecting children, adults, and schools to society.
Limitations of existing educational theories	Critiques and experiments within education: Discourse, advocacy and activism

I. THE PROBLEMS OF SOCIAL JUSTICE AS AN EDUCATIONAL CONSTRUCT

Education, as well as schooling, does not happen in a vacuum. Wherever and whenever education is practiced, social, political, cultural and contextual influences are evident. As a result, education, like social justice, has been unevenly distributed around the world (Bush & Saltarelli, 2000). The philosopher, Iris Young (1990) observed:

Providing educational opportunity certainly entails allocating specific material resources – money, buildings, books, computers, and so on - and there are reasons to think that the more resources, the wider the opportunities offered to children in an educational system. But education is primarily a process taking place in a complex context of social relations. In the cultural context of the United States, male children and female children, working class children and middle class children, Black children and white children often do not have equally enabling educational opportunities even when an equivalent amount of resources has been devoted to their education (p. 26).

In other words, educational opportunities are more than the distribution of resources. For Young, opportunities must be attuned to self respect, identity, autonomy, decision making, choices, cultural and social capital. Not surprisingly, there are no formulae or guarantees that education will lead to socially just outcomes. Thus, the foremost problem facing social justice is that it has been defined by ideas, ideologies, and theories [i.e., problems] which are divorced from the contextual dynamics for individual growth and development in an essentially open-ended world of educational opportunities.

Philosophers, psychologists, and legal scholars have responded to the world's problems by presenting *balanced* views of the world, views that simultaneously uphold external authorities, for example state power, as well as the virtues and values of individual freedoms. To a degree, educators, too, participate in upholding balance. Educators need to continuously validate their own practices, pedagogically and through leadership, while being professionally obligated to teach others the merits of all worldviews. We are obligated professionally to have a position with respect to our own practices and theories; yet, we are also expected to be objective and neutral with respect to others and to our subject matter content. To this extent, educators, too, seek to maintain balance.

However, the different sides of the balance equation create for educators a unique dynamic. On the one hand, we transmit knowledge and culture and teach restraint and other social virtues. On the other hand, we strive to teach freedom, history, and social power (see essays in this volume). If our educational objectives were limited to establishing balance, then we would not be teaching freedom, social power, or any other possibility – as the authors in this volume have defined these terms. Instead, we would be working to preserve current ideas and practices, leaving authorities and power relationships uncontested. If the purposes of education, however, are social, ethical, and political, that is, to teach others to question, critique, and act in socially just ways, we would be working to question and disrupt balance, bringing forth new ideas, as part of the dynamic processes of education. We as educators are responsible for continuously engaging with others pedagogically – not just in the delivery of already existing [i.e., balanced] answers, however satisfying the latter processes may be to these others. Hence, to re-center social justice as an educational construct requires *more than* the distribution of resources and *more than* maintaining balance. In this role, educators go beyond the limits, that is, problems, inscribed by laws, psychology, and rational philosophy. For educational leaders, it is important to understand these established limits and the social, political, and economic processes which maintain balance in order to discover our own professional powers and responsibilities to engage with others in and out of schools: that is, our possibilities.

I. A. 1. BETTER FUTURES PROMISED BY PHILOSOPHY, SOCIAL THEORIES, AND THE LAW

Unless, we as educators can destabilize current worldviews, that is, replace war with peace, replace injustices with justice, replace poverty with wealth, and replace the lack of health care with universal health care, the possibilities for social justice are limited; but, no more so than the limits derived from existing social justice theories emanating from philosophy, social theory or the law. The limits found in philosophy, psychology, and the law revolve around on-going debates between the balance of the state's police power to alleviate social injustices [e.g., child labor gender inequities] and individual freedoms [e.g., civil rights] to do "as he [sic] likes so long as he does not interfere with the liberty of others to do the same..." (Rehnquist, 2004, p. 107).

Often missing from these serious discussions, however, is the place of education. When education is debated, however, it, too, is constrained by the balance arguments. That is, there are educational theories that present stable ideas, identifiable patterns, dominant stages of development, diagnoses of readiness, etc. versus educational theories that are a matter of *endless reconstructions, ever-evolving, never-ending worlds* (Garrison, 1999), *fluid entities*, and *continuously more problems* (Rorty, 1998). The evidence on both sides of these educational debates can be persuasive, just as they are for other academic disciplines. The consequences, however, are always more intimate, immediate, and greater in education (Kemmis, 1996) than in these other disciplines. Listen to the defense of education offered by Socrates:

And if I tell you that no greater good can happen to a man than to discuss human excellence every day and the other matters about which you have heard me arguing and examining myself and others, and that an unexamined life is not worth living, then you will believe me still less. But that is so, my friends, though it is not easy to persuade you (Apology, XXVIII l. 38 ff.).

Socrates understood how difficult it is to make the educationalist argument persuasive. But let us still try.

I.A.1. A. LIMITS OF PHILOSOPHY

In philosophy, there have been many arguments over the word "justice." They begin, not surprisingly, with the search for a definition. Frederick Hayek (1976) shared his initial frustrations in his research.

The more I tried to give it [i.e., justice] a definite meaning, the more it fell apart—the intuitive feeling of indignation which we undeniably often experience in particular instances proved incapable of being justified by a general rule such as the conception of justice demands (p. xi).

Continuing, he wrote,

It is not pleasant to have to argue against a superstition held most strongly by men and women who are often regarded as the best in our society, and again a belief that has become also the new religion of our time (and in which many of the ministers of old religion have found their refuge), and which has become the recognized mark of the good man" (p. xii).

To Hayek, we live in an unpredictable and spontaneously ordered world; therefore, any theory of social justice is only a mirage. Worse than a mirage, however, is the ever-present danger of living without freedom in a so-called "just" system. For Hayek and many other philosophers, freedom is a first principle of civilization, not justice as measured by balance, stability, and predictability.

Another philosopher, Karl Popper (1945), described the absence of freedom as "the enemy of open systems," citing both Plato and Marx as prime movers of closed-system thinking which made justice synonymous with their conceptions of ideal societies. In so doing, Popper argued that Plato and Marx aligned justice to a fixed and deterministic set of beliefs governing everyone's daily and future actions. Plato conceived of justice as a fundamental and natural principle of all ordinary lives inside of a just society. He rejected *real* world behaviors that invoked the natural right of the strong (p. xx), unlimited self-assertions (p. 32), and encroachment on others' rights to function freely (p. 128). These were unjust "habits of mind" (p. 142) which occurred in imperfect people and in imperfect political systems, falling outside of his Republic. Plato made justice a natural consequence of *all actions* in a just society and the product of individuals' *free* "habits of minds" (p. 142) so that everyone freely chooses a just life and everyone is fully protected from any wrongdoings inside the just society.

Plato and Marx offered powerful arguments on behalf of their totally just systems. To Hayek (1979), however, it is impossible for everyone in society to agree *freely* on a particular law or effect unless one lived in a totalitarian state that demanded that everyone see propositions in the same way. The conditions under which Plato established freedom were ideal, a utopia, based on human and societal perfection as real possibilities. To understand Plato, the ideal and the real must become one and the same concept. There is no room for imperfections as far as behaviors or choices. Reason becomes an all-encompassing reality.

Hayek (1976) and Popper (1945), however, saw human conditions and societal imperfections as realities. In their real worlds, free choice could and has been replaced by totalitarian regimes. Hayek described how rules, including local laws, would have to be passed in order to guarantee societies' promises.

> To succeed …government would have to do more than merely ensure that the conditions affecting the positions of the individuals were the same for all which necessarily depend on its actions. It would have to control effectively all the external conditions influencing the success of an individual's efforts. And conversely, freedom of choice would lose all importance if somebody had power to determine, and therefore would know, the opportunities of the different individuals (p. 10).

Further, according to Hayek (1976),

> There are many bureaucratic regimes that certainly follow the rules and are utterly predictable, and some are undeniably just. A Hegelian state run by impeccable universal class, would be just by any standards in administering existing rules fairly (p. 106).

That is not the freedom or justice that any of us as freedom loving people can subscribe to.

A.1. B. JUSTICE IS ESSENTIALLY AN OPEN EMPIRICAL QUESTION

The eighteenth century Scottish empiricist David Hume (1777/1952) asked, "Are there any marks of a distributive justice in the world (p. 157)?" To which he himself responded affirmatively, negatively, and in a "medium between affirmation and negation" (p. 157). Thus, for Hume, justice was an open-ended, empirical question, not an already developed, *a priori* theory accessible through reason [or faith] alone.

Similarly, for William James (1891/1968), the American pragmatist, the most important philosophical divide throughout history has been the debate between "the one" and "the many," which extended to debates among rationalists and empiricists, secularists and religious authorities, and moderns and post-moderns. For James, the test of any theory rested on its practical utility. If an answer [i.e., "the one" or "the many"] did not make a practical difference, then either explanation might be acceptable. Conversely, only if the consequences of a particular theory mattered would there be a *real* philosophical problem in terms of deciding which explanation should prevail.

Following this logic, the question *what matters* would be different for different people over time and space. No one fixed worldview, e.g., Plato or Marx, would have an absolute claim to a privileged position over another worldview. Differences would be debated and even fought over, again and again. In such a world, pragmatism is consistent with liberal definitions of justice. That is, as long as a person's [or peoples' collectively] actions did not harm others, then individuals should be free to make decisions and act accordingly. Thus, the validity or truth of a theory of justice is left to *others* to judge for themselves according to the merits of the arguments as well as the consequences. Here James speaks more like an educator who is charged with teaching people how to think, and in thinking, freedom emerges as a necessary component of justice for both the actors and those acted upon. However, this is not a freedom based on teaching fixed or known first principles of civilization, but rather a freedom that emerges pedagogically and critically through mutually beneficial human interactions. Thus, freedom or social justice as an educational construct becomes a practical social theory of action.

Such views were supported by philosophers writing from many different traditions – which was exactly what James had asserted was the "cash value" of pragmatism. For example, Marcuse (1970), a critical theorist, argued that reason presented a false reality and that revolution required an "aesthetic-erotic dimension [which] comes to mind almost spontaneously" (p. 68). It is a "qualitative difference" (p. 69) in terms of dispositions, relationships, and institutions in contrast to the way we currently live. Elster (1995) suggested a modest, heuristic role for empirical findings in questioning fixed, normative approaches to justice. Postmodern theorists also seek to create space and disrupt the hold of rationalism. Usher and Edwards' (1996) paraphrased one of the leading postmodern thinkers, Jean-Francois Lyotard, as follows:

> …'consensus' like the 'social totality' is outmoded. Justice can only be built around the recognition of the variety that exists in language games and consensus is localized to players of particular language games (p. 183).

I. A.1.C. CONTEMPORARY JUSTICE THEORIES: A "PRACTICAL" NEW BALANCE?

A more contemporary idea of justice has surfaced as *cosmopolitanism* (Hayden, 2002; Appiah, 2006). Simply put, cosmopolitanism means universality plus difference (Appiah, 2006). The world presents itself with peoples of different cultures living in nation-states, some of which function better than others. Appiah (2006) has argued that solutions have to be found in *decent* policies, governance and institutions (p. 169). Yet, others disagree, (see also Marcuse, 1970; Diamond, 1999) arguing that philosophy, policies, governance, and institutions are themselves the problems [i.e., hegemonic policies, proximate causes, and practices] and only by transforming, if not also erasing them can humanity hope to ever achieve *social* justice.

For Appiah (2006), however, cosmopolitanism provides real answers by going to the "why" of the world's problems-which means going beyond good intentions, conversations, and what he called "shallow pond" solutions that "save the same children over and over again" (p. 167).

Whether the solutions offered be of the shallow pond type or not, when justice has been considered variously as philosophy, social theory, law, morality, religion, etc., the necessity of theory has been at the center of the debates. Nevertheless, *social* justice theories have *not* yet been sufficient to eliminate real world problems, whether of tribal, ethnic, or national conflicts, local or national poverty, the environmental health of our planet, or the lack of universal health care. Relative to human development and progress, the litany of social, political, and economic problems, some rising to the level of *injustices* (see Roberts, 2005), may be as great today as they have ever been in recorded history. Hence, we must ask, why has the *necessity* of theory failed us?

One response is to challenge Appiah (2006) on whether cosmopolitanism provides real answers in today's world. Hayden (2002) pointed out that the most prominent theory of justice to date, by Rawls (1971, 1999), is essentially a domestic theory, applicable to advanced western societies only. Rawls accepted this criticism. Yet, this admission has not limited others from universalizing his theory to the world as a whole, as if it were cosmopolitan, as if life were how Plato saw it inside of his Republic.

In opposition, Neuhaus (1988) argued that

> Whether we are aware of it or not, we are each participants in a particular historically contingent tradition, and those who flit betwixt and between in order to develop a more 'universal' perspective are indulging in a frivolous model of pseudo-cosmopolitanism (p. 66).

Unfortunately, world events, especially those in the first decade of the 21st century, seem to have reverted back to Rawls' theory which privileges the west in terms of justice and democracy. We can read in op-ed pieces (e.g., David Brooks, Thomas Friedman, *New York Times*) and foreign policy journals and see US-UK foreign policy being enacted in terms of a "clash of civilizations," a world divided by progressive [i.e., western] and backward cultures [i.e., Islamic and other non-western cultures] (Harrison, 2006).

How can social justice as an educational construct disrupt on-going world policy debates? Education and educators are not even at the policy-making tables. While we can acknowledge political, economic and social crises that rise to more immediate concerns, that take priority over education in cases of war, violence, and terrorism, we must also assert that history and current events are replete with repeated incidents of war, violence, and the most serious of human and social problems, such as child abuse, child labor, child prostitution, poverty, disease, hunger, potable water, and sexual abuse. None of these problems has been solved by other disciplines. Political science, economics and social theory responses to real social and political problems, that have ignored education, are, therefore, not *ipso facto* more appropriate, i.e., valid theoretically. Why then have the alternative empirical options of education not been re-considered as a viable if not the *better social justice response*? Can we begin to articulate what that response would be? Before we do, however, there are still more problems, limits, that will need to be addressed.

I. A. 1.D. THE RATIONAL POWER OF FEAR: PSYCHOLOGICAL GUARANTEES

There are theories of justice that emphasize freedom, cultural values, choice, and unpredictable consequences. Conversely, there are justice theories that look to universal principles and higher authorities-secular and sectarian-for ethical and spiritual guidance. Along the many paths to social justice, there are hard and soft versions for each of the different theories. How one sees the tensions between individual freedoms and the powers of state authorities largely determines the kind of social justice definition that is promulgated. That is, where one finds a comfortable balance largely determines the definition.

Sigmund Freud (1962) saw antagonistic tensions between individual freedom and community:

[The] replacement of the power of the individual by the power of the community constitutes the decisive step of civilization.... The first requisite of civilization, therefore, is that of justice (p. 42).

Freud may have been driven by the Hobbesian psychological fear of a state of nature – a fear that is pervasive in many parts of the world, and, according to Bush and Saltarelli (2000), readily evident inside some schools:

The fear to act because of the constant threat of punishment is transformed into a subconscious, cultural predisposition not to act. It becomes better to ignore, forget, or selectively see the world, than to live with the corrosive omnipresence of fear. In such settings, the school system can be a force for change by sustaining hope, courage, and imagination in the minds of students. However, for the large part, under the conditions described above, the regime's efforts to control the population involve the subordination of all public institutions – especially schools – to its political objectives. Both the content and the process of schooling become a means through which the regime attempts to shape ideas and affect behaviour in ways that glorify its own project and inculcate obedience. Violence or the threat of violence within the school becomes an essential ingredient in this process. While dissent may remain in hidden forms within schools, the overarching form of response is silence (p. 26).

Postmodern thinkers, who are also fearful of domination and oppression, de-center everything from the role of the human subject to disciplinary practices to concepts that begin with capital letters as in rational with a capital "R" (Biesta, 2006).

One influential line of thinking holds that democracy needs rational individuals who are capable of making their own free and independent judgments. This idea, which was first formulated by Enlightenment philosophers more than two centuries ago and has remained influential up to the present day, has led to the belief that it is the task of schools to `create' or `produce' such individuals. It has promoted the idea that schools should make children `ready for democracy' by instilling in them the knowledge, skills, and dispositions that will turn them into democratic citizens" (p. 119).

In the name of Rationalism, it could be argued that educators – even in western democracies - have not been able to take the fear out of pedagogy as theory or as educational leadership. Implicit in this analysis are limitations with respect to governance and social control. That is, the very processes of schooling as a rational function have been imposed upon educators with respect to theory development, structures, policies, and practices, including discipline and testing. For example, we ask, how do we treat the immature, child mind and still teach the possibilities for social justice, i.e., how do we give the child the priority of freedom (Strike, 1989)? How do we balance obedience and restraint with a child's capacity of exercising his/her free will; for, without a sense of freedom to learn, education is mechanical and routine (see Rusk, 1929, pp. 176-177)? How do we do all this inside institutions and organizations that deny justice to administrators and teachers (Strike, 1989)? These questions go to the very heart of liberal justice definitions grounded in the western philosophy of Enlightenment and Rationality (Biesta, 2006). How do we, as educators, remove the capital letters, and fear, from our teachings?

I. A. 2. CONSTITUTIONAL PROMISES: A LEGITIMATE BALANCING ACT?

With respect to guaranteed futures, national constitutions seek to position education as a basic or fundamental right under their state responsibility. However, when those charged with state responsibility can not or do not protect education or other rights, citizens may legitimately question the authority behind constitutional promises. This state of affairs introduces the philosophical concept of *public justification* (http://plato.stanford.edu/entries/justification-public, retrieved June 1, 2007).

The idea of public justification translates into the fact that a regime can be judged to be legitimate based on whether its policies are perceived as reasonable from an individual's perspective. Under the criterion of public justification, the gap between constitutional promises and realities become apparent. There is not only a distance between "what is" and "what should be" in a nation-state, but there is also a realization that national governments are not seriously addressing educational issues. That conclusion is easily transferable from nation-states to local school authorities, including administrators and teachers. In fact, this conjunction was implicitly revealed by Bush and Saltarelli (August, 2000) in their report titled "The two faces of education in ethnic conflict." They wrote:

> Education is often used as a panacea for a broad spectrum of social ills, from racism to misogyny. While the impact of such initiatives has been mixed, their starting premise is the same: that formal education can shape the understandings, attitudes, and ultimately, the behaviour of individuals. If it is true that education can have a socially constructive impact on intergroup relations, then it is equally evident that it can have a socially destructive impact (p. 9).

The authors conducted their research for the Innocenti Center under the auspices of UNICEF. While their conceptual framework focused on ethnicity, they acknowledged other possible causes of conflict, violence, and hatred, such as history, economics, bad governance, cultural identity, ideology, politics, religion, and skin color. And while they themselves made no mention of national constitutions, rather, they focused on United Nations' international efforts, their examples of schools and schooling being used for hatred and violence are compelling. Still, it is worthwhile to note what constitutions have to say about the promises of education.

Education, in most societies, the United States being an exception, is protected by national constitutions. The term, education, appears twenty-nine times in the Chinese constitution, including five as the titles of Articles in its Constitution. In today's volatile world, there are approximately 210 constitutions among the 219 nations listed in the UNESCO data-base. Most contain explicit promises to protect and extend education. While it is beyond the scope of this investigation to make a *prima facie* case of inequities based solely on constitutional provisions, it is evident that nations make constitutional promises publicly to their citizens, and that their citizens can then judge for themselves whether these promises are true or false depending upon how it affects them and their families.

At one end of the world community are the examples of the Sudanese states of Darfur, and the nations of Chad, and Afghanistan- where human tragedies are occurring daily. In the Sudan, youth illiteracy in 2004 was at 74.6 percent, among the highest in the world. Yet Article 12 of the 1998 Sudanese constitution reads

> The State mobilizes its official resources and the popular institutions for combating illiteracy and ignorance, strengthening educational systems, and promoting science, research, scientific cooperation and facilitating access to education and research. It also encourages all forms of arts and seeks to encourage society to adopt religious values, piety, and activities beneficial to social development.

In nearby Chad, where many refugees from Darfur have fled, the constitution has one short article, 35, devoted to education that states that elementary education is free, compulsory, and a fundamental right for all citizens. Neither of these two constitutions reflect the educational realities experienced by the citizens in the Darfur states.

In Afghanistan. Article 220 of the 2001 constitution calls for "suitable environments for the education of girls as well as boys." Yet, recent reports from Afghanistan, however, describe how dangerous life is for girls – and their families – to be educated – even when their studies involve memorizing passages from the Quran (Constable, 2006).

> Children's education was once touted as an exceptional success in this struggle new democracy. Within two years of the 2001 overthrow of the Taliban…, officials boasted that 5.1 million children of both sexes were enrolled in public schools (p. 24).

Continuing civil war has forced many Afghani children back into their homes. A UNICEF representative was quoted as saying "With all that the children of Afghanistan have gone through, to expose them to this kind of violence is appalling (Constable, p, 26).

Consistent with Bush and Saltaratelli's (2000) thesis, some constitutions speak explicitly about protecting ethnic differences and building national unity. Section 75: Congress: No. 17 of the Argentine Constitution states: "To guarantee respect for the identity and the right to bilingual and intercultural education…". No. 18 calls for "…progress of education…university educational plans…". No. 19 states: "To enact laws referring to the organization and basis of education consolidating national unity…". Other national constitutions focus on child-parent relationships and the educational responsibilities of parents; others emphasize subject areas or ideologies. But what constitutions cannot do is guarantee the ideals contained in their educational articles and provisions.

As a result, national constitutions are both problems and possibilities as we will see later. Beyond constitutions, however, is how judges interpret local laws in relationship to constitutions, that is, how the law reaches a balanced response. On one side of this issue, Rehnquist (2004) cites a dissent written by Supreme Court Justice Oliver Wendell Holmes, illustrating a strict reading of the constitution:

> …my agreement or disagreement has nothing to do with the right of a majority to embody their opinions in law. It is settled by various decisions of this Court that state constitutions and state laws may regulate life in many ways which we as legislators might think as injudicious, or if you like as tyrannical, as this, and which, equally with this, interfere with the liberty to contract…. The liberty of the citizen to do as he likes so long as he does not interfere with the liberty of others to do the same, which has been a shibboleth for some well-known writers, is interfered with by school laws, by the Post Office, by every state or municipal institution which takes his money for the purposes thought desirable, whether he likes it or not…. A Constitution is … made for people of fundamentally differing views, and the accident of our finding certain opinions natural and familiar, or novel, and even shocking, ought not to conclude our judgment upon the question

whether statutes embodying them conflict with the Constitution of the United States [108 U/S. 75-6 (1905), pp. 107-08 in Rehnquist, 2004)

Thus, the case for a strict interpretation of the constitution is upheld, even if that standard interferes with liberal notions of justice [and freedom] – as it does daily within schools (see Strike, 1989). Yet, Rehnquist (2004) then pointed out that the notion of "equity" was added to the law in order to give the courts/judges discretion in "weighing the circumstances or context surrounding any set of facts in a case" (p. 157). For the political philosopher Iris Young (1990), this is always a matter of politics.

> ...in the myth of the social contract, the people delegate their authority to the government officials, who are charged with making decisions impartially, looking only to the general interest, and not favoring any particular interests,,, (p. 112)...

> [I]t is not simply possible for flesh and blood decisionmakers, whether in government or not, to adopt the standpoints of transcendental reason when they make decisions... (p. 114).

Yet, when it comes to decisions within organizations, in psychology, or educational theories, the question of balance has been decided by conservative proponents who find objectivity and neutrality in our structures, theories, and practices – limiting the need for questions, critique, politics, advocacy, and activism.

I. B. 1. ORGANIZATIONAL THINKING: EDUCATION AS SYNONYMOUS WITH SCHOOLS AND SCHOOLING

Educators work within powerful ideological institutions (van Dijk, 1998). Although educational reformers throughout history have not found it difficult to identify problems and contradictions within and across schools and society and between adults and children, the power of schools as ideological institutions is often depicted as benign, or at worst, as cultural reproduction (Bourdieu and Passaron, 1977; Bowles & Gintis, 1976). In reality, the situation translates into conditions that are far more dangerous.

For example, the two organizational environments that are most repressive under Hayek's criterion of rules of control are totalitarian regimes and organizations as closed bureaucracies. Dewey (1939), in fact, described education in one particular totalitarian nation, Nazi Germany.

> Its schools were so efficient that the country had the lowest rate of illiteracy in the world, the scholarship and scientific researches of its universities were known through the civilized globe..." (p. 42).

Their schools were both effective and efficient. Dewey described the practices he found inside them.

That the schools have mostly been given to imparting information ready-made, along with teaching the tools of literacy, cannot be denied. The methods used in acquiring such information are not those which develop skill in inquiry and in testing of opinions. On the contrary, they are positively hostile to it. They tend to dull native curiosity, and to load powers of observation and experimentation with such a mass of unrelated material that they do not operate as effectively as they may in an illiterate person (p. 149).

Further, what makes the Bush and Saltarelli (2000) Innocenti Center report so remarkable is that their research presents a graphic picture of the negative face of education – as schooling – by specifically identifying "peacedestroying" and "conflict-maintaining" aspects of education. In so doing, they reveal to us the dynamic power of education for both good and evil. They identified:
– the uneven distribution of education as a means of creating or preserving positions of economic, social and political privilege
– education as a weapon in cultural repression
– denial of education as a weapon of war
– education as a means of manipulating history for political purposes
– education serving to diminish self-worth and encourage hate
– segregated education as a means of ensuring inequality, inferiority, and stereotypes
– the role of textbooks in impoverishing the imagination of children and thereby inhibiting them from dealing with conflict constructively.

In the face of limitations and problems, the balance argument has not been a powerful theory of social justice, philosophically, socially, politically, or legally. The argument serves a functional purpose in helping to maintain stability of nations, communities, theories, and even individuals' mental, i.e., psychological, states. But it is not a valid theory of social justice. Therefore, it should not be surprising that Hayek, the market economist and philosopher, Popper, the philosopher of science, Marcuse, the critical theorist, Dewey, the progressive educator and philosopher, and leading postmodern thinkers [e.g., Lyotard] – all coming from different ideological positions, have arrived at the same conclusion *vis a vis* justice; namely, there is a verifiable contradiction between justice viewed totally as a state responsibility and justice that effects individuals' lives personally.

I. B. 1.A. ROLES AND RULES

Social justice, as a duty or responsibility, is not yet a part of an educator's formal job description nor is it defined as subject matter in state mandated curricula; nor is it intrinsic in instructional methods, other than those found in some critical pedagogies (Cochran-Smith, 2004). In terms of roles and functions, social justice is still outside schools and schooling.

In contrast, there are individuals who practice social justice in any field or profession-including that of education (see Bogotch, 2002; Theoharis, 2004). They do so by embracing multiple roles in addition to their formal job titles. In an obituary for the Reverend William Sloan Coffin, whose career as a Presbyterian clergy spanned tenures at Yale University and at Riverside Church in Manhattan, this duality was made explicit and real.

> Every minister is given two roles: the priestly and the prophetic. The prophetic role is the disturber of the peace, to bring the minister himself, the congregation and entire social order under some judgment. If one plays a prophetic role, it's going to mitigate against his priestly role. There are going to be those who will hate him (Shudel & Bernstein, April 14, 2006, p. 8b).

What would it take to make this duality – contradiction - more explicit for educators? How might social justice become part of an educator's professional responsibilities as well as lived daily experiences? In asking these questions, I am mindful of the liberal tenet that unless these new roles and tasks were deliberately and freely chosen, there can be no justice.

The divide in terms of roles and tasks represents the perceived separation between schooling and society. Dewey (1939), of course, never accepted this division; yet, schools as a matter of fact function apart from societies in many ways. Schooling problems have not been reinterpreted through the lenses of social or political problems. Why? Universal and compulsory education keep both children and K-12 educators away from the mainstream of daily life in communities and society. Educators, including building administrators, are often "locked down" during long periods of time for test preparations or just ordinary routines of their worklives. Educators do not as a rule or by practice visit other schools or walk the streets of their school's communities-except on rare occasions-a limitation for educators and students noted throughout the history of schools and schooling. The long hours-on and off the job- and daily routines of schooling keep system-bound educators insulated from communities and civic engagement in daily discussions or in the study of *Big Ideas*, *Complex Thinking*, and *New New Things*.

The separation of school and society is not only physical, but also educational.

> We have been negligent in coming to a sense of quickening change of life in our time and its implications for the educational process. We have not share with our teachers the benefits of new discovery, new insight, new artistic triumph. Not only have we operated with the notion of the self-contained classroom but also with the idea of the self-contained school – even the self-contained educational system (Bruner, 1966, pp. 125-126)

And,

> Many schools are like little islands set apart from the mainland of life by a deep moat of convention and tradition. Across the moat there is a drawbridge, which is lowered at certain periods during the day in order that the part-time inhabitants may cross over to the island in the morning and go back to the mainland at night. Why do these young people go out to the island? They go there in order to learn how to live on the mainland (Carr, 1942:34).

Educators themselves have not been educated in how to conduct systematic research on educational theories or practice or to do close textual analyses of

93

complex scientific, philosophical or social science theories; their curricula in postsecondary education courses focus primarily on methods and procedures-albeit very important. Therefore, the historical and contemporary debates surrounding social justice are not easily accessible or deemed relevant to either the everyday practices of educators, when procedural matters as well as the transmission of knowledge, customs, and traditions all come first.

That there are administrators and teachers who engage in social justice lessons despite these institutionalized realities of schools and schooling, there can be no doubt. Moreover, in many instances, the work of educators is the students' first and only introduction to discussions of values. An emerging and important empirically-based literature on social justice and educational leadership is beginning to provide concrete examples of these just actions by practicing educators in and around schools (e.g., Theoharis, 2004). For purposes of theory, however, these practices will need to be rigorously examined in order extract the different principles and values common to these practices. We need theory as a guideline for continuing thoughts and actions among educators, otherwise we will be left with examples illustrating activities and actions which may be categorized in a taxonomy as either just or unjust actions.

Thus, when we combine the limits of social theory and philosophy with the constraints established by roles, rules, and organizational structures, the problems for social justice as an educational construct become evident. The daily constraints placed on teachers and administrators within schools – e.g., chemistry teachers having to "check out vinegar and baking soda from the front office because something bad might happen in class" (Siberman, June, 2006, p.200) – have a chilling effect on educators [i.e., the dominance of fear] outside of school buildings, settings for social justice. More and more researchers are beginning to tell realist tales of the dark side of teaching and administration. But that is not our purpose here. Rather, we are seeking a theory of pedagogy and leadership that may guide us towards change and social justice.

Before that discussion of possibilities, however, I will address the last problem: limitations of educational theories themselves.

I. C.1. LIMITATIONS OF EDUCATIONAL THEORIES: DEVELOPMENT AND LEARNING

In general, school administrators and school teachers do not systematically test or retest educational theories. That is, practicing educators do not engage in systematic or critically grounded methods of research. What they do is a kind of informal research; they adjust their theories to fit situations. In so doing, however, the theories themselves become the standards and their practices either exceed or fall short of expectations. While educators do learn from practice and they do question authority, their relationships to theory are often not strong enough to disrupt existing theories or radically change practices, individually or organizationally.

From the beginning, educators have been introduced to a small set of theories to guide their thinking about teaching, learning, and leading. Most of the learning theories have come out of psychology. According to Jerome Kagan (1989).

We work [in psychology] with the unfortunate burden of a small number of concepts used repeatedly to refer to a large number of different phenomena; hence the same word may not have the same theoretical meaning (4).

Jerome Bruner (1990), too, acknowledged the narrowing of concepts that are evident in psychology. Given the ideology of education as a global phenomenon, "old theories and approaches are seldom discredited because they are explicitly proven false or inadequate" (van Dijk, 1998, p. 4).

The names of specific theories are often attached to the theorists themselves. The list has evolved into a classic canon: Montessori, Froebel, Piaget, Vygotski, Erickson, Kolhberg, Tyler, Bruner, Banks, Maslow, Bennis, Fullan among others. Their theories differ as well as the methods of induction and deduction that produced them. All of these theories contribute to our knowledge base in teaching and leadership. My point, however, is twofold: the theories themselves are limited and they require on-going critiques in practice.

My reading of theory, Dewey and others, tells me that educational theorists themselves often present their initial conceptual frameworks [i.e., theories] as hypotheses – derived from experiences, which call for re-testing of the ideas [by themselves and others] (see Bogotch, 2005). Erickson (1963) noted in his now classic study of adolescents, "in this sense, this is and must be a subjective book, a *conceptual itinerary* (p. 17). Tyack (1974) asserted that his historical and sociological methods "[did] violence to the kaleidoscopic surface and hidden dynamics of everyday life" (p. 4). Such statements represent a pervasive intellectual honesty among educational researchers. Similar statements found in prefaces, introductions, and conclusions are more common than not. Yet, researchers as theorists have had little or no control over how their ideas will be interpreted or implemented.

Thus, once a theory, or more accurately, a hypothesis, has been developed empirically and conceptually, there is a tendency to make it into a fixed and immutable truth rather than a hypothesis originally meant to generate further discussion and systematic replications by others, including practicing educators. When educational ideas are presented as best practices, the field of education loses the strength of practitioners' willingness to question, critique, and continuously learn. Thus, the generative line of educational ideas is stunted. Over time, educational practice is measured against the inscribed *a priori* theories [independent of immediate experiences] which were developed through empirical methods. Thus, education has moved further from direct experiences and learning from practice. In fact, direct experiences and learning from practice have become justifiable ways for educators to resist new ideas. Quite a paradox (see Britzman, 2007).

Unlike Kuhn's dynamic scientific revolutions, alternative educational theories, that is, new findings from classroom and school experiences, have not been able to challenge the existing paradigmatic theories; moreover, the dominant theories themselves have not been used generatively to test or explore new ideas or guide educational experiments. Existing theories are structurally delivered within a set of self-sealing classrooms, schools and national educational systems. For many reasons, articulated clearly in Dewey's writings, the teaching of static or outdated ideas seems to be more preferable than asking difficult questions and expecting complicated answers. Already-existing knowledge, rote memorization, overemphasis on cognitive skills, words, an emphasis on conformity and obedience have become the norms – and accountability measures - of schools, school practices, and schooling. Practices and theories persist without new skepticism and experimentation-leaving persistent doubt and critique absent from our ideas and professional practices.

The limits of our theory extend to educational institutions. We have built schools and conceptualized schooling upon the categories of age and grade levels. These have become the "abiding frameworks" as Dewey called them even though the theorists themselves offered their ideas as hypotheses not as validated, universal truths. Such theories have brought us "punishment, tracking, grading, and honors programs (Purpel, 2004/2007). The psychologist, R.D. Laing, quoting from the cultural studies of Jules Henry (1963), observed that in American schools.

> A skilled teacher sets up many situations in such a way that a negative attitude can be construed only as treason. The function of questions like, "which one of you nice, polite boys would like to ..." (p. 69).

Just as an educator must negotiate the meanings of a child's plea that some rule or action is *not fair,* so, too, must the researcher negotiate the meanings of the data by interpreting intentions and consequences, politically, socially, and, educationally. It is not unusual for a practitioner to apply a non-negotiated standard onto a whole school, grade, class, or group in the name of *fairness.* For example, I have heard a teacher saying, "because table one did not follow the rules, we will all have to put away our books and sit quietly with our hands folded in front of us for the next ten minutes." Should we attribute such practices to the lack of experience, skill, or knowledge? Or, have similar practices emerged in schools because of the structural and cultural conditions presented to teachers and administrators?

Educational leaders struggle against real institutional barriers that infect us mentally and physically. As much as we need organizations, laws, rules, and structures, we also are made individually and collectively to suffer inside them. R.D. Laing (1972) described the negative effects psychologically in terms of defense mechanisms and a defeatist mentality developed by both the people and organizations which he attributed to the lack of power.

> We act on our experience at the behest of the others, just as we behave in compliance with them. We are taught what to experience and what not to experience, as we are taught what movements to make and what sounds to emit (p. 59).

We say that children should become critical thinkers. But do schoolchildren speak out or have they been taught to follow and obey as a matter of structure and routine? How have schools taught freedom and justice? If teachers do not model such behaviors, how can they teach them? Instead, many educators look to reduce anxiety, limit ambiguities and uncertainties. In their search for best practices, educators are ready to receive, be reassured, and then as caring teachers, to reassure others. By education and disposition, educators are doers, men and women of action; educators are problem-solvers of immediate conflicts. For the most part, educators are a caring segment of a nation's population, people who enter education with ideas of making a difference, doing something enjoyable and worthwhile.

In practical terms, what separates K-12 educators from other working adults is that many of us are around students, including children, every day. To a researcher, students are data. What can we learn from interacting with them? Students are an untapped source of learning. They are, or should be, the lessons we teach. In Sizer and Sizer's (1999) *The Students are Watching*, the authors documented the insights of high school students on the daily routines in and out of class. Their insights confirmed that students are able to construct different meanings-in contrast to adults- from their interactions inside the cultures of schools and society. In this case, different may also connote better. That is, Sizer and Sizer presented students' perceptual data in constructing the processes and behaviors with meanings that could be re-negotiated between the students and educators. Unfortunately, the authors documented that the adults did not learn from their students, but rather imposed their limited set of theories onto them. As a result, instead of seeing students as bringing new and collaborative ideas to the practice of education, the students were quickly categorized into pre-existing categories of the good and bad, slow and gifted, etc.

In practical terms, this situation can be turned around with direct action (see below). The solution is a matter of elevating our professional judgments and systemic thinking about education and humanity as we work inside institutions and organizations, some of which are oppressive. School children are told to walk down the hall with their fingers on lips or raise their hands before speaking. They should also be taught that these school practices are contextual and of limited use outside of their institutional settings. If we do not teach this explicitly, then we are likely to create a society in which adults have their fingers on their lips and who defer to higher authorities as a matter of adult habit. It is left up educators not to assume or extend institutional/organizational rules and roles as if they apply to the whole of the person or to a community or to the world. Unless we make these lessons explicit to *others*, then the definitions of a good student, a good girl or boy moves uninterruptedly and unreflectively straight into society with obvious consequences (see Jacques Maritain, 1943/1960). It is the responsibility of educators to see the whole world and bring that world into focus for others. The world must be made relevant as part of the daily lessons of schools and life.

Lastly, we are taught at universities that one way to bring about systemic change is through research. Goodlad (2004) described how in writing of his classic *A Place Called Schools,* he collected over "20,000 pieces of data (data points) on each school" (p. 290).

I regard careful inquiry as necessary to gaining insights into not only the ongoing practices of human affairs but also the deeply seated assumptions that guide them. These assumptions are rarely brought to the level of consciousness by the parents, students, and teachers closely connected with the local school. Consequently, these groups are not alert to the implications for practice when politically driven reforms based on different assumptions enter into the schooling enterprise. When realization dawns, it commonly is accompanied by feelings of helplessness. The operational-commonly referred to as conventional-wisdom of the citizenry is seriously shortchanged by the neglect of its education in both formal and informal education. The educational research development community has not served its educative role in the public arena (p. 291).

If Goodlad is correct, then the problems of education have come full circle, from practice into theory. An educator, at any level, teacher and administrator, can work her/his entire career trying to solve problems – of children, parents, and communities. It is a life worth living to be sure. And, as we well know, such a life has produced men and women such as Ella Flagg Young who as Chicago's Superintendent in the first decade of the 20th century sat down with teachers to construct reading curricula (Bogotch, 2005). Elise Clapp (Stack, 2004) who with her colleagues traveled to small towns in the Appalachian mountains during the 20th century's economic depression to study a community for an entire year before writing a community-based curriculum.

How different today to see that education has been outsourced to authors of textbooks, publishers of tests, consultants, and curriculum developers who deliver packaged ideas in simple, easy-to-follow instructions. The skills and discourses become a matter of technical proficiency, classroom management, and methods, rather than a knowledge of development, implementation, and critique. This state of affairs can and does produce individuals who engage in social justice actions, but not systemically. At best, the problems of education revolve around limited projects, procedural, distributive, and liberal justice (Strike, 1989). Social justice as an educational construct, however, can be much more. That is, there are other possibilities in governance, organizations, theory, and practices (see Marshall and Oliva, 2006). The question here is whether educational researchers, teachers, and leaders can play a more effective role in creating alternative possibilities.

II. THE POSSIBILITIES FOR SOCIAL JUSTICE AS AN EDUCATIONAL CONSTRUCT

The possibilities for social justice as an educational construct require deliberate thoughts and actions. Even then, given the contingencies of problems and circumstances, there are no guarantees that our best efforts will make a difference in individual lives or in the world. We must judge our good works by results, not by intentions or words. But even our judgments may lack validity. Why?

We live in a disparate world marked by advantages as well as desperate human conditions (Young, 1990). Under more optimum conditions, naturally and artificially, there are free choices; however, there are no assurances that the decisions made, individually or collectively, will lead to social justice. In free and complex societies, education is a resource that may be used to make everyday decisions, navigate complex situations, solve problems, and secure a virtuous life. Under harsh human conditions, individuals still may choose to accept them as socially just, or they may resist, through reform, revolution or by flight (see Fanon, 1968, Nafisi, 2004).

Thus, there are possibilities for social justice in any decisions regarding full participation in society or fleeing in search of opportunities elsewhere. In the latter instance, the choices are limited; the consequences for taking actions tend to be greater, if not also dangerous. Yet despite danger and limited choices, education can potentially open the world to individuals inside closed societies (e.g., *refuseniks*). If so, then it is a mistake as well as a conceit to equate social justice with any one system of government, laws, economy, religion, etc. There are possibilities for social justice under any and all human conditions and systems of government so long as individuals are free to think and act. The pursuit of social justice as an educational construct involves constant struggles over dominant ideas, unpredictable events and consequences, and fear. Such struggles occur everywhere, not only in western-style democracies.

Under the broad heading of possibilities, I want to suggest how educators who work for social justice may overcome problems encountered inside political and social institutions, including schools. Thus, I return here to debates on the social contract, constitutional rights, extra-institutional learning, and, most importantly, to educational theories themselves. Of this I am certain: social justice as an educational construct is much more than what we currently call democratic schooling and community education, and much less than what we hold out as the ideals of progressing toward a just society and a new humanity worldwide. Whether such ideas will be labeled postmodern, romantic, radical, or quaint is not as important as our willingness as educators to recapture the best of what we have forgotten, lost and neglected.

II. A. 1. MULTIPLE DISCOURSES ON BASIC RIGHTS

Turning again to John Goodlad, the systematic and careful researcher of *A Place Called School*, he asserts in his autobiographical work *Romances with Schools* (2004) that education must be a basic right that is established by a new constitutional promise. He wrote:

> ...the need now is for a Bill of Educational Rights and an Educational Constitution intended to ensure and renew this educational heritage. But it is not, however, *only* for children. This legacy is also the strongest guarantee people could have that the moral ecology now holding us together will be strong enough to ensure the freedoms, responsibilities, and justice embedded in its democratic principles (p. 330).

While his words read like the other constitutional promises found in the examples above of Sudan and Chad and other national constitutions throughout the world,

Goodlad argued that education must be renewed as a national promise. In the U.S., this specific proposal would assume an enormous significance in that it reverses a deliberate omission by the framers of the original constitution. Yet, the very process of amending any national constitution would create political forums for new voices on behalf of educators and education in the world. While such proposals and forums leave unspecified how the status of education might avoid becoming another generation of "false promises," they would offer educational leaders an important political and moral role in the larger society. Thus, the first possibility for social justice as an educational construct is to *advocate* for a national agenda which specifies that education is a basic and fundamental right. This would bring local educators from around the globe into the spotlight of national and international politics – as part of their responsibility as educators.

That said, the distance between a romantic vision and *realpolitik* was made apparent in the writings of Michele Fine (2004), another educational researcher. In analyzing marginalization in terms of institutional/ideological dynamics, Fine identified the negative consequences of the U.S. Supreme Court's 1954 Brown decision ending *de jure* segregation of public schools:

> Within education, outraged and organized demands for justice were co-opted into bureaucratic strategies for access. Bold calls to dismantle oppression morphed into remediation and buses, which were moving/fixing bodies. A collective and responsible "us," which included everyone, converted into a deficient and needy "them," which included only African American children. The scope of justice, damage, and responsibility shriveled. The broad-based goal of justice as transformation of a system of racial inequities and White supremacy grew emaciated into a call to help Black students by "allowing" them access to White schools. Bold analyses of White supremacy funneled into targeted studies of Black student achievement (p. 507).

Fine's phrases "bold calls" and "bold analyses" highlight the irony and inadequacies of depending solely upon political strategies. In terms of struggle, "[n]either stubborn courage nor fine slogans are enough" (Fanon, 1968, pp. 135-16). Thus, the possibilities for social justice as an educational construct must extend beyond existing laws and constitutions as it moves towards a status of basic rights. Hence, as quoted in the Introduction previously (see p. 15).

> [t]he virtue of social justice allows for *people* of good will to reach different—even opposing—practical judgments about the material content of the common good (ends) and how to get there (means). Such differences are the stuff of politics (emphasis added) (Novak, 2000, n.p.).

According to Hayden (2002), "[t]he task is then to attempt to create, not presuppose the basic institutions and to implement the principles that will bring about, as far as possible, such an ideal person and such ideal cooperation" (pp. 169-70). While some radical critiques have called for dismantling institutional structures, the politics of education call for educators to work on multiple levels from constitutions to institutions to educational theories/practices. Constitutionally, the educational question revolves around legitimacy in terms of how serious and how capable the state and its officials are with respect to protecting and promoting education as a fundamental right. Educational leadership and research needs to inform the state on how to amend and enforce laws and to make it known that there will be public resistance when appropriate.

II. A. 1. A. ADDING ETHICS TO POLITICS

There are many practical approaches to politics on national and local levels. Blunden (2003) offered a theory of justice called Ethical Politics. He recognized that in today's world it was impossible to reach a universal agreement on an ethical principle. Thus, what is needed are "ethical principles governing collaboration - these *must* be agreed. Collaboration aims at *practical agreement*; theoretical agreement is generally immaterial" (n. p., Part 4). His argument was that ethical politics is "a practical field in which the tension between ideals is played out" (n.p). He further stated that

> The incompatibility between autonomy, community, equality and liberty, justice, freedom, democracy, stability and recognition have tortured the minds of social reformers and revolutionaries for centuries. [Rather] [w]hat *we* do is decided by *you and me*," in order to reflect what I claim as the genuinely human relation, *collaboration*, as opposed to the mutual instrumentalisation implied in economic theory and contemporary ethics. Whether such a move is sustainable is yet to be established (n.p.).

In the world of ethics and politics, Blunden held that the unit of analysis of social justice was activity. This point is crucial because it makes plain, again, that intentions, words, ideas, and even institutionalized practices – all of which are necessary – are insufficient for purposes of social justice. Sometimes, however, the solutions we seek do not result from our deliberate activities. Why did the Kellog-Briand Pact in the US outlawing war and the Council of the League of Nations after World War I fail and disappear while the United Nations and its member agencies struggle, yet survive? The differences in terms of words, ideas, and institutionalized practices do not explain why one effort continues and another effort disappears. What it does tell us, however, is that we need to engage in continuous political activities from generation to generation and that our efforts will be labeled socially just only in hindsight. What that means, for me, is that the educators' ideas as to what constitutes social justice actions can never be an idea of justice alone; it must incorporate and emerge from political and ethical actions. The methods of social justice research extend beyond collecting and analyzing data and move directly into leadership.

II. B. 1. WORKING WITHIN INSTITUTIONALIZED PRACTICES

In transforming constitutions, institutions, and theories-educationally, educators need to stop thinking only in terms of consciousness-raising. Real change must be made evident in the conditions of everyday life. For educators, much of their everyday lives are inside the institution of schools. Although Jean-Jacques Rousseau was no friend of institutionalized practices, he wrote in *Emile*

> There are teachers dear to me in many schools and especially in the University of Paris, men of whom I have a great respect, men whom I believe to be quite capable of instructing young people, if they were not compelled to follow established custom. I exhort one of them to publish the scheme of reform which he has thought out. Perhaps people would at length seek to cure the evil if they realized that there was a remedy (p. 8, note)

For public education to be judged by the public as legitimate, our school leaders would do well to address the practices of procedural justice whereby institutional rules, school roles, and everyday educational practices are enacted. A leader's willingness to rethink institutional rules, roles, and practices and address injustices and inequities in everyday activities is another first step towards the possibilities of social justice. Education always begins with and involves mutual interactions, that is, with how educators perceive and treat parents, children, teachers, administrators, and community members. Schools around the world will, of course, do this differentially and selectively within specific contexts and customs. Local knowledge here should take precedence. But at the same time, unless we can demonstrate to one another professionally that our own interactions are ethical and educational, then we have no basis for teaching others how to interact.

Some of the barriers to ethical practices are imposed externally. Others are self imposed. Our responsibility is to address both the external and internal. Under any and all conditions, from the closed society of absolutist regimes to democracies, there have been individuals who have presented us with clearly marked paths toward freedom and justice: from Thoreau's *Walden Pond*, Anne Frank's *Diary*, Castro's *History will absolve me*, King's *Letter from a Birmingham jail*, Nafasi's *Reading Lolita in Teheran*, Fanon's *The Wretched of the Earth,* Freire's *Pedagogy of the Oppressed,* etc. Not all of these moral treatises ring true, even to their own countrymen and women. Nevertheless, in history and modern times, we are witnesses and participants in a world that is fighting against injustices and oppression. As educators, we have an important pedagogical and leadership role to play. We can not be left out of this history, whether as teachers, administrators, or researchers. It is our responsibility to integrate this knowledge into our teaching, institutions, and theories.

II. C.1. CRITIQUES, EXPERIMENTS, AND ACTIONS IN EDUCATIONAL THEORIES

Toulmin (1972) offered this advice on the history of ideas:

> It [i.e., philosophy] can cling to the discredited research program of a purely theoretical (i.e., "modern") philosophy, which will end by driving it out of business; it can look for new and less exclusively theoretical ways of working, and develop the methods needed for a more practical ("post-modern") agenda; or it can return to its pre-17th-century traditions, and try to recover the lost ("pre-modern") topics that were sidetracked by Descartes, but can be usefully taken up for the future (p.11).

The choices offered by Toulmin, once again, speak to Hume's open-ended empiricism and James' pragmatism in terms of making a practical difference in the real world. In education, there have been and continue to be intellectual voices, albeit the minority within our own minority status, that have challenged conventional wisdom, the *status quo,* and non-educative definitions of theory. My selection here is far from being comprehensive, but collectively, the educators' voices make plain that education as theory and action is *much more* than what we have settled for in terms of teaching, learning, and leadership. The theories are often framed as open-ended questions that generate responses unique to a particular student [and to the unique educator as well]. What also emerges from these educational theories is the fact that education as a lifelong process does not close off possibilities for learning new ideas and engaging in actions, including social justice ideas/actions, limited by age, geography, or ideology. Furthermore, these theories all operate in the present, such that education is neither a passive nor future-oriented profession, but rather an intervention that makes a difference for others both now and in the future.

Confucius, the teacher asked his disciples to state their ideals of life.

"When one of them hesitated to speak, because his ideal of life was so different from those of the others, Confucius urged him on, saying, 'What does it matter? After all, each of us may speak of his own ideals'" (Wu, note 21, p. 407)

Giovanni Gentile (1922) was quoted in Rusk (1929):

[S]o that far from limiting the autonomy of the disciple, the master as the propulsive element of the pupil's spontaneity, penetrates his personality, not to suppress it, but to help its impulses and facilitate its infinite development (p. 198).

Was not Socrates, a teacher and citizen, accused of making the weaker argument the stronger (Apology), and, therefore, viewed as a threat to the moral and intellectual authority of the Athenian government? The charge against him was corrupting youth. And for such teachings, Socrates was put to death by his fellow citizens. From his death we learn what civilized societies should not do, namely assert absolute dominance over citizens by killing questions.

In *Emile*, Rousseau guided his pupil to ask questions of the world.

Having thus considered every kind of civil society in itself, we shall compare them, so as to note their relations one with another; great and small, strong and weak.... We shall inquire whether too much or too little has not been accomplished in the matter of social institutions; whether individuals who are subject to law and to men, while societies preserve the independence of nature, are not exposed to the ills of both conditions without the advantages of either, and whether it would not be better to have no civil society in the world rather than to have many such societies (p. 430).

Rousseau framed the comparative questions so as to analyze societies from different perspectives. The content of his lessons came from actual conditions in the world. The questions were empirical and open-ended, abstract and concrete, and critical and affirming. At its best, education allows us to live and work within and around differences and disagreements - even when the very acts of teaching and learning themselves may be forbidden by customs or outlawed by mandates.

In asking Emile what kind of life he will live, where he will live, what he will do, and how he is to relate to others including family, Rousseau tell us

"I have even taken care that he (Emile) should associate himself with some many of worth in every nation, by means of a treaty of hospitality after the fashion of the ancients, ...Not only may this be useful,...it is also an excellent antidote against the sway of patriotic prejudices, to which we are liable all through our life and to which sooner or later we are more or less enslaved. Nothing is better calculated to lessen the hold of such prejudices than a friendly interchange of opinions with sensible people whom we respect" (p. 435).

Confucuis, Socrates, Gentile, and Rousseau inserted education into the practices of society, expanding teaching, learning and leadership into history, morality, politics, economics, etc. Moreover, they did so with a faith in the dynamic processes of education that did not limit the responses of their students. Rousseau again on education:

Viewed as an art, the success of education is almost impossible, since the essential conditions of success are beyond our control. Our efforts may bring us within sight of the goal, but fortune must favor us if we are to reach it (p. 6).

Clarence Stone, a disciple of Cubberly during the early era of educational administration wrote:

Administration, for the person possessing executive capacity, is easy and interesting, and the results are immediate and obvious. The improvement of instruction, on the contrary, calls for exact knowledge, involves the human equation, is slow and difficult, and the results are not so evident, even to the trained observer (Stone, 1929, p. v.).

Deborah Meier (1995) echoed this tenet of open-ended educational theories:

It's thirty years since I began and twenty-one years since Central Park East opened its doors. I feel almost as far from discovering how to make a difference as I did then. That sounds foolish, given our successes. But given what I wanted to do, it's a simple fact. The puzzle isn't, it turns out, one where you can finally put the last piece in and say 'Done.' It just gets more and more complicated (p. 181).

More recently, Deborah Britzman (2007) has attempted to deconstruct the myths surrounding the educational construct of development. For her, development has become a worn out metanarrative that serves to confirm itself in practice and institutionally [inside of universities]. In contrast, Britzman argued that development is a human condition, uneven and uncertain [i.e., not unlike social justice]. "We many agree that others develop, but rarely do we wonder how our own development affects our educational imagination" (p. 1).

While I cannot critique the so-called stages of development as proposed by Rousseau, Piaget, Erickson, Kohlberg, Vygotsky, and others, I contend that each raised important exceptions to his own theories. As conceptualized, the theories themselves come alive – as hypothesis and tentative conclusions. In some instances, they may even challenge the essence of the theory as presented in the original texts. To quote Jean Jacques Rousseau in his Preface to *Emile*, (1790/1943)

> The wisest writers devote themselves to what a man (sic) ought to know, without asking what a child is capable of learning. They are always looking for the man in the child, without considering what he is before he becomes a man (p. 1).

Rousseau asked educators to deliberately "lose time" and let children be children. Yet, today we seem to be headed in the opposite direction in bringing packaged and programmed school curriculum to pre-pre-schoolers and kindergartners. As we pay less and less time to children, we are missing something significant in teaching, learning and leadership, and we are also limiting social justice possibilities from those directly in front of our faces – our students.

QUAINT OR DISCARDED THEORIES

How is it that at the beginning of the 20th century, the status of singing and music across the curriculum was considered to be the hallmark of a "world class curriculum" (Bogotch, 2005, 2006), while a century later, singing is nominally absent from the formal required course curriculum? How is it that gardening was once considered important to a child's growth, yet today it, too, is an infrequent part of curriculum-despite hunger and poverty around the world? What about the status of play? Once it was taught that "play is our best ally in bringing up children" (Johnson, 1907, p. 8). That play was "not sugar coating, but sweetening of work" (p. 18). That "[t]he contrast should not be between work and play but rather between play and "fooling" on the one hand, and between play and *distasteful* labor on the other (Johnson, 1907, p. 19).

Johnson presented data from 1901 through 1905 that play dramatically reduced truancy (p. 51). Beyond play, past curricula included collecting [stamps, coins, rocks], cooking, drawing, fieldwork, gardening, games, mechanics, dancing, etc- as both curricular and extra-curricular activities. How and why did these educational activities, practices, ideas disappear? Were there more valid theories of education that displaced them? Have we proven that standardized tests in reading and mathematics are more educational than singing and play? Why have test scores supplanted self-respect and self-esteem as educational measures of success and school accountability for both children and adults? On what scale of validity do we embrace one set of theories and discard others?

Today, the very ideas of de-schooling society or institutionalizing free schools would be labeled "quaint," "progressive," or worse. In the United States, the decade of the 1960s is perceived by many as a turning point in American educational theory. Throughout that decade, critiques of institutionalized schooling reached their apex, but are now viewed as either the high point or low point in the history of education and society depending upon one's ideology. Yet, it is not out of nostalgia that I re-present a little-known 1960s radical educator, Michael Rossman (1972). While at the University of California at Berkeley Rossman participated in the free speech and free school movements. With respect to the latter, he witnessed how young children chose to develop in environments not dominated by adults, questioning the belief that kids were uniquely dependent upon our efforts as 'adults' to *construct* the circumstances of their education for them" (p. 338).

As if echoing Ivan Illich, Rossman wrote:

This is no argument against being purposeful about the educational process, as best we can. But it is a dangerous narrowness of vision to mistake the school we construct for their [i.e., children's] actual School (p. 339).

Rossman pre-empted his critics then and now, noting how his descriptions may appear as lopsided (p. 340) or "seem a parody" (p. 341). He was deliberately writing against conventional wisdom and theory. Yet as a radical, he sought to give a minority, in this case children, a real voice.

...I don't think this business of learning from children is just a romantic fancy; nor is what we have to learn from them just some humane redecoration of the rooms of our consciousness....a culture of continual change: adults learning major life lessons from their children, who will lead them in adapting to changing conditions of the material world and of human reality...In its fullness, our conception of the nature and function of an educational system will be overturned. And in transition, each of us will constantly be confronted by opportunities for learning – for growth or for survival – for which our culture never prepared us (p. 345).

Is it not curious that the people who were educated in these liberal times are now the people who are constraining their children and grandchildren in ways they were not?

Instead of Rossman's vision of children as teachers and learners, we are confronted today with the realities of children as soldiers at war, children as prostitutes, and child as laborers in sweatshop conditions. Not only are the voices of educators in these nations inadequate, there is no social justice as a political or philosophical or educational construct helping these children or these nations develop.

To view education as solely a matter of physical and mental growth is to ignore the different world cultures with different traditions and milestones for childhood as well as for adults around the world. Everyone today is not only exposed to more information, they also have to adapt to stimuli in different ways that facilitate emerging new literacies. The changes are not just cognitive; there are dramatic physical changes, too, which are already self-evident. For example, we have instituted sponsored and coordinated activities ranging from Olympic sports to

Extreme sports [i.e., X-Games], indicating that the boundaries of young people's growth physically are constantly being challenged and surpassed. In education, through experience and experimentation, we cannot ignore how changes also occur both outside and inside institutional schools. There are new meanings to growth and development, and as educators, we do not want to underestimate the capacity of either children or adults in our professional practices. Nor do we want to underestimate the capacity of ourselves as educators.

> Because of the unpredictability of the world and the limits of human rationality, it makes sense to emphasize building capabilities of people first, encouraging them to develop ways and means for using their capabilities, than it does to develop plans and then seek the know-how and commitment to implement the plans (Sergiovanni, 1989, p. 39).

Over his long career, Jerome Bruner (1990) looked more and more beyond the limits of psychology to the discipline of anthropology in order to understand the phenomenon of how development intersects with culture and meaning:

> ...the child does not enter the life of his or her group as a private and autistic sport of primary processes, but rather as a participant in a larger public process in which public meanings are negotiated. And in this process, meanings are not to his own advantage unless he can get them shared by others. Even such seemingly private phenomenon as "secrets" (itself a culturally defined category) turn out once revealed to be publicly interpretable and even banal – just as patterned as matters openly admitted (p. 13).

Bruner's words begin to embrace Dewey's ideas on how education is always *social* and why the study of education is about problems of experience and practice. Thus, while psychological theories have continued to be the foundation of teaching and learning, education in society has expanded into sociology, anthropology, physiology, etc. as possibilities. In the world of education, both children and adults construct meanings, individually and collectively. But if the theories we use to interpret educational practices speak only to the separate stages from childhood to adulthood, to distinct worlds, to isolated functioning minds, and to institutional and organization thinking, then the theories themselves become *the problem for education* limiting *the possibilities for social justice.*

If we let philosophy, psychology, or the law limit what we can learn from education, then we become like Rawls, the pre-eminent justice philosopher, who saw children as unable to discern intentions and motives of others (p. 411). He ignored what happens with, to and around children [and any other citizen who does not meet the criteria for participating in the *original position*]. In other words, we, too, come to ignore dynamic educational processes so as not to disrupt our own theories of teaching and learning. Rawls' "excuse" for omitting education was that children are included in his theory through the rights granted to parents and guardians (p. 446). My argument is that educators must erase such excuses in others and from themselves. Unfortunately, it is not self-evident in our theories that children are the center of educators' constructions of reality (see Sizer and Sizer above); likewise, the constructions of parents and guardians remain distinct and separate as well. In short, the separation of schools from society reinforces these distinct and narrow views of ourselves, others, and the world around us.

WHY NOT?

Why not replace our cluttered, busy lives governed by forgettable and insignificant routines with new ideas regarding education based on child and adult development? How come the new CEO of Toys R Us, who transitioned from his role as Executive VP for Best Buy, stated that his greatest challenge is "grappling with children growing out of toys faster and preferring gadgets". While his purpose was to understand marketing and sales, his insights were derived from careful attention to children/customers changes in terms of growth and development. If we could follow that path, more accurately, if we could follow our own unique and individual paths in education, then the possibilities for educational reforms would emerge inside our practice as teachers, leaders, and researchers.

Illich (1971) among others argued that "most learning happens casually, and even most intentional learning is not the result of programmed instruction" (p. 12). His own solutions, that is, extra-institutions of convivial and voluntary networks were written three decades before the advent of the worldwide web. To date, no educational reform, from the standards' movement to standardized testing, has tested the bonds of institutionalism from inside out. Why not?

Today's digital technology has accelerated not only the pace of learning, but it has also nullified space and power relationships between theorists and readers, students and teachers. The processes of teaching and learning in today's world, especially for children and adults who have mastered digital communications, has turned linear and sequential school lessons upside down.

> In the digital world, texts are mobile and changeable. I can move a digital text around the world in an instant. Space offers no resistance to bytes on the Internet. A few nanoseconds is all it requires to circle the globe.... If digital texts did no more than disperse themselves more efficiently and ubiquitously than paper, the analogue author [define] would perhaps be expanded. But the temporal instantaneity of digital texts undermines their spatial stability. Embodied in computer files, digital texts subsist in space only at the whim of the reader. The author of the digital text loses the assurance of their spatial continuity. Pages of digital text have the stability of liquid (Poster, 2001, p. 92).

Within and beyond technology, transformational learning experiences happen accidentally and spontaneously – as a matter of activity. As an activity, education reinforces existing ideas and creates new ones, that is, it is experiential and experimental (Biesta, 2006, p. 106). Education is formal and informal, the latter coming with "the unexpected question" (Illich, 1971, p. 17). Educational theory requires that we "engage in what we learn" (Biesta, p. 94). That "engagement with" is different from "solutions to" in that we engage questions and critique rather than with advanced knowledge of the outcomes (Usher & Edwards, 1996, p. 209). The educators' questions of when, where, how, and why are dependent upon relationships, contexts and life's circumstances. For the educator and the learner, life itself is presented as on-going empirical questions to be discovered and rediscovered anew (Patri, 1917) – as theory and practice.

II.C.1 DIRECT ACTION: BRINGING EDUCATION AND SOCIETIES OUT OF BALANCE

In modern times, *Refusniks* around the world hold study groups to keep past ideas alive, to question and challenge state authorities, to promote literacies, to engage in intellectual and aesthetical activities, to make the weaker arguments the stronger, to teach *Lolita in Teheran*. These activities are not just theoretical; neither are they just practical. Rather, they are necessary for life. Why else would oppressive regimes outlaw literacy, terrorize educators, destroy schools? The appropriate responses in each of these situations are educational: teachers teach and people learn.

Martin Luther King in his *Letter from a Birmingham Jail* was explicit on the connection between teaching, learning, leadership, and research. In his letter, he outlined a four step plan for thought and action. Step one was the collection of the facts. That is, it becomes necessary to distinguish between real injustices and the fact that there are negative outcomes in everyone's life which are not injustices. For King, the end of step one was the realization that "...we were the victims of a broken promise." In this essay, too, we began with constitutions as broken promises. It was part of our first problem of social justice as an educational construct.

Step two was negotiation, the kind of interactive processes described here in the social justice theories of Young, Hayden, Deutsch, and Blunden. It must become evident to educators that the meaning of social justice can pre-suppose the processes of negotiations. It is precisely this omission that brought philosophy and social theories of justice into theoretical doubt in this essay.

Step three is something we must re-consider for education. King called step three, self-purification. He described the necessity for the intensive workshops whereby participants wrestled with difficult questions as well as the underlying principles of non-violence. The questions were personal self-reflections on how each person could accept the mental and physical treatment they would surely endure. For King, this step paved the way for step four, a moral transformation. As I read King's description, I recognized the questions asked by Socrates, Rousseau, and others challenging students, societies, and, most significantly, themselves to take political and ethical actions. I also thought how different King's step three was from the content of teacher education programs, leadership preparation programs, and professional development experiences in which we participate. That is, it is rare to hear either pre-service education or in-service workshops described as being intense and self-reflective or transformative. But that is precisely what was required for personal and institutional transformation in the civil rights movement in the U.S. The demands for excellence inherent in the theories of Dewey, Bruner and others speak to the difficulty of educational interventions described by Biesta (2006). To use King's metaphor, educational leaders must steel themselves professionally to face criticisms which include bigotry and physical violence. The school official, too, whether administrator or teacher, must be steeled professionally to engage in leadership roles in society, inside and out of the educational organization.

Lastly, step four was direct action. For King, this direct action was in terms of leadership and research as a matter of choice extending beyond the formal job descriptions of teaching and administering. Too many educators have not gone beyond analyzing problems of injustices as they exist institutionally as well as socially. Like the caring citizen in Appiah's "shallow pond," educators save the same child over and over again without coming to an analysis of the "why" of the child's problem. For many children, the problem resides elsewhere. The direct action to which King refers goes beyond more negotiations. The problem goes beyond measuring student achievement on standardized tests. Yet before educators can make the leap into direct action, we must return to self reflections and negotiations in order to educate ourselves and societies of the worth and power of education. As educational leaders, we have made this omission too easy for others to impose their will upon us by not entering into hard negotiations or direct actions.

III. CONCLUSION

I began by questioning why and how philosophers and social theorists who write about social justice have ignored educators and education. I argued that this omission invalidates their theories of justice- or, at least, opens them to a new educational critique. Even when education was asserted to be a fundamental right of individuals, constitutionally protected, its actual theories, processes, and practices were left out of serious discussions and debates of social problems. In other words, although education may be asserted to be a necessity of life, it has been positioned outside societal and cultural debates only to be inserted-by fully developed rational adults who are already educated, thus privileged - after society had been established.

My thesis was that education is a basic necessity of life; it is not outside any social relationship or any society. Education is not, as Rawls and others hold, prior to the *original position* or social contract. Any thought, action or outcome that rises to a valid criterion of social justice requires the immediate presence of education, for children as well as for adults.

At the same time, I argued that none of the processes or outcomes of education or social justice were guaranteed. What that means is that education and social justice are always in transition. Its concepts and processes are never fixed or permanent or complete. Thus, while the relationship between education and social justice is necessary, the outcomes will always be contingent on natural and social factors. Education greatly improves the possibilities for achieving positive social justice outcomes and *vice versa*.

Central to my argument was that much of the literature on social justice emanating from the West relates to the concept of democracy. Yet if education is in fact transformative at the individual, community, and national levels, then we must also envision social justice in non-democratic settings – in order to test our power in the real world. What positions educators-at every level- to use their powers are the professional relationships with *others*, who are different. Until educators recognize our unique position in terms of extending privileges and freedoms to others-within schools and outside in the community, we will not see why it is our obligation to promote social justice constitutionally, institutionally, or systematically.

It is precisely the differences of educators-as a legitimate representative of the other and a minority voice- that gives educational leadership the power to make the here and now of education a significant voice inside institutions, policies, laws, and practices. By transforming teachable moments into socially just moments [through questions, critique, and experiments], the disparate histories of races, classes, and genders may be seen in the contexts of today's struggle for people to learn.

> Educational plans, policies and practices are always framed by contexts which stretch from the intimacy and immediacy of local circumstances to reach and intersect with broader social frames, nationally and internationally, communally and globally. There are the products of struggle, and they give rise to still further struggles for a better education for a better world (Kemmis, 1996, p. 213)

The theory and practice of education cannot and should not erase history; rather it should be privileged inside history in terms of making social justice a reality for today's and tomorrow's generation. Privileging the minority voices of educators who work in the present has the potential for becoming the most effective remedy to injustices past, present, and future.

What exactly is this leadership and research agenda? Michael Rossman (1972) does not name it, but he does describe its power and possibilities:

> There are newer modes aplenty, and reason to use them. Any frontier movement ought to be reflexive, ought to turn the full force of understandings about educational process now available to us upon its own operations and serve as the laboratory for it own best experiment, making possible a different order of business....I don't know how to name it. It has to do with being involved together, interdependent on the edge of an uncertain future; and with levels of consciousness, allegiance, and commitment (pp. 342-343).

For sure, social justice has been and will continue to be a mirage, a false or broken promise, a ruse, or any number of negative concepts more closely associated with injustices than to the meanings of justice. In this essay, I have rejected intimidation and coercion socially and politically, while also rejecting theories based on a psychology of fear. I have rejected epistemologies of certainty and determinism, but only when they limit the possibilities of social justice as an educational construct. Organizationally, I have argued against the limits of distributive and procedural justice as well as against social justice in terms of achieving balance.

Justice and social justice are much more, especially with respect to the aims of education. While I will not give up on the ideals of world peace, I believe that fighting for education as a basic right of each and every person is a more realistic social justice goal. Lastly, I cannot imagine limiting social justice to only those nations which are said to have democratic governments. In today's world, education and nation-building – not democracy and nation-building - are reciprocal processes.

FENWICK ENGLISH

TOWARDS A THEORY OF SOCIAL JUSTICE/INJUSTICE

Learning to Lead in the Social Cage

Cornel West (1999) has remarked of our times:

> We live in the midst of a pervasive and profound crisis of North Atlantic civilization whose symptoms include the threat of nuclear annihilation, extensive class inequality, brutal state repression, subtle bureaucratic surveillance, wide spread homophobia, technological abuse of nature and rampant racism and patriarchy (p.251).

West's trenchant summary anchors the focus of an increasing number of educational leadership preparation programs in university centers. Indeed, the term *social justice* has become the bell weather slogan of many educational leadership programs, and like an advancing hurricane over warm water, shows increasing volume in professional publications (Shoho, Merchant & Lugg, 2005). New books are already appearing on the topic (Marshall and Gerstl-Pepin, 2005; Marshall and Oliva, 2006). Many educational graduate programs have adopted the concept as a guidepost to shape and connect their courses, incorporating them into program vision and mission statements (McDonald, 2005).

While there is certainly a long history of social injustice within the profession regarding its exclusion of women, minorities, and persons with different sexual orientations (Blount, 1998; 2005; Gonzalez, 2003; Kumashiro, 2002; Lugg , 2003; Tillman, 2004); not to mention supporting policies and practices which were based on genetic determinism and eugenics, racism, sexism and class discrimination (Bartee, Beckham, Gill, Graves, Jackson, Land, Williams & Parker, 2000; Bowles & Gintis, 1976; Chen, 1980; Cortina & Gendreau, 2003; Daniels, 1974; Gould, 1981; Kevles, 1995; Kluger, 1977; McLaren, 1986, 1994; Sizemore, 2005; Young and Lopez, 2005), a problem arises when one contemplates constructing a curriculum around the concept, particularly a curriculum which is responsive to some of the outcome requirements, for example, of NCATE in accrediting practices. More importantly than NCATE are probing questions of the graduates of our preparation programs.

Beyond making them historically aware of the policies and practices which have defined, implemented, and perpetuated social injustice in schools, what actions would they take to not only undo them, but work towards re-conceptualizing what

Ira Bogotch et al. (eds.), Radicalizing Educational Leadership: Dimensions of Social Justice, 113–146.
© *2008 Sense Publishers. All rights reserved.*

schools do to create a more socially just society in the future? In-other-words, to illustrate social injustice we have to look backwards. But our graduates are not going to work in the past. So it isn't enough to work to *undo* socially unjust practices such as tracking and grouping which reinforce race and gender biased classes, or doom students of color to the most mind numbing instructional strategies in rote forms of teaching based on research rooted to standardized test scores (Oakes, Gamoran & Page, 1992; Kohn, 2000; Parker, 2001).

The more complex question surrounding making social justice a thematic anchor and connector of an educational leadership program is the requirement to create within a theoretical framework in which the effects of a curriculum can be empirically assessed, and which can serve as an holistic and heuristic model by which graduate students can engage in a gestalt view/approach to leading schools and school systems in very different directions than before.

Our students have to be more than complainers, whiners, protestors or simplistic change agents who try and erase the most obvious forms of social injustice which schools historically have perpetuated such as ability grouping which reproduces the distance between the haves and have nots in the larger society, or protest the use of standardized tests which make possessing certain forms of cultural capital an advantage in the competitive race for grades in schools. Such practices reproduce cultural inequities and economic advantage and disadvantages for entire classes of people (English, 2002; Lucas, 1999; Parker, Kelly & Sanford, 1998).

So this essay is not a criticism of the rich and increasingly thick descriptive research, both quantitative and qualitative, which have lent contextual portraits of the embedded beliefs and practices which have since the beginning of public schooling in the U.S., perpetuated so many forms of socially regressive, punitive, and race-gender-and sexual orientation based discriminatory practices which continue in a variety of forms in public education. Rather, it represents a line of inquiry regarding creating a theoretical framework which moves beyond finding ways and means of erasing them to more fully understand whether socially unjust practices are built into the brick and mortar of society as, for example, in the U.S. Constitution which from the beginning embraced slavery, to more temporal forms of social injustice based on scientific racism (Mehler, 1999; West, 1999, pp. 55-86) and which were then adopted to fit schooling beliefs and practices (Oakes, Gamoran & Page, 1992; Sapon-Shevin, 1994; Parker, Kelly & Sanford, 1998).

WHY CURRENT STANDARDS FOR THE PREPARATION OF EDUCATIONAL LEADERS ARE INADEQUATE AS IT PERTAINS TO SOCIAL JUSTICE

Current standards for educational leaders are centered on the ISLLC standards and are hegemonically connected to NCATE policing via accreditation. The term social justice does not appear in the standards at all. A close examination of the standards and indicators reveals that they are almost exclusively centered on *schooling interiorities*, that is, practices within schools regarding resource allocation and vague notions of equity. There is nothing in the standards that would propel educational leaders to engage in a discourse outside of the school or school system in the larger socio-economic arena to confront social concepts, beliefs and practices which perpetuate social injustice (English, 2005). These are the critical *exteriorities* and the differentiation between them is what Carolyn Shields (2004) has called the difference between "transformational" vs. "transformative" leadership.

At best the ISLLC standards might be used to prepare educational leaders to question certain inequitable practices in schools. However, I have argued elsewhere, that there is nothing in the standards which would propel leaders prepared by such standards to question larger socio-economic practices nor even the pervasive Jim Crow laws by which racial segregation was practiced legally in public schools for many years (English, 2005). The current ISLLC standards are a-theoretical in that they represent no coherent theoretical base except the doctrine of efficiency (English, 2003). Such standards cannot be the foci for the creation of a theory of social justice/injustice, nor were they ever promulgated to deal with social justice or injustice. The standards are not only a-theoretical but pseudo-scientific (English, 2004).

Understanding these differences amounts to preparing future educational leaders to find more effective means of combating forms of social injustice as they are encountered, or searching for deeper patterns and meanings which continue to produce a variety of forms of social injustice in the larger society and in the schools which are embedded in it. It ought to be remembered that some forms of social injustice which are now recognized were once promulgated and advocated by those ostensibly pushing for reforms which were supposed to combat privilege and prejudice, as for example in the efforts which led to the creation of the Scholastic Aptitude Test (see Lemann, 1999). However, once implemented some of these reforms perpetuated the problems they were intended to resolve with higher failure rates for large groups of culturally and racially diverse persons (see Young, 2003).

I argue in this essay that current efforts to incorporate the concept of *social justice/injustice* in educational leadership preparation programs is based on a number of questionable assumptions, not the least of which is a theoretical hiatus which robs our efforts of the power to engage in social transformation instead of merely tinkering inside of schools and engaging in what some critics have called incorporating the "the culture of resentment" in such efforts (McCarthy & Dimitriadis, 2005, pp. 321-335).

THE ISSUE OF THE "CULTURE OF RESENTMENT" IN THE ISLLC STANDARDS

The "culture of resentment" refers to an approach in which the "incorporation and mobilization of racial identities...the tasks of educating about group differences, and the management of diversity" (McCarthy & Dimitriadius, 2005, p. 324) are incorporated into practices which are centered on containment and restriction (p. 329). "Resentment" as a concept can be traced to Nietzsche's (1966) *The Natural History of Morals* in which the process of identity construction is directed outward towards those hostile or opposed to one self (McCarthy & Dimitriadis, 2005, p. 325). The world outside is conceived in extremely hostile terms where great effort must be directed to consolidate exceptionalities into a more cohesive and communal group. We see such visions of hostilities and perceived social threats in Murphy's (1999) AERA address and later UCEA publication *The Quest for a Center: Notes on the State of the Profession of Educational Leadership* (pp. 6-10), and replete in the ISLLC standards (Hessel & Hollway, 2002) in which school administrators facilitate the creation of a "vision of learning" that is shared and supported by the school community for "all students to acquire the knowledge, skills, and values necessary to become successful adults " (p. 31); and a school administration is one which ensures "management of the organization, operations, and resources for a safe, efficient, and effective learning environment" (p. 59); where effectiveness is assessed by ensuring that school leaders, "maximize the efficiency of the collection and analysis of these data and will be sure not only to ask the right questions but also to ask the right people" (p. 79). The school leader also is one that "eliminates actions of outsiders that interfere with teaching and learning" (p. 98).

As McCarthy & Dimitriadis (2005) emphasize, that such a discourse "provides imaginary solutions to groups and individuals who refuse the radical hybridity that is the historically evolved reality of the United States...The dreaded line of difference is drawn around glittering objects of heritage and secured with the knot of ideological closure" (p. 326). As lines are drawn around those groups that evoke from us hostile moral evaluations and perceived threats, social justice cannot become strategies for containment, restriction or homogenization cloaked over as they are in the ISLLC standards with such phrases as "facilitates processes" (Hessel & Holloway, 2002, p. 20); acting "upon appropriate theories and models of organization" (Hessel & Hollway, 2002, p. 22); "assuring safe and supportive learning environments" (Hessel & Hollway, 2002, p. 23); bonding "students, staff members, parents, and the community in the work of the school (Hessel & Hollway, 2002, p. 36); in order that, "All stakeholders must be willing to revisit the vision and, in the recursive process of school improvement, ready to create a new vision responsive to change" (p. 43). Such phraseology surrounds the implicit metaphor sketched out by McCarthy & Dimitriadis (2005) as the idealism of resentment, a twenty-first century form of racial condescension which "targets the black and Hispanic minority poor of America's inner cities, who are seen as the tragic ballast weighing down the forward motion of the ship of state" (p. 329).

My line of argument in this essay is that if educational leadership preparation programs are to instruct their graduates to engage in the kind of change which Carolyn Shields (2004) has called *transformative*, social justice has to be conceptualized as more than "being against" or protesting or complaining about assumptions and practices which are unjust, unfair, and/or discriminatory on criteria which serve to marginalize or erase the viewpoints of persons who are poor, of color, or of a non-heterosexual orientation. *Transformative leadership* is about calling into question the larger societal assumptions and practices which relegate schools to the role of reproducing them inside. *Transformative leadership* is concerned with schooling exteriorities (English, 2005). *Transformational leadership* is centered on schooling interiorities.

My position is that preparation programs have to do more than work to erase the most obvious and harmful effects of social injustice in the schools. They also have to position future leaders for roles as *transformative agents* of larger social change.

In order to do this we need at least a theory of social power to undergird our work. To that end I have turned to the work of Michael Mann (2003, 2004), an historical sociologist whose scholarship represents a postmodern outlook on the work of understanding social power.

I seek a theory or theories of social power in order to:

- Create systematic curricula in preparation programs;
- Provide the basis for empirical investigation and evaluation of those programs;
- Provide graduate students with an empirical framework by which to analyze, act upon, and evaluate the impact of their actions in schools and school systems, as they work to create more socially just educational environments for children;
- Provide graduate students with the means to anticipate continuing forms of socially unjust practices, and to understand the relationship between schooling interiorities and exteriorities in this process;
- Provide graduate students with a cognitive map of the process of how socially unjust policies and practices keep being produced in the larger society, their causes and effects, and how such policies and practices are reflected and reproduced in the schools.

CONSIDERATION OF A THEORETICAL FRAMEWORK TO VIEW SOCIAL JUSTICE IN GRADUATE PROGRAMS

John Dewey (1929) once said that "Theory is in the end... the most practical of all things" (p.17). Thomas Kuhn (1996) remarked that the function of a paradigm (theory) was that it made sense of data which had been gathered, otherwise all of it had equal value (p.15). Without an adequate theory from which to engage the concept, the instructor ends up teaching about protest movements (social action); social activists and their lives; (Martin Luther King, Cesar Chavez, Mother Jones), or famous law cases such as *Brown v. Board* (Kluger, 1977). While these curricular topics help the student see the past forms of social injustice and how they were or were not remedied by social action, there are few generalizations that serve to help the student anticipate or perhaps even predict how forms of social power will continue to create inequities in the larger social spheres that impact the schools. Without a sense of understanding the forces at work and how they actually form and interact, the future educational leader is unable to anticipate the manner in which legislation, elections, and national, regional, or local conflicts will manifest themselves around school practices and programs.

The most common theoretical foci in use in teaching social justice appear to be critical theory (see Kellner, 1989), critical race theory or CRT (see Parker, 1998; Parker and Lynn, 2002), queer theory (Hall, 2003; Young and Lopez, 2005), or a theory of justice and oppression advanced by Young (1990). While the latter theory has been explored in teacher education (see McDonald, 2005, pp. 421-2), it has inherent limitations which have triggered this essay. First, Young's (1990) theory of justice and oppression does not deal systematically with how social power comes to be developed in human societies in the first place. Young's (1990) theory simply begins by acknowledging that there are inequalities in such power between groups and that some groups use it to oppress others, "based on race, ethnicity, or

117

class" (as cited in McDonald, 2005, p. 422). Such approaches mask the actual complexities at work in which social power is constructed, supported, and extended, and furthermore, present possible solutions as being based on forces or factors which have been or are repetitive in nature.

Michael Mann (2003) has approached the notion of social power from a different perspective. One of the shortcomings in our current approaches in teaching about social justice in the classroom is how to develop a curriculum that predicts and anticipates how the larger social mechanisms already in place work to perpetuate and extend forms of social power which result in social injustice. We have to move beyond whining, protesting, and lamenting how forms of social injustice keep re-occurring, to one in which we have a much clearer and improved understanding of larger social processes and how schools, as part of that process, reflect, react, reproduce, forms of social injustice or justice as the case may be:

Here are Mann's (2003) major premises:
– societies are constituted of multiple overlapping and intersecting sociospatial networks of power;
– Societies are not unitary. They are not "open" or "closed" because they are not totalities;
– Because there is no system, there can't be sub-systems, dimensions, or levels of such a totality. Because there is no whole, social relations cannot be reduced to some "ultimate" level. There is "no bounded totality" (p. 1);
– Because there is no social system, there is no "evolutionary" process within it;
– Because there is no totality, individuals are not constrained by social structures, class, status, political power or abstractions such as "the economy" (p. 4).
– Multi-causality is the feature marking social power and social life. What this means is that social events or trends have multiple causes. Mann (2003) avers that "…we distort social complexity if we abstract one, or even several, major structural determinants" (p. 4);
– "Societies are messier than our theories of them," says Mann (2003). He notes that Marx and Durkheim were aware of this phenomenon. Max Weber, Mann says, dealt with the complexity of social life by resorting to "ideal types" (p. 4). Mann's approach is similar to Weber's and he makes only the modest claim that he is searching for a "proximate methodology" rather than any ultimate or unitary one.

Mann (2003) deals with the human variable by indicating that "power is a means to other goals" (p. 6). Humans seek power to accomplish goals so Mann does not examine power as a resource. "Resources are the media through which power is exercised" (p. 6). Power, according to Mann is "the ability to pursue and attain goals through mastery of one's environment" (p. 6). Power contains two dialectical aspects says Mann. They relate to a *collective aspect* which exists where humans band together to accomplish joint aims, or a *distributive aspect* where one person is attempting to carry out his will over another despite resistance encountered. In turn each of these can be either exploitative or functional.

Mann (2003) describes a general developmental line to understanding the development of social power. It is illustrated in *Figure 1.*

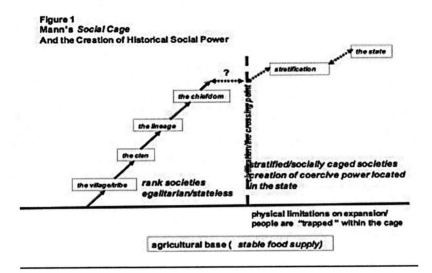

Figure 1
Mann's *Social Cage*
And the Creation of Historical Social Power

In viewing the movement of some societies into those which would be called "civilized," the characteristics of which, according to Mann (2003) are the creation of three social institutions: writing, a ceremonial center, and the city (p. 38), their existence results in a "jump" in development, and when combined with the creation of fixed borders into which human beings are contained and constrained, a comparatively rare event happened, that is, a transition to social stratification and the state. A very similar progression/differentiation has been created by Jared Diamond (1999) in *Guns, Germs, and Steel* (pp. 268-9).

Mann (2003) estimates that in the creation of human villages over the entire globe in total human history, that the number of human societies that became "civilized" was "probably under ten" (p. 38). Most human societies preferred to remain egalitarian, and unless forced by unusual physical circumstances, would not normally take the next steps to social stratification where coercive power could then be embodied in "the state." Mann (2003) uses the metaphor of the "social cage" to describe this rare phenomenon. The low probability of the transfer from a "rank society" into a "stratified society" is represented in *Figure 1* by dotted lines indicating the movement towards "civilization" as Mann has defined it.

Mann (2003) then differentiates between extensive and intensive and authoritative and diffused forms of power. Intensive power is the capability of organizing humans into tight groups and command a "high level of mobilization or commitment from the participants" (Mann, 2003, p. 7). Extensive power has the capability of organizing large groups of humans over "far-flung territories in order to engage in minimally stable cooperation" (Mann, 2003, p. 7). Two other forms of power are *diffused* and *authoritative* While the latter spread in an spontaneous or unconscious way, the former is "willful" and requires obedience (Mann, 2003, p. 8). These forms of power, categorized as "ideal-typical" forms comprise the "reach" of power.

Mann's (2003) analysis of social power centers on *social stratification* because it is with this variable that a society exhibits the "dual collective and distributive aspects" by which "human beings achieve their goals in society" (p. 10). But he examines social stratification without the usual Marxian assumptions regarding a symmetrical or unitary structure. Asserting that "human beings are social, not societal" (Mann, 2003, p. 14). Mann insists that social processes utilize "interstitial emergence" resulting in confederations of overlapping networks and that further, as social power assumes different functions, they are "promiscuous," that is, multiple social networks come into being. These then become the organizing means for the creation of institutions beginning the process of institutionalization and create even more interstitial networks. As human beings pursue their goals they use four sources and organizations of power to attain them.

The first is *ideological power*. This form of power represents the formation of symbols, signs and meanings which impose upon humans a framework of sense making into which people perceive the world. These lead to norms which are shared understandings of how people are supposed to act in regards to one another. People who come to monopolize forms of ideological power through transcendent organizations which emphasize "sacred" forms of authority come to exercise social power. The church is an example of a transcendent organization and its adherents can develop a separate community apart from the rest of the social structure.

The second source of power is economic. In this area, Mann rejects the development of classes. Groups of people come to dominate control over the production, distribution, exchange and consumption of goods. While the development of classes is important, Mann rejects Marxian notions that "Classes are the motor of history." Mann identifies four phases of class development and relations— latent, extensive, symmetrical, and political, and he does not hypothesize that the production function is basic to all of the forms of economic exchange (Mann, 2003, p. 24). Mann does accept two of Marx's tenets under the umbrella *circuits of praxis* (Mann, 2003, p. 25). The first is that there is at one end a mode of production of large groups of people who are laboring in an enterprise. At the other end are many humans involved in networks of exchange. Groups are defined in relationship to these antipodal ends as "classes," but the extent to which they are extensive, symmetrical or political determines the extent to which there is a tight linkage between "intensive local production and extensive circuits of exchange" (Mann, 2003, p. 25).

The third form of power is military. Its character may be said to be *concentrated-coercive*. The fourth type of power is *political,* that is, *state power*. Mann avers that whereas military, economic, and ideological power can be configured in any kind of social relationship no matter where it is located, state power must be centralized. These four sources of social power: ideology (as transcendent power); economic (as circuits of praxis); military (as concentrated-territorial); and state (as centralized-territorial) can be combined in many different interactions and configurations over time.

Since Mann (2003) rejects social symmetry because he proffers that the multiplicity of social relationships and networks are "too complex for any general theory" (p. 30), he does examine the history of the development of social networks in historical contexts. He does this because he believes that the only empirical test which can be developed of social power is an historical one. And the creation of social power historically is largely accidental. Mann (2003) rejects comparative sociology as very useful because there are "so few comparable cases" (p. 30).

Societies are not self-contained units to be simply compared across time and space. They exist in particular settings of regional interaction that are unique even in some of their central characteristics (p. 30).

Mann argues for a "confederal" as opposed to a unitary notion of society (p.16). As he searches for the basis of an empirical approach to social power, he examines the historical record looking for an uneven set of "jumps" because "power capacities have developed unevenly" (p. 31). So history does not repeat itself. Mann argues:

Precisely the opposite: World history develops. Through historical comparison we can see that the most significant problems of our own time are novel. That is why they are difficult to solve (p. 32).

At this juncture it may appear that Mann (2003) has evoked a rationale that would or could be employed to argue against the possibility of an empirical theory even being developed. But some reflection would indicate that while the development of social power may be configured accidentally, neither is it random. An empirical theory would begin to raise such issues as: (1) what are the forces or events that lead to certain social configurations of power, and; (2) what have been the consequences of those configurations?

SOCIAL POWER AND SOCIAL STRATIFICATION

In coming to terms with the development of social power in human societies, Mann rejects evolutionary models as well, partly because they stem from assumptions about unitariness. But he does offer a definition of *the state* that is important. Crediting Weber he defines *the state* as:

a differentiated set of institutions and personnel embodying centrality, in the sense that political relations radiate outward to cover a territorially demarcated area, over which it claims a monopoly of binding and permanent rule-making, backed up by physical violence (p. 37).

To crystallize the idea of the creation of social power, Mann employs the term "social cage" as a metaphor (p. 38) (See *Figure 1*). The development of "civilization" is much more problematic. Examined in empirical/historical terms, Mann (2003) indicates that for a human community to qualify as "civilized" it had to have three social institutions: a ceremonial center, writing, and a city (p. 38). Within these borders humans were contained "behind clear, fixed, confined social and territorial boundaries "(p. 38).

The emergence of civilization according to Mann represents a small percentage of the total possible dwelling places where humans lived. Standing in contrast to some of the prevailing notions of human development, Mann (2003) indicates that most human societies did not "evolve," but "devolved," that is, once reaching a place where a state could become possible with the attendant social stratification, they refused to collectively move into this rank. One of the stark differences between so-called "civilized" and "non-civilized" societies was that the later escaped from the kind of social compacting which led to the "social cage" which created the conditions for permanent and coercive power (p. 39).

In examining the potentiality for teaching social justice (or injustice as the case may be), if a society has rejected the creation of permanent, coercive power in a human situation where authority was "freely conferred, but recoverable," it would not resemble anything like the one in which school leaders work today. Our social structure is densely compacted, or to use Michael Mann's (2003) metaphor, "socially caged" (p. 38). The "social cage" is marked by "civilization, stratification, and the state" (p. 69).

In reviewing the emergence of the state and social power, Mann (2003) stipulates that, "There were no general origins of the state and stratification. It is a false issue" (p.49). Mann (2003) attacks liberal theory on the grounds that it locates social inequality in the differences between individuals. Stratification, however, as he insists, is a *social process* and originally had little to do with genetic differences (p. 50).

Social stratification, according to Mann, may be marked by these characteristics:
- the source of hierarchy resides in representative authority that is not unitary (p.53); social elites have rarely been unitary and they have not often given away power that they could not recover (p. 67);
- collective power came before distributive power, rank societies preceded stratified societies (p. 53), but there is no good theory which explains how social ranks became stratified (p. 62), and not all rank societies evolved into stratified ones (p. 67);
- the state originated in warfare, but human evolution carried it forward to other pacific functions (p. 55);

So far, Michael Mann's (2003) premises challenge these notions of the development of social power:
- The kind of social power we see in institutions today was a rare occurrence in history, so rare, that "no quantitative study of the origins of states" will be adequate because "there is no known overall population of original or 'pristine states...thus one cannot sample from that population" (p. 57). In fact, Mann (2003) indicates that the number of human societies that actually developed into the kind which are dominant today, were originally so small in number that "we might be unable to establish any generalizations" based on statistics because the number of variables exceed the number of cases (p. 341);
- Social power as it exists within a stratified society cannot be conceptualized as unitary or even as a system. It is properly conceptualized as a confederation of overlapping networks. Such a view of the reification of a sort of an immutable, monolithic "state" is a myth and has also been discussed by McCarthy &

Dimitriadis, 2005, p. 322). According to Mann (2003), the configurations of these networks is the result of accidental or idiosyncratic forces involving four sources of power: ideological; economic; military; and political. This possibility is especially challenging in that a theory of social justice/injustice would seemingly have to embrace linkages of causality or at least hypotheses about them to the larger social forces which have created them. But, if Mann (2003) is correct, that "no laws are possible in sociology" (p. 341), what then remains for teaching future school leaders about social justice/injustice? Are such matters purely idiosyncratic? If they are, the basis for moving to correct or change them must rely on creating alternative forms of political power as the nexus of alteration. And, how then can educational leaders anticipate or predict newer forms of social justice/injustice if no laws are possible?

- It is reasonably clear in Mann's delineation of the development of social power stemming from the creation of the historical "social cage," that social stratification (e.g. civilization) and the creation of a centralized state did not necessarily embrace much of what constitutes the agenda for social justice activists today. For example, some ancient civilizations were not necessarily homophobic and accepted same-sex relationships, as for example the Greeks and Chinese, and even among Arab men on pilgrimage to Mecca (Tannahill, 1982, pp. 88, 178-9; 285-6). In ancient Sparta, homosexual relations were recognized as valid in the legal code of the times (Guttentag & Secord, 1983, p. 47) and lesbian relationships were not discouraged by the state (Guttentag & Secord, 1983, p. 48). Slave trading was practiced by nearly all ancient cultures (Hine, Hine, & Harrold, 2006, p. 29). In fact, when Europeans first came to Africa somewhere in the early 1400s, they discovered the slave trading had been going on for several centuries among the extant Islamic states and involved trade in both white and black persons (Hine, Hine, & Harrold, 2006, p. 29). At the time there was no concept of racial solidarity, which did not develop until the eighteenth century (Hine, Hine, & Harrold, 2006, p. 31).
- When it comes to racism Mann (2003) notes, "We find slavery extraordinarily repugnant, and we tend to expect moralizing to legitimate it. Racism seems to fit the bill, but racism is a modern concept not an ancient one. Slavery in the ancient world did not need much justification" (p. 214) where even in six-century Athens when the sale of children was finally abolished, a male guardian could still sell an unmarried woman who had lost her virginity into slavery (Guttentag & Secord, 1983, p. 46). So critical race theory and queer theory, for example,(see Young and Lopez, 2005, pp. 348-50) would not have been necessary in pre-Christian and/or pre-modern societies as an agenda for social change. Cornell West (1999) however, indicates that he believes that ancient Greek ideals of beauty as captured in "Greek ocular metaphors" once crystallized with enlightenment (modernity) thinking, worked to cast black persons and their bodies as inferior and ugly (p. 71).
- Mann (2003) does not deal with gender relations. But since it is an important aspect of contemporary social justice/injustice efforts within educational leadership, it is important to consider how the unequal relations between the sexes originated and in what forms it continues in educational leadership. The

123

imbalance of women in educational leadership roles has been the attention of extended scholarship (Blount, 1998; Brunner, 1999; Shakeshaft, 1987; 1999) and continues into current times (Kowalski & Brunner, 2005).

- When it comes to economic power, Mann (2003) rejects the Marxist metanarrative of society conceptualized in a unitary or symmetrical manner. Instead, Mann (2003) envisions "societies are series of overlapping and intersecting power networks" (p. 77). As such he rejects the idea that there is an "obvious, formulaic, general patterning of the interrelations of power sources "(p. 523). Mann (2003) does not even see class relations as constituting a force of history until classical Greece, and then only within the city states. On-the-other-hand, while rejecting orthodox Marxism, Mann (2003) contends that a second kind of class structure was critical, that is the creation of a "single, extensive, and political ruling class" (p. 529). The creation of such an upper class "was a decisive phase in world-historical development" (p. 529). He called what occurred the creation of a "ruling-class nation" (p. 530).
- Perhaps one observation of Mann's (2003) deserves to be quoted in full because of its importance for incorporating the idea of social justice/injustice in the courses/curricula of educational leadership and because of the importance of the role of schooling in perpetuating an array of existing social problems:
- There is, thus, a simple answer to the question of why the masses do not revolt—a perennial problem for social stratification—and it does not concern value consensus, or force, or exchange in the usual sense of those conventional sociological explanations. The masses comply because they lack collective organization do do otherwise, because they are embedded within collective and distributive power organizations controlled by others. They are organizationally outflanked (p. 7).

TOWARDS DEFINING A THEORY FOR SOCIAL JUSTICE/INJUSTICE BASED ON SOCIAL POWER

In laying the groundwork for a theoretical base which is at least partially empirical, connected to a larger narrative which is descriptive and even predictable is a daunting task, especially given Mann's admonition (2003) that "no laws are possible in sociology" (p. 341). Mann (2003) does indicate, however, that patterns can be discerned as long as it is remembered that the "sources of change are geographically and socially 'promiscuous'—they do not all emanate from within the social and territorial space of the given 'society'" (p. 503). Mann (2003) and McCarthy and Dimitriadis (2005) dispel the image of a single, unitary state. They present the boundaries of the state as porous, and with the internet, exceptionally so. But even in the past, no power network within any given society could "fully control or systematize social life as a whole, but each can control and reorganize certain parts of it" (Mann, 2003, p. 506). Mann (2003) rejects traditional Marxism:

Thus theories that assign the state's main function as the regulation of its internal 'civil society'—whether this is seen in functional or in Marxist class-struggle terms—seem simplistic (p. 511)

That this is so hinges upon Mann's (2003) observation based on Skocpol's (1979) work that there are two autonomous determinants of social power. They are the structure of social classes and the second, the external ordering of the states. As Mann (2003) notes, "Because the external ordering is autonomous of class structure, so is the state irreducible to social classes" (p. 514).

Without moving into a discussion of how Mann's (2003) four sources of power produced the various configurations of social power his lengthy work describes, I want to take those four sources and apply them to educational leadership preparation programs. In so doing, my purpose is to ascertain if a description of them can shed any light on more effective ways of teaching and assessing our success in dealing with sources and practices of social injustice in schools and in the larger society in which they are located.

Figure 2 shows the historical development of four kinds of social injustice which comprise its focus (Shoho, Merchant & Lugg, 2005; Marshall & Oliva, 2006) which are racism (white supremacy and slavery); homophobia (homosexuality including gay/lesbian/bisexual and transgendered orientation) sexism (gender discrimination), and classism, i.e., cultural supremacy based on the presence of a class structure centered on wealth.

The first area in which *social justice* issues arise is racism and white supremacy. A form of racism which has been especially painful in U.S. history, the cause of its most destructive war was chattel slavery based on race. Racism, *viz.* legalized white supremacy for the purpose of the sale and exploitation of human beings based on their race, was a part of U.S. life from 1619 (Hine, Hine & Harrold, 2006, p. 32) to 1865 when the U.S. Constitution was amended to prohibit slavery, a period of nearly 250 years in which slavery was part of the fabric of American life.

The practice of slavery stretches back into ancient times. One of the spoils of war was the acquisition of slaves to perform the work not especially appealing to the conquerors. While not necessarily based on race, the social position of slaves was important when the practice became race-centered. For example, Aristotle posited that the "true slave" was a victim "derived from an innate deficiency in their beauty and inner virtue of the soul" (Davis, 1966, p. 70). Aristotle believed that from the moment of birth some human beings were "marked out for subjection, others for rule. The natural slave lacked the moral and intellectual freedom to make decisions in the light of deliberative judgment" (Davis, 1966, p. 70).

I have already indicated that Cornel West (1999) talked about racism being present in "Greek ocular metaphors" (p. 71). These metaphors, as represented in Greek ideals concerning human beauty and proportion, were elevated to a metanarrative during the period of European classical revivalism. They set the representational standard for observational beauty. When the African was compared to this ideal, a racial binary was created. The African was ugly, with "horrid Curles" and "disfigured" lips and nose (Jordan, 1968, p. 8). Furthermore, the darkness of the skin for Englishmen contained a color binary also attached to beauty. Elizabethan Englishmen thought of a beautiful woman with a very white face and neck with red cheeks. Shakespeare himself in Twelfth Night used the white lily and red rose metaphors (Jordan, 1968, p. 8). And the color black had an emotional content in

English which conveyed an attitude of "[partisan color, the handmaid and symbol of baseness and evil, a sign of danger and repulsion" (Jordan, 1968, p. 7).

Figure 2

Evolution of Contemporary Social Justice Themes
Within Michael Mann's Four Forms of Social Power

Forms of Social Power	B.C.	0-1499 A.D.	1500-1599	1600-1699	1700-1799	1800-1899	1900-1999	2000-200?
			The rise of modernity					
ideological power								
political power								
economic power								
military power								

In the ancient world (the column marked B.C.) *Figure 2* shows that slavery was widely practiced in nearly all early civilizations (Davis, 2006). While it was not necessarily racial, it did often involve whole groups of people such as the ancient Hebrews, who were both slaves and practiced slavery. Many Native American tribes also practiced slavery, with the Lower Chinook of the Washington coast having two or three slaves per family (Niethammer, 1977, p. 181). Slavery is represented in the *Old Testament*. The practice of slavery in ancient times involved all four forms of social power (triangles 1-4). Jesus used the concept of slavery in speaking to the Pharisees indicating that a person who committed a sin became a bondservant (slave) of sin (Davis, 1966, p. 84, from John 8:31-35). And within Biblical texts of Genesis 9 and 10 was contained the story of Ham, who was punished by God after the flood by looking upon his father's nakedness. Jordan (1968) indicates that the writings of the early church fathers referred to the curse as a rationale for the dark skin of Ham's children. Jordan (1968) indicates the specific references to this connection were found in Talmudic and Midrashic texts where "Noah told Ham, "your seed will be ugly and dark-skinned" (p. 18). Early Christian fathers such as Saint Thomas Aquinas could state that slavery was opposed by some principles, but was in harmony with other Christian teachings (Davis, 1975, p. 43).

In the next time period shown in *Figure 2* (0-1499) we begin to see the presence of race in slavery as a factor. Racial differences were important markers in the Arab world. According to Davis (1966) African slaves were ostensibly more numerous in Mameluke Egypt than they were in the Roman Empire (p.50). In the Tang Dynasty (618-907) in China, the connection between slavery and race was visible. The Chinese associated race with inferior peoples such as Koreans, Turks, Persians and Indonesians and the darker-skinned peoples were decidedly second-class (Davis, 1966, p. 51). The first European enslavement of Africans occurred in 1441 by the Portuguese. Davis (1966) indicates that a race riot occurred in Cairo in 1498 when a sultan permitted the marriage of a Black arquebusier to a white slave woman. And, according to Hine, Hine, and Harrold (2006), it was not until the 1600s that the European centered Atlantic slave trade attained the same proportion as the trans-Sahara slave trade (p. 30).

The third column (1500-1599) now shows that slavery had become nearly fully racialized. Spain joined Portugal as a great slave trading nation. Slavery was driven by economic concerns and the need for cheap labor in growing first sugar and then tobacco, rice and indigo in Spanish America and the Caribbean. It is estimated that nearly 60% of the 11,328,000 African slaves transported to the Americas went to Spanish or Portuguese colonies (Hine, Hine, & Harrold, 2006, p. 32). The economic profits were so huge that other militarily powerful European nations also became involved, notably the Dutch, English and the French. After 1713 the sea power of the English overwhelmed the Spanish and French, and the English came to dominate the slave trade, carrying approximately twenty thousand African slaves per year to the Americas with a peak in 1790 when fifty thousand were transported (Hine, Hine, & Harrold, 2006, p. 33). Davis (2006) indicates that by 1820 nearly 8.7 million slaves had been taken from Africa for the New World, the majority for the West Indies and Brazil.

The development of cheap slave labor fueled the industrial revolution in England with the triangular trade in which Africa became a market for cheap English manufactured goods which were exchanged for slaves. Slaves were then taken to the West Indies and exchanged for sugar which was then shipped to England. So the racism that become synonymous with slavery dominated all four forms of power advanced by Michael Mann (2003) until its abolition. But the attitudes affiliated with racial slavery were now reinforced by the rise of science in the enlightenment which reinforced white notions of supremacy. And slavery continued in the U.S. as powerful economic and political interests maintained and reinforced it, while the nation struggled to contain its expansion. What is important today as part of the agenda for social justice is white attitudes towards Blacks and other minorities, as well as the legacy of scientific racism which replaced Biblical justifications.

Cornel West (1999) proffers that the European "Age of Enlightenment" (1688-1789) constitutes the rise of modernity, beginning with Rene Descartes (1596-1650) who began to assert the links of reason to God. The rise of reason did not occur in a cultural vacuum. It was laced with the thinking of the times, and while it challenged the authority of the church in temporal affairs, it also yielded to the cultural norms of the times regarding beauty and norms of objective physicality which cast Black people as inferior. That this occurred is the result of the primacy of observation in science and its penchant for evidence. Prediction and explanation rested on observation and data. It produced what has been called "the normative gaze," (West, 1999, p. 75). Within the "normative gaze" came the rise of white supremacy (West, 1999, p. 76). White supremacy was bolstered by the origins of a variety of taxonomies and classification systems on which the inferiority of Africans was part and parcel of their construction.

Perhaps the most notable example of the construction of such classification schemes was proposed by Carolus Linnaeus (1707-1778) a Swedish botanist often called the originator of modern scientific classification (Jordan, 1968, p. 484) who divided human kind into four types: Homo Europaeus, Homo Asiaticus, Homo Afer, and Homo Americanus. While Linnaeus did not rank these four types, it is clear in his description of them where they fell. He ascribed to Homo Europaeus such adjectives as, "gentle, acute, inventive" (West, 1999, p. 78) and to Homo Afer terms such as, "crafty, indolent, negligent, governed by caprice" (West, 1999, p. 78).

It was not long before those working in the classification and categorization of animals began to conceptualize what has come to be called "the great chain of being" (Jordan, 1968, p. 219). The "great chain of being" was a metanarrative which became firmly implanted in the Age of Enlightenment. Such a metaphorical stair case arranged the animals by some characteristics in lines all the way to God. Man was superimposed on the chain somewhere in the middle, but it was the all important ranking of men that became the basis of white supremacy. Johann Blumenbach (1752-1840), called the father of anthropology, had no problem in placing white Europeans at the top of the human ladder (Jordan, 1968, pp. 222-3).

Finally, reverting to the notion that Africans were also slaves, and with a long history of viewing slaves as inferior on so many counts all the way back to Aristotle, the African was ranked lower on the great chain and closest to the ape. As Cornell West (1999) has so prophetically indicated European ideals of beauty came to be incorporated into "science" as categorizing humans on the basis of facial and other anatomical characteristics. The fact that the "great chain of being" mirrored rankings in social power and status between human groups at the time was an alternative hypothesis not explored or not taken seriously (Jordan, 1968, p. 227). The great chain of being also placed the African as inferior and such inferiority was "natural," i.e., supported by observation and by evidence. It became the corner stone of scientific racism.

At the root of scientific racism is the faulty notion that people of different races all have the same "actual and imaginary characteristics of that race" (Mayer, 2001, p. 262). Early scientists and popularizers of scientific thinking were engaged in the construction of "typologies" for races. That this view is incorrect has been advocated by the evolutionary biologist Ernest Mayer (2001) who indicates that typologists should be replaced by a "populational approach in which each individual is considered on the basis of his or her particular abilities" (p. 262). However, the history of scientific racism clearly shows that in the construction of ideas regarding intelligence, the typological mindset was still at work in the ranking of the races. Foucault (1983) indicates that such a methodological perspective was attributed to the enhanced powers of observation in the scientific process (p. 125).

Beginning with the work of Francis Galton (1822-1911), who applied mathematics to heredity, beginning with the study of famous men derived from a sample of distinguished men of his times. He found that a large proportion were blood relatives, leading him to the conclusion that heredity governed talent and character (Kevles, 1995, pp. 3-4). With the categorization schemes in place, an increasing number of early scientists mirrored the analogy in the "great chain of being" following the precepts of measuring skulls, looking in human facial characteristics for criminals, all of which have been shown to be false by contemporary science (see Gould, 1981).

The construction of the I.Q. test and its early proponents were deeply immersed in eugenics and racism (Kevles, 1995, pp. 127-147). Such ideological categorizations lent "scientific evidence" to Jim Crow laws which embraced miscegenation, political and economic segregation/oppression (Woodward, 1974) and lent credence to engage in forced sterilization of Africans in many states.

The popular book *The Bell Curve* (1994) by Herrnstein and Murray which attempted to resurrect all of the old typological shibboleths about I.Q. and heredity, indeed mirror the "great chain of being," anchored not by facial characteristics, but by a single, unitary core measure, the I.Q. (Semali, 1997, p. 164).

There were echoes of past scientific racist arguments over I.Q. from former Professor Henry E. Garrett, a psychology professor at Columbia University in New York who argued that "racial differences are facts that cannot be wiped away by social or political theories or by 'freedom marches,' for they are hereditary and follow the laws of genetics" (Osofsky, 1967, p. 512). Garrett argued that African Americans were inherently inferior based on data from I.Q. tests. He singled out the U.S. Supreme Court's 1954 decision *Brown v. Board* as an example of the false doctrine of equalitarianism (Osofsky, 1967, p. 516).

White supremacy is still argued on so-called scientific grounds by Charles Murray, who is on the payroll of the American Enterprise Institute. The publication with Richard Herrnstein (1994) was an attempt at showing since the destiny of every person in society is set at birth genetically, government attempts "to ameliorate economic and social inequality" was a waste of resources (Conason, 2003, p. 138). The blatant misuse of statistics in *The Bell Curve* cost Murray a relationship with the Manhattan Institute. According to David Brock (2004) "the Right had spent more than $1 million promoting Murray alone" (p. 47).

One of the true believers of Murray's notions of IQ and genetic determinism is Rupert Murdoch, conservative media mogul and owner of the Fox TV Network (Brock, 2004, p.174). Murray (2005) penned an op-ed piece in the *Wall Street Journal* following the impact of Hurricane Katrina in New Orleans in which he railed against politicians who were reacting to the large numbers of African Americans shown being forced from their homes because of the calamity in the broken levees. In the same theme from *The Bell Curve* (1994) Murray indicates that the "government hasn't a clue" about what to do. These people (he never calls them Black):

> We already know that the programs are mismatched with the characteristics of the underclass. Job training? Unemployment in the underclass is not caused by lack of jobs or of job skills, but by the inability to get up every morning and go to work. A homesteading act? The lack of home ownership is not caused by the inability to save money from meager earnings, but because the concept of thrift is alien. You name it, we've tried. It doesn't work with the underclass.

The genetic determinism which lies behind Murray's opinions is the kind of white racism being funded by the Right wing think tanks. It is also indicative of a recent work entitled *Human Accomplishment* (2003) in which Murray classifies the great human achievements from 800 B.C. to 1950. As he reviews human accomplishment in the sciences, philosophy, music, visual arts, literature, he indicates the countries from which they hail. In his astronomy inventory, he cites 124 "significant figures," of which none are indentified as African though two are identified from Egypt (apparently Egyptians are not Africans). Of the 193 significant figures in biology, none are from Africa (or Egypt). In chemistry, of 204 significant figures, none are from Africa. In the inventory of significant figures (n=85) in the earth sciences, one is from Africa. Of the physics inventory, of the 218 significant figures in physics, none were from Africa. In mathematics, of 191 significant figures, Murray cites none from Africa. In the inventory for medicine, of 160 significant figures, two were from Africa. In technology, of 239 significant figures listed, none were from Africa. Murray (2003) presents inventories of significant figures for Chinese, Japanese and Western art. No category for African art was a part of his inventory. He includes categories for Arabic, Chinese, Indian, Japanese, and Western literature, none from Africa. Works such as these are representational of white supremacy based on genetic determinism. Jared Diamond's (1999) Pulitzer Prize winning work, *Guns, Germs and Steel*, provides a different rational for human accomplishment, much more in line with Michael Mann's perspective.

First, Diamond indicates that "racist explanations" while most everywhere publicly repudiated as the basis for so-called "civilization," (except in Japan and some other countries) he explains:

> The objection to such racist explanations is not just that they are loathsome, but also that they are wrong. Sound evidence for the existence of human differences in intelligence that parallel human differences in technology are lacking...as I shall explain in a moment, modern 'Stone age' peoples are on

the average probably more intelligent, not less intelligent, than industrialized peoples (p. 19)

But Diamond (1999) also confesses that, "Until we have some convincing, detailed, agreed upon explanation for the broad pattern of history, most people will continue to suspect that the racist biological explanation is correct after all" (p. 25). It is this racist explanation that is heavily funded by the political right which also represents the viewpoints of conservative capitalistic elites. They represent the exercise of politics and economics in Michael Mann's model. But mostly these works are attempts to propagate the ideology of racial superiority based on genetic determinism (see also Smith, 2006).

For example, in his book on *Human Accomplishment* (2003) Murray declares, "Brain size is reliably correlated with IQ..."(p. 289). After reviewing all of the data in various attempts to relate brain size to intelligence, Gould (1981) shows that Arthur Jensen (1979, pp. 361-362) supported such a claim but that the actual correlation was about .30 and that there was a .25 correlation between I.Q. and physical stature. Jensen concluded that there was "no causal or functional relationship between stature and intelligence" and did not explore the fact that larger brains would be commensurate with taller persons (p. 108-9). "Scientific" attempts to show racial superiority by dent of brain size have so many anomalies as to be meaningless (see Gould, 1981, pp. 71-112).

White supremacy is a doctrine which has long roots in the Western psyche, all the way back to Aristotle. And Murray is not alone in its advocacy in various forms. A recent infamous example is former U.S. Secretary of Education Bill Bennett's radio talk show remark that, "...if you wanted to reduce crime, you could, if that were your sole purpose, you could abort every black baby in this country, and your crime rate would go down" (Borja, 2005, p. 6). Bennett is also a fellow right wing traveler supported by the Heritage Foundation (Brock, 2004, p. 354) who is part owner of a consulting group that provides services to inner city school systems (Borja, 2005, p. 6).

WHITE SUPREMACY AND SOCIAL INJUSTICE

An effective preparation program which is aimed at confronting the ideology of white supremacy has to do more than work at the abolition of grouping and tracking in the schools, or gifted programs that are based on assumptions of genetic superiority (Sapon-Shevin, 1994; Smith 2006). What has to occur is a full scale analytical de-construction of western science as embodied in modernism and how it came to dominate the ideology of superiority, locating and objectivizing the "normative gaze" which is based on the assumption of inferiority of Africans and/or other persons of color. White supremacy has long roots in European history beginning with the concept of the "white man's burden" based on the idea that European civilization was superior to all others.

In short, the white man had rights to all the wealth of the world because he carried the burden of a superior civilization on the road to solving all the

problems of mankind. Whatever was necessary to exercise this right—
murder, rape, kidnapping, torture, genocide—could be rationalized under this
self-imposed mandate. This wave of European imperialism... found its roots
in a combination of ethnocentric intellectual tradition, a newly energized
'scientific racism,' and the perceived demands of world trade (Mohawk,
2000, p.170)

Such an attitude still exists in the cultural tools used to select "leaders" for
university programs in educational leadership. It means that we have to thoroughly
examine the means by which we identify future administrators such as the
Graduate Record Exam, which has a long history of discrimination against women
and persons of color. The snobbism and racism which prevails in academe
regarding admissions connected to such tests is a legacy of the "scientific racism"
of the past.

White supremacy continues to be the hot point of contention in racial relations.
It even manifested itself within the abolitionist movement (see Davis, 1983, pp. 70-
86). It was identified in the Report of the National Advisory Commission on Civil
Disorders released in 1968 following urban rioting in the nation's cities as a major
cause of civil unrest (p. 235). It remains alive and vibrant even today as Walter
Allen (2005) indicates, there is a choice between warring ideologies. On the one
hand is the vision of great opportunity which is nearly unlimited. On-the-other-
hand, "is the belief in and commitment to the ideas of racial supremacy" (p. 22).
The continued subjugation of African Americans and Latinos economically is
justified politically by the continued ideological support trumped up by right wing
think tanks supporting genetic determinists such as Charles Murray or racists such
as Dinesh D'Souza who have argued for the repeal of civil rights legislation
(Conason, 2003, p.139). D'Souza was reportedly paid $483,023 in salary from the
American Enterprise Institute before moving on to the Hoover Institute (Brock,
2004, p. 351).

What Michael Mann's (2003) theoretical network of forms of social power
would indicate is that there are strong connections between ideological, political
and economic power, and that university educators must begin to take the activities
of the right wing think tank noise makers much more seriously than they have
in the past. While university based scholarship continues to dominate serious
academic discourse, the larger public media outlets controlled by conservative
elites are spending enormous sums to propagate the continued ideology of the
"wholesale subjugation of women, gays, and lesbians; and most especially and
centrally of the deeply antidemocratic and dehumanizing hypocrisies of white
supremacy" (West, 2004, pp. 13-14).

HOMOPHOBIA

Another area which has been part of the social justice agenda has been that of confronting homophobia and the accepted normativity of heterosexism (Koshoreck &
Slattery, 2006; Kumashiro, 2002; Shoho, Merchant & Lugg, 2005). Homophobia
was first coined by George Weinberg in 1972. It refers to the extreme contempt or

rage some people had when encountering homosexuals (lesbians, gays, bisexual, transgendered, transsexual or intersexual persons). This definition now includes derisory comments, excluon and/or violence, sometimes referred to as "bashing".

The practice of homosexuality in a variety of forms is likely to have been part of humanity's total trajectory, although written records did not come into existence until 3000 B.C.(Tannahill, p.18). Taylor (1996) believes that the Neolithic period (Stone Age) was the birthplace of homophobia and notes that the Old Testament, which was reflective of farming life, "is stiff with it" (p. 163). Taylor observes that among domestic farm animals homosexual behavior is often observed. But from the eyes of the farmers it was not functional behavior for reproductive purposes (p. 163). It was therefore to be avoided.

There is certainly abundant evidence in the ancient world that homosexuality was practiced. In the 6th Century B.C., the island of Lesbos was home to the famous poet Sappho who practiced *charis*, which included music, art, poetry and romantic lesbian love (Walker, 1983, p. 534).

Both ancient Greek and Roman societies contain long histories of same-sex liaisons and practices, notably in Greek man/boy relationships (Foucault, 1986, pp.193-228) or specifically in Sparta where lesbian (called tribadism) relationships were common (Tannahill, 1980, pp.84-100). Taylor (1996) comments "The sixteenth-century Spanish were outraged by the widespread homosexuality and transvestism that they found among the indigenous peoples they conquered in the Americas" (p. 17). Europeans also were shocked by African sexual mores in the seventeenth and eighteenth centuries:

> The extent of nakedness; the free use of sexual jokes, allusions, and symbols, the apparent ease with which sexual partners could sometimes be exchanged— in a word—the different standards of behavior—convinced Europeans that Africans had no standards, no morals, no restraints (Genovese, 1976, p. 458).

In North American Indian tribes, homosexuality was often respected as a valid life choice. In the Mohave tribe, a lesbian was called a hwame and "took a male name and wore male clothing if she needed it for riding and hunting. A hwame was accepted into all male activities but could not become a tribal head or war leader" (Niethammer, 1977, p. 230). Hwames sometimes took wives. In the Kaska tribe located in Canada, lesbianism was sometimes encouraged if there were too many girls. A girl was taken aside and raised like a boy. Niethammer (1977) notes that some of these girl-men became outstanding hunters (p. 230).

Foucault (1985) notes that while Plato condemned certain relationships as "contrary to nature," he enjoyed same sex relations as a youth and was most worried about males who assumed female roles in sexual relations. This was most likely the subject of discussing what "contrary to nature" meant in practice (p. 222). Homosexuality in ancient Rome also was common. Many of the emperors were bi-sexual. It was rare when one was completely heterosexual as was the case with Claudius (41-54) (see Grant, 1985, p. 33). Plato's attitude towards male homosexuality based on Biblical interpretation is quite different than female homosexuality which is mentioned only once (in a disputed passage by Paul in Romans 1:26) in

Scriptures (McNeill, 1993, p. 85). What is so homophobic about male homosexuality is that in a male dominated society, assuming the role of the subordinate (female) sexual partner is viewed as "one who had betrayed not only himself but his whole sex, dragging his fellow men down with him in his voluntary disgrace" (McNeill, 1993, p. 86).

The decline of Rome and the rise of the Christian church began to re-define sexuality and sexual relations between humans. Michael Mann (2003) examines Christianity's rise as an example of the *ecumene*, the rise of a transcendent power as a religion "of the book" (p. 301. This transcendent ideological power cut across class lines and it was diffuse rather than of the authoritative kind. Mann (2003) observes that:

> Christianity was a form of ideological power. It did not spread through force of arms; it was not for several centuries institutionalized and buttressed by the power of the state; it offered few economic inducements or sanctions. It claimed a monopoly of, and divine authority for, knowledge of the ultimate " meaning" and "purpose" of life, and it spread when people believed this to be true (p. 302).

Mann (2003) avers that Christianity provided solutions to the five great contradictions to the Roman Empire, one that was better than the empire itself. These were:
- Universalism vs. particularism
- Equality versus hierarchy
- Decentralization versus centralization
- Cosmopolitanism versus uniformity
- Civilization versus militarism (pp. 306-7).

The result was an *ecumene*, a universalistic, egalitarian, decentralized, civilizing community (p. 307). Although Christianity would later incorporate all of these contradictions within itself, the religion required communication and literacy to be advanced.

But Christianity also re-cast not only heterosexual relations as "unseemly, degrading and shameful" (Tannahill, 1982, p. 143), but homosexuality was condemned as well. The metaphor of "sodomy" was employed based on the city of Sodom in Genesis 19, 4-11). The *Old Testament* does not refer to the sins of Sodom as being homosexual. Rather, it says that the sins were those of "pride and inhospitality" (McNeil, 1993, p. 68). Later, in the first century A.D., Tannahill (1980) indicates that Philo of Alexandria "expressly interpreted the story of Sodom in homosexual terms" (p.155). The early church fathers adopted this version of the fall of Sodom (McNeil, 1993, p. 75). St. Thomas Aquinas was particularly harsh and condemning of homosexuality as a violation of the laws of God regarding procreative sex. To engage in same sex acts was obviously not for procreation. And because the church fathers believed that such perversions were extreme in the sight of God, they ran the risk of provoking earthquakes, famine and pestilence (McNeil, 1993, p. 83). Homosexuality was therefore a threat to the state. And the state took steps to protect itself by passing draconian legislation that has persisted into modern times.

The church's ideology concerning homosexuality was similarly used during the Nazi rule in Germany to sentence homosexuals to the death camps. It is estimated that perhaps 220,000 perished as a result. Even if they survived the death camps they were not entitled to any recompense as other survivors because in Germany they were still identified as "criminals" (McNeil, 1993, p. 83). As for lesbians, in Christian Europe, their sexual orientation was regarded as "'a crime without a name,' and they were sometimes burned alive without trial" (Walker, 1983, p. 536).

Figure 2 (circles 1, 2) shows that homophobia and oppression for LGBTQ persons was first ideological in Christian writing and Church practices, and became political when Christianity became the religion of the state. Laws and decrees were then passed which were designed to protect the state from such transgressions that would anger God and provoke natural disasters, similar to that which befell Sodom and Gomorrah. Foucault (1990) indicates that up to the end of the eighteenth century (circle 8 in *Figure 2*) there were three codes which governed sexual relations between humans: "canonical law, the Christian pastoral, and civil law" (p. 37). The code governed "debauchery, adultery, rape, spiritual or carnal incest, but also sodomy, or the mutual caresss" (p. 38).

But as with the concept of white supremacy, and as we shall see in the continued gender discrimination/subordination of women, homophobia became the doctrine of the rise of modernity in the categorization and medicalization of "contrary sexual sensations," the term used by Carl Westphal in 1870, which according to Foucault (1990) transformed homosexuality from a type of sodomy into a "kind of interior androgyny, a hermaphrodism of the soul" (p. 43). What was important about this re-configuration was that the homosexual was now *a type*, a *species.* Sexual "perversions" were now given names as sub-types or species of "abnormalities". Foucault (1990) cites Richard Krafft-Ebing (1840-1902) who wrote *Psychopathia Sexualis* in 1886 and mentions others who began to categorize other distinctive abnormalities in sexual practices. Foucault (1993) points out that the process of medicalization in the name of science produced "a natural order of disorder" (p. 44) which inevitably produced "the medical examination, the psychiatric investigation, the pedagogical report, and family controls" (p. 45). The exercise of this power "questions, monitors, watches, spies, searches out, palpates, brings to light" (p. 45) deviancies from the heterosexual couple.

Foucault (1990) summarizes the rise of science as contradictory. On the one hand, it was focused on some forms of rationality to come to know and understand that which it was studying. The contradictory development was a "systematic blindness: a refusal to see and to understand...a stubborn will to nonknowledge" (p. 55). Scientific studies of sexuality tried to shed light on sexual practices, simultaneously failing to confront "age- old delusions" (p. 55). While sexual practices had long been a concern of the state since Roman times, the rise of the medicalization of sexual practices made "sex [become] a matter that required the social body as a whole, and virtually all of its individuals, to place themselves under surveillance" (p. 116). While such surveillance was first practiced on middle class families in the "psychiatrization of sex," it was later expanded to all social classes at the end of the nineteenth century (circle 10 in *Figure 2*) (Foucault, 1990,

p. 126). The overriding ideology which developed was that "Our sexuality, unlike that of others, is subjected to a regime of repression so intense as to present a constant danger" (Foucault, 1990, p. 128).

It is this transcendent posture that has carried well into our own times. Homphobia has been an agenda of the right-wing think tank writers and right wing press corps, nobtably Rupert Murdoch's newspapers and the Fox Network (Brock,2004, p.174) as well as talk show pundits. In 2003 the conservative *Washington Times* ran an article that a course at the University of Michigan was aimed at "How to be Gay," when in fact it was an examination of the evolution of the social, literary and media perspectives on homosexuality. This false charge was subsequently repeated on FOX news, MSNBC and even CNN (Brock, 2004, p. 182). Far right psychologist, Dr. James Dobson, who works for Christian fundamentalist ministries wrote in his book *Bringing up Boys* released in 2002 how to prevent homosexuality (Brock, 2004, p. 195). Brock (2004) comments:

...these Christian rightists, with their polemical biblical interpretations and pseudosocial science, have come to stand for what it meant to be a politically committed Christian in the United States (p. 195).

Both Jerry Falwell and Pat Robertson blamed "Abortionists, feminists and gays and lesbians" for the 9/11 attack on the World Trade Center (Brock, 2004, p. 194; Hart, 2004, p. 27). FOX news columnist Sean Hannity has been particularly noted for gay bashing and for promoting a drive to prevent gay marriage (Brock, 2004, p. 272).

An examination of historically "great figures" in history, particularly the arts couldn't be ignored even by AEI author Charles Murray (2003) who revealed that many were either bi-sexual or homosexual (p. 287). In an examination of greatness in his book by the same title, Simonton (1994) commented that while it would be difficult to know exactly how many famous persons were homosexual or bi-sexual, it was quite likely that those who were strictly heterosexual would be the marginals (p.169). The reason may be:

...eminence and sexual marginality may be the result of a third factor underlying both attributes: To attain the highest success, a certain amount of personal independence is essential. To conform to all the dictates of one's culture is to condemn oneself to creative mediocrity. In fact empirical studies show that creativity is linked with autonomy, or even a radical anticonformity (p. 169)

In contrast, Simonton (1994) observes that because a nation's leaders are expected to observe all of social expectations, they usually lead "the most sexually conforming lives" (p. 170). This trend is not expected to lessen in the future and would apply to educational leaders.

However, the continued homophobia which is prevalent on certain news channels and media outlets, the far right and the Christian right, continue to promote an ideology that is rooted in Biblical misinterpretation/exaggeration which is then through political activism manifested in political power. It is the same source for white supremacy, and for our next area of social injustice, sexism.

SEXISM, GENDER DISCRIMINATION

Tannahill (1982) indicates that "at some stage during the Neolithic era, man took over the dominant role and learned to use every available means to sustain it" (p. 45). She speculates that perhaps the source of the domination of men over women began with the construction of the taboo associated with menstruation. Up to a certain point, the sexes were about equal. But something occurred to change this to produce "the kind of assurance, arrogance, and authority that spring...from the kind of blinding revelation—beyond argument, beyond questioning—that was later to be experienced by the prophets of the *Old Testament* and the saints of the New" (p. 47).

Taylor (1996) agrees that the Neolithic period was the time "that the position of women deteriorated" (p. 153). He believes that the rise of agriculture in the lives of humans was partly to blame. First, as animals were domesticated, alternatives to breast milk became more available to human babies. This meant that more children could be raised in quicker succession than before. Shortening the period of lactation also meant that women could conceive children again much more rapidly, since prolonged lactation also performed a natural form of contraception. Taylor (1996) cites the work of Roger Lewin (1993) who notes that women who lived in hunter-gatherer societies ovulated on the average about 158 times during their lifetimes, compared to modern women who on the average ovulate 451 times (p. 264).

As women raised more children they became "ever more tied to hearth and home in the process" (p. 9). Similarly, the archaeological evidence appears to show that the management of herds of animals, notably cattle, became associated with the work of men (Taylor, 1996, p. 172). It became obvious that only one bull was necessary to keep a herd going, and that the control of the bull in relationship to cows along with the rise of property, lead to a sexual inequality between men and women. Taylor (1996) speculates that, "Early farming societies were probably the first to formulate rape laws, not so much to protect women as to defend property and lines of inheritance" (p. 175).

There are several popular, contemporary explanations for the emergence of the dominant/subordination pattern between men and women. One is evolutionary biology in which the biological facts are presented in which "males evolved to compete for scarce female eggs; females have evolved to compete for scare male investment" (Wright, 1994, p. 63). Wright claims that science wins in a contest with cultural explanations because, "It is a simpler and more potent theory (p. 46). The more active role for men suits an evolutionary explanation for the relationships between the sexes. Women have to be picky so they are more reluctant to engage in sexual relationships. This places them in a more subordinate role in human reproduction.

Jamake Highwater (1990) offers the cultural explanation by stipulating that "sexuality is shaped by social forces. Far from being the most natural force of our lives, it is, in fact, the most susceptible to cultural influences" (p. 6). Highwater (1990) posits that the bodies of women...serve as social symbols of the important boundary markers between the group and outsides" (p. 12). In this situation, "female chastity...as the means of guarding against the intrusion of 'strangers' upon a kinship-based society, in which clear biological lines of descent are of great importance" (p. 12). Virginity is an important concept in a patriarchal system. Highwater (1990) believes that what makes human society human is that human females are different than females of other species. Their sexuality is not regulated by hormonal inputs of the estrual cycle. They may choose to engage in sexual relationships "on the basis of social and psychological factors" (p. 49). This mean that "sexual intercourse [was] not simply a means of reproduction, but an aspect of culture" (p. 50).

> As long as female sexuality remained a central impetus of the human community women retained their role as the prime spiritual movers of humankind (Highwater, 1990, p. 50).

The cultural evolution which brought females from the dominant role to a subordinate are recounted by Highwater (1990) as first the result of Greek civilization in which "the authority of women was give over to a feminized male earth spirit" (p. 77).The dominance of men over women was embodied in patriarchal religions such as Judaism and Christianity which share some of the same myths and practices.

Walker (1983) has declared that, "Fathers of the church were earnest woman-haters" (p. 921). She quotes numerous examples including from the *Catholic Encyclopedia* which stated, "The female sex is in some respects inferior to the male sex, both as regards body and soul" (Walker, 1983., p. 921). Hart (2004) says that, "Beyond Genesis, the Bible overflows with passages demonizing women" (p. 164). Women were blamed for the existence of sin and mortality. Hart (2004) indicates that "wife-beating was allowed by Church law and took place at every level of society: (p. 167). In the 1650s men could beat and kill their wives without fear of retribution; but, for a woman who killed her husband, she would be burned at the stake (Walker, 1983, p. 924). Even the Black church, which Michael Dyson (2004) indicates "has been at the forefront of every major social, political, and moral movement in black culture" (p. 237) has "failed to be just and fair with gender relations" (p. 240).

Sexist thinkers often profess that female subordination is the "natural" order of things, or is "a divinely ordained biological mandate" (Walker, 1983, p. 927). Charles Murray(2003), the genetic determinist, points out the supposedly biological basis for the fact that on his lists of outstanding human accomplishments, men are better abstract thinkers and this explains why there have been no female musical composers of the first rank in the world (p. 290). In the case of female scientists, says Murray, they have made their reputation in concrete rather than abstract work (p. 290). He leaves little doubt regarding his own biases in the matter. Taylor (1999) demurs:

It is often assumed that men made all the great cultural advances while women looked on, with their babies at the back of the cave. But we have good reason to believe that some of the most crucial inventions enabling human development were made by women. The seemingly trivial invention of the papoose or baby-sling, around 1.8 million years ago, I argue, was critical in enabling a longer and more intense period of infant brain development, culminating in the emergence of language (p. 20).

Sandra Bem's (1993) commentary on the support for the dominance of men as the "superior sex" is prescient:

Until the mid-nineteenth century, this naturalness was typically concerned in religious terms, as part of God's grand creation. Since then, it has typically been conceived in scientific terms, as part of biology's—or evolution's—grand creation (p. 1)

Gender discrimination in education has a long history which has been recounted elsewhere (see for example Blount, 1998; Brunner, 1999; Shakeshaft, 1987; 1999). It remains a formidable obstacle to correcting the imbalance of men and women in senior administrative roles in education. Recent attacks by right wing think tank spin meisters against a mélange of alleged deficiencies in educational leadership preparation such as the Broad Foundation and Thomas B. Fordham Institute's *Manifesto for Better Leaders for America's Schools* (2004) are really about reducing female leadership of the schools.

When the *Manifesto's* anonymous authors advocate "opening up" educational leadership positions to former business CEOs, ex-generals and other private sector persons, all of these fields have much lower records for women in leadership positions. In 2003, there were only eight women in Fortune 500 CEO slots (Jones, 2003; Sellers, 2003). When such arguments are advanced to "open up" leadership, it may be conveniently pushed aside that education awards more doctorates to women (66%) than eight other professional fields including business, which awards only 38% of its doctorates to women (Characteristics of Recipients of Earned Doctorates, 2003).

The recent study by Arthur Levine (2005) of educational leadership programs financed by conservative interests in which he advocated the elimination of the Ed.D. degree is similarly gender biased. Furthermore, the qualifications advocated by the Board and Thomas B. Fordham Institute's document fits the masculinized versions of administrative leadership and recommends little to no teaching experience as necessary. This also works against women because they typically bring more classroom experience to leadership positions than men (Brunner, Grogran & Prince, 2003, p. 6).

CLASS AND CULTURAL DISCRIMINATION

America has always prided itself on its social fluidity and mobility. *The Economist* (2005, June 11) reported that a study by Joseph Ferrie, an economic historian at Northwestern University examined the census from 1850 to 1920 and found that in the U.S. 80% of unskilled men had moved up to higher-paying jobs compared to only 51% in Britain (p. 32). For a quarter of a century after World War II, American income growth was somewhat evenly spread over the nation. But this trend has been dramatically changing.

> Since 1979 median family incomes have risen by 18%, but the incomes of the top 1% have gone up by 200%. In 1970…the bottom fifth received 5.4% of America's total national income and the richest fifth got 40.9%. Twenty-five years later, the share of the bottom fifth had fallen to 4.4% but that of the top fifth had risen to 46.5% (*The Economist*, 2005, July, p. 12).

The income gap is growing in America. In 1968, for each dollar white's earned, blacks made about 55 cents of that same dollar. Thirty years later, blacks earned 57 cents of the same dollar. As Collins and Yeskel (2005) point out, "At this pace, it would take 581 years for blacks to achieve parity with whites in terms of income" (p.40).

> In 1976, the wealthiest one percent of the population owned 20 percent of all the private wealth. By 2001, the richest 1 percent's share had increased to over 33 percent of all household financial wealth…The top 1 percent of households now has more wealth than the entire bottom 95 percent (Collins & Yeskel, 2005, p. 51).

In 2002, nearly 34.6 million people lived in poverty. This was 1.7 million more than in 2001 (Schaefer, 2003, p. A14). Collins and Yeskel (2005) point out what they term "the wheel of misfortune" in America (p. 85). Fueled by the kind of scapegoating advanced by Charles Murray's op-ed piece on the "underclass", divided communities, extreme individualism and escapism create a cycle in which Americans experience longer working hours, rising personal debt coupled with large monied interests in politics. There is a loss in political participation which continues to shift the influence to large corporations and big investors that lead to rule changes that favor the top 1%. The gap in income is the result of greater economic inequality.

Coupled with this "wheel of misfortune" is the right-wing anti-tax movement which is paradoxical because the right wing doesn't want all government influence shrunk. What they desire are the withdrawal of tax support for the "Opportunity State":

> …the government programs that foster social justice and broaden wealth and opportunity for all Americans. They also aim to weaken the elements of government that regulate corporations to protect workers, the environment, and community interests. Their vision of limited government could be characterized as a 'Watchtower State'—with our tax dollars paying only for military, police, fire, and property-rights protection (Collins & Yeskel, 2005, p. 99).

Michael Mann (2003) rejects orthodox social stratification theory (p. 11). He does so because it is based on notions of social symmetry he does not believe are accurate, autonomous nor homologous (p. 13). His theory rejects the assumption that "the driving force of human society is... institutionalization" (p. 15). He envisions power as a series of interactions of four sources: ideological, political, economic, and military. Social development proceeds through these interactions which are, for the most part, accidental.

THE CHALLENGE OF THEORY DEVELOPMENT: SOURCING FORMS OF SOCIAL INJUSTICE BASED ON SOCIAL POWER

A formidable challenge in attempting to develop a theory of social justice instead of relying on the current approach which is to characterize them somewhat separately, is that Mann (2003) insists,"...there is no obvious, formulaic, general patterning of interrelations of power sources" (p. 523). What this means in searching for a theory Mann makes clear:
- His analysis cannot support "historical materialism";
- Economic power relations do not assert themselves as a finality of the last instance;
- History is not a discontinuous success of modes of production;
- Class struggle is not the motor of history (p. 523)

Mann (2003) sees his power sources weaving in and out of history. The process of developing social power has been through "accidental conjuncture...internally uneven, and geographically shifty" (p. 524).

On-the-other-hand, Mann (2003) does see some patterns: He admits that social power does develop when "a society [becomes] characterized by a single, extensive, and political ruling class. The history of that class is similar to that of the nation. (p. 529), and "classes cannot exist as social actors unless people similarly positioned in relation to economic-power resources can exchange messages, materials, and personnel with each other" (p. 530). These interactions could not exist "until infrastructures gradually developed to allow for the diffusion among them of common education, consumption patterns, military discipline, legal and judicial practice, and so forth" (p. 530). But Mann (2003) concedes that his study is a "theoretical disappointment" [because]:

> History seems just one damned thing after another. If the damned things are patterned, it is only because real men and women *impose* patterns. They attempt to control the world and increase their rewards within it by setting up power organizations of varying but patterned types and strengths. These power struggles are the principal patternings of history, but their outcomes have often been close-run (p. 532).

Jared Diamond (1999) puts it similarly when he notes, "History followed different courses for different peoples because of differences among peoples' environments, not because of biological differences among peoples themselves (p. 25).

A theory of social justice cannot therefore be based on a "single factor" or "single structure" concept. Mann (2003) indicates that he has not written an historical account, rather he wrote a "developmental account of an abstraction, power," and it is not evolutionary in that there are no "immanent tendencies of society" that lead to higher phases from earlier, lower ones (p. 538).

If Mann (2003) is correct than these propositions may be applicable in the development of a theory of social injustice. Because it is clear that what we now consider forms of social injustice as forming an agenda for correction and change, a theory dealing with social justice has to be one (at least historically) that deals with the formation of *social injustice*. Here is what Mann's (2003) work indicates:

- social injustice is not caused by the same interplay of forces in every society over time;
- social injustice is not evolutionary. Some forms of social injustice now considered as such were not always considered so (sex discrimination; homophobia, slavery);
- social injustice is neither unitary nor solely structural even if it becomes institutionalized;
- social injustice does not follow patterns, nor is it's "motor" primarily economic, nor is it confined to or spread by forms of advanced capitalism;
- social injustice has been rationalized within early science (homophobia, white supremacy [racism] as genetic determinism) and continues in science with sex discrimination (educational opportunities, genetic determinism).

It seems to me at this point that what Mann's (2003) analysis of the creation of social power from the beginning to A.D. 1760 has shown is that the main source of social injustice this essay has examined (white supremacy, homophobia, gender discrimination and class/culture gaps) has been primarily ideological, with white supremacy and sex discrimination existing in ancient times; both of these forms, along with homophobia, reinforced and advanced the rise of Christianity; and, then were given additional ideological transcendent power in the intermingling with modernity, which while anti-clerical in some respects, continued to use age-old metaphors and stereotypes in the newly emerging "scientific" disciplines of the Age of Enlightenment beginning with Rene Descartes.

The presentation in this essay indicates that the basis of social injustice has been reflected in the state and its politics after its acceptance in the larger population's religious mythologies and early taxonomic development of the budding "sciences." Economic policies and in some cases military practices followed the ideological and political power sources. Evidence of these connections comes from a new book on Hitler's Third Reich (Evans, 2005) which indicates:

> The dictatorship worked best in areas where the peculiarities of German Christianity matched the prejudices of the new system—penalizing, for example social 'outsiders' of all kinds, from homosexuals

to gypsies. He also makes a great deal of the race question, and shows that this was by no means only about Jews. The 1930s were filled with efforts to purify the race, encourage a high birth rate among the most 'Aryan' in the ethnic German population and stamp hard on anything that smacked of race defilement, including abortion, prostitution, and homosexuality (The Economist, 2005, October 29, pp. 87-88)

What Mann's (2003) scholarship has shown is that forms of social injustice arise in human beliefs because "we cannot understand (and so act upon) the world merely by direct sense perception. We require concepts and categories of *meaning* imposed upon sense perceptions" (p. 22). These beliefs are the "master motivators" for political power, and that economic and military sources serve to reinforce such "master motivators." As Mann (2003) comments, those who can monopolize such claims have an inside track to social power. He quotes Durkheim who indicates that:

> Shared normative understandings are required for stable, efficient social cooperation, and that ideological movements like religions are often the bearers of these (Mann, 2003, p. 22)

These relationships are shown in *Figure 3*. Ideological power has occupied a role of primacy of creating social cohesion.

> ...religion's boost to urbanization and civilization was its ability to provide a rational integration of diverse and new social purposes through more abstract, ethical values (Mann, 2003, p. 126).

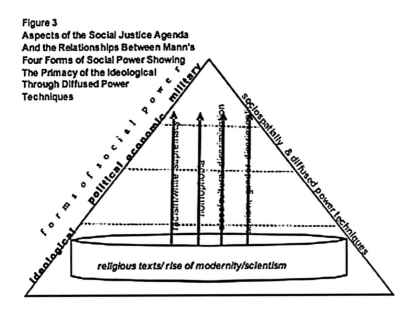

Figure 3
Aspects of the Social Justice Agenda
And the Relationships Between Mann's
Four Forms of Social Power Showing
The Primacy of the Ideological
Through Diffused Power
Techniques

Mann (2003) gives the power of ideology the most important role to the formation of social power in human societies, a role which has been:

> ...normally neglected in theories of origins. Neither state nor social stratification originated endogenously, from within the bosom of existing systemic 'societies' (p.127)

Eugenie Samier (2002) has also recounted the scholarship of Max Weber who rejected Marxist interpretations of such relationships by:

> Propos[ing]a historical explanation in which ideas and ideals, as well as material conditions, can act as independent forces in bringing about socioeconomic change. 'Very frequently the 'world images' that have been created by 'ideas' have, like switchmen, determined the tracks along which action has been pushed by the dynamic of interest (p. 28, From Weber, 1946, p. 280).

IMPLICATIONS FOR EDUCATIONAL LEADERSHIP PREPARATION PROGRAMS

For educational leadership preparation programs centered on eliminating forms of social injustice in the schools and then in the larger society, Mann's (2003) scholarship would suggest that the battleground for change lies not only or even solely in attacking unjust social practices in schools, nor in the larger society where, for example, recent scholarship has shown a strong correlation between poverty, racism, and incarceration rates for African-American males (Andrus, 2005-06), but lies within attacking the ideas which lie behind them, to use a Weberian term also used by Mann, "the switchmen who have laid the tracks along which the dynamics of interest have been projected (Samier, 2002, p. 28; Mann, 2003, p. 28) . The elimination of class differences has to be attacked with political strategies, which are in turn connected to notions of white supremacy rooted in genetic determinism (ideology). And, more ominously, sources of social injustice which are deeply embedded in the religious ideologies governing social practices which continue into present times. Religion clearly has been a two-edged sword in the battle for social justice in the nation's history.

On-the-one hand, Christianity has been the wellspring of abolitionism in the work of William Lloyd Garrison (Mayer, 1998) where slavery was attacked directly as violative of Divine Providence, even as other Christian leaders wrote defenses of slavery using the Bible as a source (Davis, 1975; Palmer, 1967); Jordan, 1968, p. 17). Slavery was not only a threat to a whole range of white mental models of the "natural" arrangements among humans, it also threatened the status of males as superior to females. It can be argued reasonably well that female suffrage began in the abolitionist movement and that it was as threatening to the existing political order as the message regarding slavery (see Davis, 1983, pp. 30-45).

As an example, Davis (1983) has presented the case of the Grimke sisters from South Carolina who after lecturing on the evils of slavery received a pastoral letter from the Council of Congregationalist Ministers of Massachusetts which severely rebuked them for placing the divinely ordained role of womanhood in danger and which created "dangers which at present threaten the female character with widespread and permanent injury" (p. 41).

Religious narratives in Scripture have been used for and against a variety of social practices. Lincoln (White, 2002) noted this paradox when he said in his Second Inaugural Address, "both [sides] read the same Bible and pray to the same

God.; and each invokes His aid against the other. It may seem strange to ask a just God's assistance in wringing their bread from the sweat of other men's faces; but let us judge not that we be not judged" (p.18).

In examining the impact of Christianity on the practice of slavery in the U.S., Genovese (1976) also commented upon the dual-edged nature of its ideological impact. On-the-one-hand, Christianity called upon the slaves to be obedient to their masters. On-the-other-hand, Christianity also made it apparent to the slaves that there were:

> ...moral limits of submission, for it placed a master above his own master and thereby dissolved the moral and ideological ground on which the very principle of absolute human lordship must rest (p.165)

This contradiction within Christianity of its "struggle to reconcile freedom with order, the individual personality with the demands of society," (Genovese, 1976, p.166) became the moral catalyst for abolitionism and the civil rights movement, and it lead to the "creation of a protonational black consciousness" (Genovese, 1976, p. 168).

We are presented with the same contradiction in confronting the continued narratives of social injustice from religious sources and from "scientism" proffered by the genetic determinists such as Charles Murray (2005) and William Bennett (2005). A theory of social injustice must openly confront such sources if educational leaders are to become *transformative*, not only taking on issues which are internal to schools (transformational), but reaching into the larger society and finding the sources which perpetuate socially unjust practices there as well.

What Mann's (2003) work thus far does is confront the matter upon which a theory of social justice/injustice might be constructed. There is sort of a "good news, bad news" with Mann's (2003) treatise. The "good news" is that forms of social injustice which concern us today in schools and in the larger society are not the result of historical determinism, that is, processes which will be repetitive over time if certain circumstances come into being. There are no such junctures of regularity. So the distinctive forms of social injustice we are facing are not in that sense predictable. The "bad news" is that if forms and forces of social injustice are not predictable and largely accidental (though some can appear so by running on for centuries), we would have to move towards a theory which was based on rooting out the mental models which often anchor socially unjust practices. These are also embedded in the economic system and protected by political power.

Mann's (2003) work emphasizes to me that supreme importance of paying attention to the ideologies which provide the rationale for continued racial, gender, and sexual orientation discrimination. While educational leaders have to work towards social justice by rooting out discriminatory patterns and practices which represent prejudice and scientism, we have to attack the core of the problem which is anchored in our culture and the attendant mythologies which define and support them. Since many of these are religious, it makes the confrontation between religious fundamentalism and science in the current battle over intelligent design even more important (Morowitz, Hazen, & Trefil, 2005).

Intelligent design is another belief structure which is faith-based. There is no theory being tested here. No theory was being tested with the perpetuation of slavery, white supremacy, gender discrimination or homophobia. These are ideologies and as Shils (1968) has noted, "no great ideology has ever regarded the disciplined pursuit of truth...as part of its obligations" (p. 73). The connection from these ideologies to the political and economic systems within Mann's (2003) model is obvious. Schooling is representative of the political power of the state.

Learning to lead in Mann's (2003) "social cage" is a huge challenge, since schools represent the institutionalization of the prevailing ideologies, the current politics, and the dominant economic interests which are all highly interconnected. What Mann (2003) does is provide school leaders with a more accurate map of the terrain to be contested and underscore its importance in the grand design of things. It clearly re-defines the scope and sources of opposition to the attainment of the four forms of social injustice described in this essay. More importantly it erodes any defense of them by asserting they are "natural," or "destined" in some way to be "true" by divine revelation or more earthly historical materialism. If social injustice is an accident it can be undone by negating the ideologies which offer them succor, and by education which will ultimately alter the political system which perpetuates them. This is the formidable task confronting programs of educational leadership at the dawn of the 21st century. We are burdened by an accreditation system which contains what Shields (2004) has called "pathologies of silence," right-wing money which is aimed at wresting the preparation of educational leadership away from universities and a socially activistic agenda, and a resurgence of white racism (genetic determinism), homophobia, and the re-masculinization of educational leadership positions, notably in the principalship and the superintendency where the numbers of women are increasing after a long period of gender discrimination. While the forms of social injustice might be historical accidents (because as Mann points out civilization was an accident leading to the creation of the social cage), the opposition to these forms of social justice are not accidental. I believe that a *theory of social injustice*, and the forms of power which perpetuate them, represents a firmer fulcrum for discovering deeper implications of erasing them in a postmodern world.

JONATHAN JANSEN

THE CHALLENGE OF THE ORDINARY

OF COURSE WE *SHOULD*

The normative claim that social justice should be central to thinking about educational leadership makes enormous sense in world that is not only deeply divided, but increasingly unequal. The further claim that we need to rethink social justice in ways that connect powerful ideas, theories if you will, to changing educational practice is especially attractive to those of us who see schools and leadership as important sites of struggle for radical change.

It should come as no surprise, as the collection of papers in this book show, that we are up against it. Killing those we despise has become normative in the political minds of both the powerful and the marginalised. Framing those who are weakest as the architects of their own disgusting state is not simply the project of the political Right, it has become commonsense in all societies, rich and poor. Sustaining privilege for the few at the expense of the marginalized is justified even in societies emerging from long periods of colonialism and racism. Any counter-hegemonic project that seeks to rethink social justice and reframe educational leadership is, without question, confronting the enormous power of ordinariness, the commonsense about power, inequality and violence.

I am not sure though that enumerating theories of social justice will begin to challenge and transform this pervasive commonsense about the way the world is, and indeed, the way it should be. Not that such courageous attempts to open-up powerful ideas long resident in the social sciences are not valuable. I found in this collection forgotten wisdoms and even crucial insights into understanding schools and society anew. We are indeed in danger of reifying dangerous ideas which insist that the social sciences and educational work have little to say to each other, and that educational practice is best understood on its own instrumental terms. This is dangerous thinking, and the book succeeds in making this point.

ORDINARINESS

What I am concerned about, however, is what Seymour Sarason once called the behavioural and programmatic regularities of the school. Take testing, for example. The current pervasiveness of testing, everywhere, in rich and poor countries, has assumed such a powerful logic that to even begin to yell that teaching, of any kind, has been reduced to constantly preparing students for endless tests and examinations is to be stared at. "When will my child learn anything if this whole

Ira Bogotch et al. (eds.), Radicalizing Educational Leadership: Dimensions of Social Justice, 147–155.

year is about testing," I foolishly asked at a packed meeting of middle class parents listening to the school leaders tell us over and over again how little time there was between testing episodes. A pin did drop, and I heard it.

I have yet to encounter social theories that openly and directly grapple with the ordinary, the everyday, and the commonsense. Let me say what I mean. As one trained in a well-known graduate school in North America I was inducted into educational thinking via the social sciences. I was treated to theories of the state in the politics of education; to new sociologies of schooling in sociology; to ethnographic studies of school communities in anthropology; to theories of justice in philosophy; and to labour market theories of education in economics. My professors were critical theorists, in the broadest sense of the term, and some were well-known Marxists who became famous for books like *Education as Cultural Imperialism* in earlier decades. This was theoretical nirvana for me, coming from the oppressive conditions of apartheid society.

But there was a problem: I was also a teacher, and as much as I revelled in these powerful theoretical ideas, it simply did not connect to my daily experiences inside schools. Try as I did, I could not see the connection between radical economics and school change. I certainly understood the social science claims, and I had the benefit of good professors, but how does this translate into a change project? This was not clear even through the writings that made most sense to me, that of Paulo Freire and his struggles to make new meanings with peasants through education in the north east of Brazil.

Schools are powerful organizations; they have their own rituals that include and exclude; they respond to external intervention with suspicion; they follow rules; they are paid for by parents who buy into the logic of personal accumulation; they contain teachers who as servants of the state "implement" new curriculum policies because that is what is required; they appoint principals who ensure that all segments of this complex machine continues to enforce these regularities and to deal, harshly if necessary, with any threats to organizational inertia.

I anticipate the criticism that this is far too deterministic a picture of what happens inside schools. There are courageous teachers and inspirational principals whose work flies in the face of orthodoxy and who bring to bear, in very practical ways, a broader and more liberating understanding among their learners of what education is for. These teachers and leaders, often the same persons, make concrete connections between schools and society, regarding the school fence as an illusion of separateness when in fact these two spheres of human struggle feed into and feed off each others. I delight in acknowledging these activists, and I know many. There are two major problems that should caution us in getting carried away with these nonetheless admirable and hopeful accounts of those who practice social justice inside their classrooms.

The first problem is that these teachers and leaders are unlikely to recite social theory, or even be aware of such profound work in the social sciences. They often draw on strong personal convictions about inequality; they are sometimes influenced by unusual biographical experiences; they sometimes only change as they begin to teach and lead, becoming sensitive to and conscious of the fact that schools work to maintain social difference; and they sometimes, as in poor countries, come through terrible teacher preparation programmes in which social justice, to put it bluntly, was not a module.

The second problem is that such teachers remain a minority. They stand out, precisely because they are bent on resisting commonsense. But they are worn down by the sheer scale of administrative minutiae and managerial impositions that everyday narrows the space for liberatory pedagogy. They are overwhelmed by complying colleagues and stifling work conditions that keep schools the same and ensure that the regularities of schooling grind over from one day to the next. Schools do not change as a result of such teachers and leaders, even though their micro-impacts on individual learners are often very significant.

DISCONNECTION

How then does one proceed, given the importance of theory and the ordinariness of schooling? It seems to me that a crucial first step is to acknowledge the contemporary disconnect between social theories and the practice of education. This by the way is not to ignore the fact that their have been theorists who have tried to make radical theory connect with what happens inside schools; here I think of the inspiring work of Munir Fasheh in the Palestinian territories, of Marilyn Frakenstein in the United States of America, of Paulo Gerdes in Mozambique, and so on.

The problem in much of this resisting work, though, is that they are expressed as the creation of curricular and pedagogical alternatives to what exists rather than the challenge and collapse of what keeps such new thinking on the margins of the everyday business of schooling. It is for this reason, also, that such alternatives tend to recede into social oblivion, given the enormous power of the ordinary and the regular inside schools and, for that matter, inside universities.

The next step for me is to bring to light the powerful ways in which schools sustain themselves as organizations. We simply do not know enough about the myriads of ways in which commonsense is imposed on and generated through the ordinariness of schooling. Here are some questions that must be probed by social theory if it is to gain any traction for social justice in the ordinariness of schooling.

QUESTIONING COMMONSENSE

How did testing become such a powerful tool in oppression, in confirming over and over again that those who succeed are those with the social capital as well as the material goods that almost perfectly predict a straight correlative line between resources and performance? Why does testing, in such contexts, not produce outrage?

How did curriculum become such a mockery of social justice? How did science and mathematics gain such prominence inside schools and in society? How did these subjects become emptied of any social conscience and deployed in the narrow logics of accumulation? How did culture and the arts become marginal so quickly in the curriculum of many societies?

How did teachers become part of the problem? Why do teachers buy into this role of "implementers" even when it goes against their own commonsense of what is required inside schools and classrooms? Why do teachers not resist more? What is it about teachers in many societies that when such acts of resistance occurs, it tends to be about their own narrow interests—teacher salaries—rather than a contestation about knowledge and curriculum?

How did teaching become so mechanised? Why is it that student teachers scorn social justice and prefer to be immersed in learning about the techniques of teaching and testing, believe it or not, rather than in the social purposes of education?

WHAT SUSTAINS INJUSTICE?

Just before he died, Edward Said listened attentively to a panel of progressive South African scholars and activists recite stories about racism in post-apartheid society. Said stood up at the end and posed a disruptive question: "do not tell me that there is racism in your country; tell me what sustains it."

This is the challenge facing radical social science which, as the collection of articles correctly points out, tends to protest what happens inside schools but does little to understand why what happens continues to roll over ordinarily from one day to the next. Until we understand what keeps schools and their citizens continuing as they do, there is little that social theory can say to unhinge such commonsense.

But there is another dilemma for social theory as it observes and engages schooling; it is, all too often, a one-way account of schools and classrooms. School-level activists, like the ones cited above, tend to seek to "apply" social theory in schools, to give Freire or Gramsci or Apple meaning in struggles over curriculum and pedagogy. This is important, but lacks dialectical authority.

It is crucial that we develop fine-grained studies of how schools function to sustain the ordinary and then to connect this back to the task of engaging existing theory and also making new theory on the basis of what happens inside schools. Until this two-way conversation between theory and practice happens as far as schooling is concerned, there will continue to be the social disconnect which I referred to earlier.

Unfortunately, writing about schooling is split into camps: those who write about what happens inside schools as important but atheoretical accounts of the day-to-day logics of schooling, like Jeannie Oakes' immensely important work on tracking; and those who write about schools from the distance of social theory without a grounded sense of what sustains everyday practice, as in the earlier works of Henry Giroux and his followers. I still feel that calling schools names and giving teachers labels hardly begins to change what they do against the grain of commonsense.

We should of course begin by documenting much more comprehensively the work of those who resist, who lead and teach against this grain of commonsense. But we must write not only to acclaim, and this is necessary in schooling cultures all over the world that only recognise teachers and leaders who "turn around" schools on the basis of test scores. It is however also important in new research to understand what it is in the DNA of educational institutions that makes it so hard to make the marginal the mainstream.

It is a humbling task for theory and practice. I have just come off a seven-year assignment as the first black Dean of Education of a virtually all-white faculty in a conservative white South African university that has existed for one hundred years. I worked very hard with a team of outstanding fellow leaders and academics, and wonderfully receptive students, to begin to change the racial balance of staffing, the racial and gendered balance of students, the ideologically conservative curriculum, and the stiflingly silent and compliant institutional culture where dissent or different thinking could end careers.

Much had changed, but I am more and more convinced that after I left, things tended to revert to the same olds forms and habits of thinking and doing; the ordinary wins again? What is it that makes change so difficult? Why is it so easy to revert to old forms even when the benefits of the new appeared so obvious? Was it always naive to think that one unit, an education school even with its own campus, would be able to go in a very different political direction when it was simply one of nine schools in an overwhelmingly white and conservative administration? Where does the power lie that sustains this conservative model of teacher preparation and educational life?

UNDERSTANDING FROM THE INSIDE, AND OUT

This should be the basis for new theorizing, and I am not convinced that relying only on received theory, however venerable the ideas and the personae that once yielded such ideas, can begin to grapple with what happens inside schools and universities. It is a sobering thought that those who often write most eloquently about schooling have never been teachers or principals or administrators; they have not worked the shifts, felt the moods, challenged the system, and been disciplined by it. There is something about working inside schools that gives a very different sense of the emotional, psychological and political nature of these environments than when one writes from a distance.

I am not suggesting at all that the only authentic voice for theories of schooling and theories of justice can come from the experience of teaching and leading in schools; not at all. The only point is that there are limits to what can be understood, and therefore changed, when there is not a direct experience of this political space called the school.

In sum, social theory needs to shed light on the broad functionalities of schooling as they reproduce and resist change; but new ways of doing social theory needs to take its cue from what sustains the ordinary and therefore what cancels out spaces and possibilities for social justice to gain traction in the everyday existence of a place called school. Such hard theoretical labour between theory and practice and practice and theory still needs to be done.

My problem with pursuing social justice and thinking about social justice in the hard surfaces of educational institutions is that it is very difficult to achieve these ends without being immersed in practice. Over the past seven years I have worked with white South African school principals who lead against the grain of what happens in almost every other white school in this post-apartheid state.

Here are white principals and communities still smarting about loss; the loss of privilege that only recently made it possible to accumulate resources at the expense of the black majority of schools and students and teachers; the loss of power that made it possible to enforce decisions that kept schools white and excluded black students who sought entry to superior facilities; and the loss of place that made it possible to secure preferred standing and status in the social and political machinery of a racist society.

Yet these white principals took on the challenge of change and made their schools places where black teachers could be hired not in the marginal and somewhat predictable subjects of African languages, but in the mainstream subjects of the physical sciences and accounting. They changed their schools to encourage black enrolments but without losing the critical mass of white students so that in this space racial encounter and engagement could be pursued as they prepared young people for a democratic country still struggling with racial divisions and racial inequalities. They broadened the curriculum to bring in a wider span of social, political, economic and cultural experiences without diluting what the tests required of official knowledge. And they worked hard to bring in white and black parents to share spaces and decisions even as their schools struggled with defying the odds.

No doubt one of the goals of this research was to recognize and acclaim these white principals who defied their own biographies and, in many ways, their own conservative communities during the early transition from apartheid. But then the hard work began around two fundamental questions:
– how does one bring enough detail, nuance and variegation to bear on these leading practices in ways that challenge schools everywhere, that majority of schools—black and white—for whom this kind of leadership labour would be a completely foreign experience?
– how does one think through these experiences of leading against the grain in ways that influence and shape existing theoretical wisdom, but even goes beyond received theory to create new ways of theorizing about social justice and the schools.

The existing theoretical landscape was not very helpful here, for I could find little that connected counter-race thinking, schools and change within the context of one of the most dramatic social transitions of the twentieth century. The existing valorisations of leadership was of black leaders going back to black schools with great charisma to take back their schools; or of white leaders from working class communities returning to the poverty and disillusionment of the poor to inspire hope and change. And the stories remained fixed on the biographical, and failed to lay the table for systemically thinking about change in schools everywhere.

What our research pointed to were some fundamentals that constitute early groundwork for rethinking leading for social justice in ways that promised fresh theoretical insights.

BIOGRAPHY AS TRANSGRESSIVE MATERIAL

We realised that changing schools for social justice must begin with making explicit the biographies of principals, teachers and students. It is fruitless coming into schools with formal theory about social justice for the tendency is to shy away, to fall back on the instrumental and the everyday. But there is something appealing about reflections on biography, on how we got to where we were. An example from a related context makes the point.

For years at the University of Pretoria where, until recently, I taught and led as Dean, we wondered how to introduce social justice thinking to conservative white students at this former bastion of Afrikaner nationalism. In the undergraduate class sat hundreds of mainly white women students interested in careers as teachers in early childhood education. Like most student teachers, they wanted a compendium of teaching techniques, strategies for implementing the new government's outcomes based approach to education, schema for assessing learning outcomes, and of course the modalities of how to establish your own educare or preschool centers. Any hint of talking about the past or talking about justice to those who had just lost power and were losing privilege, would be end and pedagogical venture abruptly. They would sit politely and listen, but the engagement would end right there.

A colleague then came up with a plan. Ask these white student teachers to go to their homes and interview the black domestics, those older women who often raised them as children, who kept their homes whether the mothers worked or not in this patriarchal community, and who left her own children and family in townships or rural areas to on site for the sake of these white children who were now young adults at university. The students responded to this with great excitement, the chance to interview "Sanna" at home. They loved Sanna, in that racial paternalistic way, that made such a learning project very exciting.

Parenthetically, to understand what is at play here requires a bit of background on the cultural politics of Afrikaner community. White Afrikaner children, unlike their white English counterparts, are taught to respect any adult through elaborate gestures and forms of greetings that typically address the adult, whether known or not, as "Oom" (Uncle). It is a warm and generous gesture, one that recognises the other adult as extended family even though there are of course no biological bonds to such a person; in fact, it could hail a complete stranger. The problem is that this gesture was reserved for whites, and so in the home a much older woman, known to the white children from birth, is called by her first name "Sanna."

The students return excitedly with their data, they interviewed Sanna about her culture and her language and he religion, all safe topics that reinforce difference for these second generation children of apartheid. What followed was a dialogue with the lecture that looked like this:

- "Wonderful, so you have data on Sanna's life. Now, what is Sanna's last name surname)?"

This creates some consternation, for it never occurred to these white young people that like any other ordinary human beings, Sanna must have had a last name. Nobody knows the last name of their domestics in this large class. It was always *Sanna*. Here was a mix of disrespect and disinterest rolled into one; the point need not be made directly, the student teachers begin to realize what is going on.

- "Is Sanna her real name, her first name?"

Further consternation. Of course it is Sanna. The students go back to find out, and then learn that the domestic has a completely different registered name, say, *Tshepiso*. But because whites did not want to be burdened with the awkwardness of black names, they gave an Afrikaans sounding name whether or not this was the first or second name of the domestic worker. The students then go back home again and this time discover that Sanna is really Tshepiso Morake. Again, the point need not be pushed here, as reality slowly dawns on these white children as biographies pry open unpleasant truths.

- Does Sanna have a family?
- Who looks after Sanna's children when they are with you?
- Where does Sanna live?
- How long does it take Sanna to get to work?
- What does it cost Sanna to get to work?
- What does your family pay Sanna?
- Is Sanna the only breadwinner in her family?
- Would you invite Sanna's teenage children over to your home?
- What languages does Sanna's children speak?
- Where does Sanna's children go to school?
- Are their schools similar to or different from yours?
- Why do you think this is the case

These seemingly innocent questions about human lives are in fact, in this context, powerful invitations into a dialogue about social justice. And the natural attractiveness about biography provides rich material for critical pedagogy, yes, but also for social theory.

This rather extended case study is raised to show that a potent theory of social justice in schools must start with who we are, with where we come from, with whom we relate, and with how we relate to those around us. It could, in other words, deploy the ordinariness of biography as transgressive material in the schools and classrooms of our societies. This kind of transgressive recapturing of the everyday is what needs to be foregrounded in theoretical work on education for social justice.

MESSINESS AS LIVED EXPERIENCE

Second, we realised that regnant theories assumed emotional wholeness, leadership perfection, single-mindedness, clarity of purpose, unflinching commitment, linear change. This is a particularly American conception of goodness in schools and in teachers and in leaders. It is an ethnocentric state of mind that cannot deal with ugliness existing alongside aspiration.

Our studies on leadership showed white principals changing slowly as they became more comfortable and more assertive with respect to the practice of social justice in their schools. Even as they forged ahead with change they unwittingly used outdated if not offensive language when describing black children and their cultural preferences. While they were fighting apartheid, nobody taught them the new lexicon for engaging this new democracy. Their fears, instilled over a life time and inherited over three centuries of white racism, shine through even as they open the doors of their school to black teachers and black students. Their attempts at bringing together cultural traditions is clumsy, at first, as they more from added-on representations of culture to genuinely engaging race, identity and power through the new presence in their white schools. It is precisely this awkwardness, the stumbling, the wrong words and the anxieties about change that attract and endear these white leaders to us as a largely black research time. In them we see our own likeness and our own fragility; and in their examples of courage against the grain of what other white principals were doing (trying to keep their schools white) and what white communities were expecting, we find hope.

But show me a theoretical framework particularly in the critical tradition that begins to grapple with this imperfect practice. There is none, for what critical theory does is to stand self-righteously at the other end of this struggle and declare the impossible ideals that real practising teachers and principals—the ordinary ones—must but simply cannot attain without working through the ruins of a troubled past, a testing present, and a future from which the lifeblood of hope is drained by the burden of the everyday.

Witness the fate of the turnaround principal in John Merrow's documentary series on troubled schools for PBS television. A white principal from the high performing middle class schools is trained as a 'turnaround specialist' and assigned to a troubled black school to improve performance. As he begins to make small progress in laying the foundations of respect, compassion and care within this dysfunctional school the bureaucracy suddenly swoops on him with a single message: the only thing that matters, the ubiquitous bottom line, is the test scores. His energies at laying lasting foundations for change is suddenly diverted towards the routines of drill-and-practice in the narrow-minded quest to raise test scores in the shortest time possible. Of course he fails. Where is the theory that grapples with such realities?

REFERENCES

Introduction References: Part One: What can social justice educators learn from the social sciences?

Buchanan, A., & Mathieu, D. (1986). Philosophy and justice. In R. L. Cohen (Ed.), *Justice: Views from the social sciences* (pp. 11–46). New York, NY: Plenum Press.

Brooks, J. S., & Jean-Marie, G. (2007). Black leadership, white leadership: The moiety structure of an American high school. *Journal of Educational Administration.*

Dantley, M. E., & Tillman, L. C. (2006). Social justice and moral transformative leadership. In C. Marshall & M. Oliva (Eds.), *Leadership for social justice: Making revolutions in education* (pp. 16–30). Boston: Pearson Education.

Cohen, R. L. (1986). *Justice: Views from the social sciences.* New York, NY: Plenum Press.

DeMarrais, K., & LeCompte, M. D. (1999). *The way schools work.* New York: Longman.

Di Quattro, A. (1986). Political studies and justice. In R. L. Cohen (Ed.), *Justice: Views from the social sciences* (pp. 85–116). New York, NY: Plenum Press.

Evans-Pritchard, E. E. (1946). Applied anthropology. *Africa, 16*, 92–98.

Furby, L. (1986). Psychology and justice. In R. L. Cohen (Ed.), *Justice: Views from the social sciences* (pp. 153–204). New York, NY: Plenum Press.

Gibbs, J. C. (1987). Social processes in delinquency: The need to facilitate empathy as well as sociomoral reasoning. In W. M. Kurtines & J. L. Gerwitz (Eds.), *Moral development through social interaction.* New York: John Wiley.

Lerner, M. J., & Whitehead, L. A. (1980). Procedural justice viewed in the context of motive theory. In G. Mikula (Ed.), *Contemporary topics in social psychology* (pp. 219–256). New York: Springer-Verlag.

Marshall, C., & Oliva, M. (2006). *Leadership for social justice: Making revolutions in education.* Boston: Pearson Education.

Nader, L., & Sursock, A. (1986). Anthropology and justice. In R. L. Cohen (Ed.), *Justice: Views from the social sciences* (pp. 205–234). New York, NY: Plenum Press.

Rawls, J. (1971). *A theory of justice.* Cambridge, Massachusetts: Belknap Press of Harvard University Press.

Rescher, N. (1972). *Welfare: The social issues in philosophical perspective.* Pittsburgh, PA: University of Pittsburgh Press.

Rytina, S. (1986). Sociology and justice. In R. L. Cohen (Ed.), *Justice: Views from the social sciences* (pp. 117–152). New York, NY: Plenum Press.

Schacht, R. L. (1970). *Alienation.* Garden City, NY: Anchor Books.

Scheurich, J. J., & Skrla, L. (2003). *Leadership for equity and excellence: Creating high achievement classrooms, schools, and districts.* Thousand Oaks, CA: Corwin Press.

Schmidt, S. L. (2003). More than men in white sheets: Seven concepts to the teaching of racism as systemic inequality. *Equity & Excellence in Education, 38*(2), 110–122.

Soltan, K. (1986). Public policy and justice. In R. L. Cohen (Ed.), *Justice: Views from the social sciences* (pp. 235–268). New York, NY: Plenum Press.

Wiser, J. L. (1983). *Political philosophy: A history of the search for social order.* Englewood Cliffs, NJ: Prentice-Hall.

Worland, S. T. (1986). Economics and justice. In R. L. Cohen (Ed.), *Justice: Views from the social sciences* (pp. 47–84). New York, NY: Plenum Press.

Wolcott, H.F. (1999) *Ethnography: A way of seeing.* Lanham, MD: AltaMira.

Introduction References: Part Two: What can social scientists learn from the study of education?

Apple, M. (1979). *Ideology and curriculum*. New York: Routledge.

Bojer, J. (2000). Children and theories of social justice. *Feminists Economics, 6*(2).

Deutsch, M. (1985). *Distributive justice: A Psychological perspective*. New Haven, CT: Yale Press.

Erickson, E. (1963). *Childhood and society*. New York: W.W. Norton & Co.

Foster, W. (1986). *Paradigms and promises*. Amherst, NY: Prometheus Books.

Freedom House. (2005). Retrieved from http://www.breitbart.com/news/2005/12/20/051220134942.8w8uaqyp.html

Giroux, H. (1988). *Teachers as intellectuals*. Grabby, MA: Bergin & Garvey.

Hayek, F. (1976). *Law, legislating and liberty: The mirage of social justice* (Vol. 2). Chicago: University of Chicago Press.

Illich, I. (1971). *Deschooling society*. New York: Harper & Row.

Miron, L. (2006). *A conception of performative ethnography* (Unpublished manuscript).

Noguera, P. (2003). *City schools and the American dream*. New York: Teachers College Press.

Novak, M. (2000). Defining social justice. *First Things, 108*(December), 11–13.

Roberts, R. (2005). *Injustice and rectification*. New York: Peter Lang.

Shklar, J. (1990). *The faces of injustice*. New Haven: Yale University Press.

Chapter 1 References: History as a Way of Understanding and Motivating Social Justice Work in Education

Blount, J. M. (1998). *Destined to rule the schools: Women and the superintendency*. Albany, NY: SUNY Press.

Blount, J. M. (2005). *Fit to teach: Same-Sex desire, gender, and schoolwork in the twentieth century*. Albany, NY: SUNY Press.

Callahan, R. (1962). *Education and the cult of efficiency*. Chicago: University of Chicago Press.

Cremin, L. (1990). *American education: The metropolitan experience, 1876–1980*. New York: Harper Colophon.

Cremin, L. (1982). *American education: The National experience, 1783–1876*. New York: Harper Colophon.

Cremin, L. (1972). *American education: The colonial experience, 1607–1783*. New York: Harper Colophon.

Cubberley, E. P. (1919). *Public education in the United States*. Houghton Mifflin.

Dewey, J. (1916). *Democracy and education: An introduction to the philosophy of education*. New York: Macmillan.

Dewey, J. (1900, 1990). *The school and society; The child and the curriculum*. Chicago: University of Chicago Press.

Diamond, J. (2005). *Collapse: How societies choose to fail or succeed*. New York: Viking.

Diamond, J. (1997). *Guns, germs, and steel: The fates of human societies*. New York: Norton.

Dougherty, J. (2004). *More than one struggle: The evolution of black school reform in Milwaukee*. Chapel Hill: UNC Press.

English, F. (2005, November). *Towards a theory of social justice/injustice: Learning to lead in the social cage*. Paper presented at the annual meeting of the UCEA, Nashville, TN.

Harbeck, K. (1997). *Gay and Lesbian educators: Personal freedoms, public constraints*. Mauldin, MA: Amethyst Press.

Loewen, J. (1996). *Lies my teacher told me: Everything your American history textbook got wrong.* Touchstone.

Mahoney, K. (2004). *Catholic higher education in protestant America: The Jesuits and Harvard in the age of the University.* Baltimore, MD: Johns Hopkins University Press.

Rousmaniere, K. (2005). *Citizen teacher: The life and leadership of Margaret Haley.* Albany, NY: State University of New York Press.

Shoho, A., Merchant, B., & Lugg, C. (2005). Social justice: Seeking a common language. In F. English (Ed.), *The SAGE handbook of educational leadership: Advances in theory, research, and practice* (pp. 47–67). Thousand Oaks, CA: SAGE Publications.

Tyack, D. (1974). *The one best system: A history of American urban education.* Cambridge, MA: Harvard University Press.

Tyack, D., & Hansot, E. (1982). *Managers of virtue: Public school leadership in America, 1820–1980.* New York: Basic Books.

Zimmerman, J. (2002). *Whose America? Culture wars in the public schools.* Cambridge, MA: Harvard University Press.

Chapter 2 References: Toward a Transformational Theory of Social Justice

Akbar, N. (2002). The psychological dilemma of African American academicians. In Jones, L (Ed.), *Making it on broken promises: African American male scholars confront the culture of higher education* (pp. 30 – 41). Sterling, VA: Stylus Publishing, LLC.

Beachum, F. D., & McCray, C. R. (2004). Cultural collision in urban schools. *Current Issues in Education, 7*(5). Retrieved from http://cie.asu.edu/volume7/number5/

Behr, T. (2005). Luigi Taparelli and social justice: Rediscovering the origins of a "hollowed" concept. *Social Justice in Context, 1,* 3–16.

Bennett, L. (1984). *Before the Mayflower: A history of Black America* (5th ed.). New York: Penguin Books.

Blanchette, W., Beachum, F. D., & Mumford, V. (2005). Urban school failure and disproportionality in a Post-Brown era: Coincidence or Conspiracy. *Remedial and Special Education, 26*(2), 70–81.

Blassingame, J. W. (1979). *The slave community: Plantation life in the Antebellum South.* New York: Oxford University Press.

Bolman, L. G., & Deal, T. E. (2001). *Leading with soul: An uncommon journey of spirit.* San Francisco: Jossey-Bass.

Brantlinger, E. (2001). Poverty, class, and disability: A historical, social, and political perspective. *Focus on Exceptional Children, 33*(7), 1–19.

Brown, K. (2004). Leadership for social justice and equity: Weaving a transformative framework and pedagogy. *Educational Administration Quarterly, 40*(1), 77–108.

Bush, L. V. (1999). *Can black mothers raise our sons?* Chicago: African American Images.

Cunningham, W. G., & Cordeiro, P. A. (2003). *Educational leadership: A problem-based approach* (2nd ed.). Boston: Allyn & Bacon.

Dantley, M. (2002). Uprooting and replacing positivism, the melting pot multiculturalism, and other impotent notions in educational leadership through an African American perspective. *Education and Urban Society, 34*(3), 334–352.

Dantley, M. (2005). African American spirituality and Cornel West's notions of prophetic pragmatism: Restructuring educational leadership in American urban schools. *Educational Administration Quarterly, 41*(4), 651–674.

Darder, A., Baltodano, M., & Torres, R. D. (2003). Critical pedagogy: An introduction. In A. Darder, M. Baltodano, & R. D. Torres (Eds.). *The critical pedagogy reader* (pp. 1–21). New York: Routledge.

Delgado, R. (1990). When a story is just a story: Does voice really matter? *Virginia Law Review, 76,* 95–111.

Dyson, M. E. (1997). *Race rules: Navigating the color line.* New York: Vintage Books.

Dyson, M. E. (2004). *The Michael Eric Dyson reader.* New York: Basic Civitas Books.

Dyson, M. E. (2005). *Is Bill Cosby right? Or has the Black middle class lost its mind?* New York: Basic Civitas Books.

Dyson, M. E. (2006). *Come hell or high water: Hurricane Katrina and the color of disaster.* New York: Basic Civitas Books.

DuBois, W.E.B. (2003). *Souls of Black folk.* New York: Barnes & Noble Classics.

Eagleton, T. (1990). *The ideology of the aesthetic.* Oxford: Basil Blackwell.

English, F. W. (2003). *The postmodern challenge to the theory and practice of educational administration.* Springfield, IL: Charles C. Thomas.

English, F. W. (2004, Spring). Undoing the "done deal": Reductionism, ahistory, and pseudo-science in the knowledge base and standards for educational administration. *UCEA Review, 46*(2), 5–7.

Epps, E. G. (2005). Urban education: Future perspectives. In F. E. Obiakor & F. D. Beachum (Eds.), *Urban education for the 21ˢᵗ Century: Research, issues, and perspectives* (pp. 218–234). Springfield, IL: Charles C. Thomas.

Fraser, N. (1997). *Justice interrupts: Critical reflections on the "postsocialist" condition.* New York: Routledge.

Freire, P. (2000). *Pedagogy of the oppressed.* New York: Continuum.

Fullan, M. (2001). *Leading in a culture of change.* San Francisco: Jossey-Bass.

Gewirtz, S. (1998). Conceptualizing social justice in education: Mapping the territory. *Journal of Education Policy, 13*(4), 469–484.

Ginwright, S. A. (2004). *Black in school: Afrocentric reform, urban youth, and the promise of hip-hop culture.* New York: Teachers College Press.

Giroux, H. (1997). *Pedagogy and the politics of hope: Theory, culture, and schooling.* Boulder, CO: Westview.

Gorski, P. (2006). The unintentional undermining of multicultural education: Educators at the crossroads. In J. L. Landsman & C. W. Lewis (Eds.), *White teachers/diverse classrooms: A guide to building inclusive schools, promoting high expectations, and eliminating racism* (pp. 61–78). Sterling, VA: Stylus.

Harro B. (2000). The cycle of socialization. In M. Adams, W. J. Blumenfield, R. Castaneda, H. W. Hackman, M. L. Peters, & X. Zuniga (Eds.), *Reading for diversity and social justice: An anthology on racism, anti-Semitism, sexism, heterosexism, ableism, and classism* (pp. 79–82). New York: Routledge.

hooks, B. (2003). Confronting class in the classroom. In A. Darder, M. Baltodano, & R. D. Torres (Eds.), *The critical pedagogy reader* (pp. 143–150). New York: Routledge.

hooks, B. (2004). *We real cool: Black men and masculinity.* New York: Routledge.

Kailin, J. (2002). *Antiracist education: From theory to practice.* New York: Rowan & Littlefield.

Katz, J. (1995). Advertisement and the construction of violent white masculinity. In G. Dines & J. Humez (Eds.), *Gender, race and class in the media: A text reader.* Thousand Oaks, CA: SAGE Publications.

Kunjufu, J. (1993). *Hip-hop vs. MAAT: A psycho/social analysis of values.* Chicago: African American Images.

Lipitz, G. (2002). The possessive investment in whiteness. In P. S. Rothenberg (Ed.), *White privilege: Essential readings on the other side of racism* (pp. 61–85). New York: Worth Publishers.

Lynch, K., & Baker, J. (2005). Equality in education: An equality of condition perspective. *Theory and Research in Education, 3*(2), 131–164.

Marshall, C., & Gerstl-Pepin, C. (2005). *Re-framing educational politics for social justice.* Boston: Allyn & Bacon.

McLaren, P. (1994). White terror and oppositional agency: Towards a critical multiculturalism. In D. Goldberg (Ed.), *Multiculturalism: A critical reader* (pp. 45–74). Cambridge, MA: Blackwell.

Mukhopadhyay, C, & Henze, R. C. (2003). How real is race? Using anthropology to make sense of human diversity. *Phi Delta Kappan, 84*(9), 669–678.

Myers, L. J. (1988). *Understanding an Afrocentric world view: Introduction to an optimal psychology.* Dubuque, IA: Kendall/Hunt.

North, C. (2006). More than words? Delving into the substantive meaning(s) of "social justice" in education. *Review of Educational Research, 76*(4), 507–535.

Obiakor, F. E., & Ford, B. A. (2002). *Creating successful learning environments for African American learners with exceptionalities.* Thousand Oaks, CA: Corwin Press.

Obiakor, F. E., & Beachum, F. D. (2005). Developing self-empowerment in African American students utilizing the Comprehensive Support Model. *Journal of Negro Education,* 74(1), 18–29.

Obiakor, F. E., Obiakor, P. H., Garza-Nelson, C., & Randall, P. (2005). Educating urban learners with and without special needs: Life after the *Brown* case. In F. E. Obiakor & F. D. Beachum (Eds.), *Urban education for the 21st century: Research, issues, and perspectives* (pp. 20–33). Springfield, IL: Charles C. Thomas.

Patton, P. L. (1998). The gangstas in our midst. *The Urban Review, 30*(1), 49–76.

Perry, T. (2003). Up from the parched earth: Toward a theory of African-American achievement. In Perry, T., Steel, C., & Hilliard, A. G. (Eds.), *Young gifted and Black: Promoting high achieving among African-American students* (pp. 1–108). Boston: Beacon Press.

Powell, K. (2003). *Who's gonna take the weight?: Manhood, race, and power in America.* New York: Three Rivers Press.

Rogers, W. G. (2000). The power in our community: Finding solutions to our problems. In S. F. Battle & R. Hornung (Eds.), *The State of Black Milwaukee* (pp. 121–138). Milwaukee, WI: The Milwaukee Urban League.

Rothstein, S. W. (1996). *Schools and society: New perspectives in American education.* Englewood Cliffs, NJ: Prentice Hall.

Scheurich, J. J., & Young, M. D. (1997). Coloring epistemologies: Are our research epistemologies racially biased? *Educational Researcher, 26*(4), 4–16.

Schmidt, S. L. (2003). More than men in white sheets: Seven concepts to the teaching of racism as systemic inequality. *Equity & Excellence in Education, 38*(2), 110–122.

Sergiovanni, T. J. (1992). *Moral leadership: Getting to the heart of school improvement.* San Francisco: Jossey-Bass Publishers.

Shields, C. M. (2004). Dialogic leadership for social justice: Overcoming pathologies of silence. *Educational Administration Quarterly 40*(1), 111–134.

Snarey, J. R., & Walker, V. S. (2004). Primary values and developing virtues of African American ethics. In V. S. Walker & J. R. Snarey (Eds.), *Race-ing moral formation: African American perspectives on care and justice* (pp. 130–146). New York: Teachers College Press.

Sidorkin, A. M. (2002). *Learning relations.* New York: Peter Lang.

Starratt, R. J. (2004). *Ethical leadership.* San Francisco: Jossey-Bass.

Strike, K. A., Haller, E. J., & Soltis, J. F. (1998). *The ethics of school administration* (2nd ed.). New York: Teachers College Press.

Villegas, A. M., & Lucas, T. (2002). *Educating culturally responsive teachers: A coherent approach.* Albany, NY: State University of New York Press.

Wade, R. (1964). *Slavery in the cities: The South 1820-1860.* New York: Oxford University Press.

West, C. (1994). *Race matters.* New York: Vintage Books.

West, C. (2004). *Democracy matters: Winning the fight against imperialism.* New York: Penguin Press.

Wijeyesinghe, C. I., Griffin, P., & Love, B. (1997). Racism curriculum design. In M. Adams, L. A. Bell, & P. Griffin (Eds.), *Teaching for diversity and social justice: A sourcebook* (pp. 82–109). New York: Routledge.

Yeo, F., & Kanpol, B. (1999). Introduction: Our own "Peculiar Institution": Urban education in 20ᵗʰ century America. In F. Yeo & B. Kanpol (Eds.), *From nihilism to possibility: Democratic transformation for the inner city*. Cresskill, NJ: Hampton Press.

Young, I. M. (1990). *Justice and the politics of difference*. Princeton University Press.

Chapter 3 References: Freedom and Justice: Conceptual and Empirical Possibilities for the Study and Practice of Educational Leadership

Aronowitz, S., & De Fazio, W. (1997). The new knowledge work. In A. H. Halsey, H. Lauder, P. Brown, & A. S. Wells (Eds.), *Education: Culture, economy, society* (pp. 193–206). New York: Oxford University Press.

Ayers, W. C., Hunt, J. A., & Quinn, T. (Eds.). (1998). *Teaching for social justice*. New York, NY: Teachers College Press.

Ayers, W. C. (1993). *To teach: The journey of a teacher*. New York, NY: Teachers College Press.

Ayers, W. C., Klonsky, M., & Lyon, G. (Eds.). (2000). *A simple justice: The challenge of small schools*. New York: Teachers College Press.

Babbitt, I. (1924). *Criticism in America: Its function and status*. New York: Harcourt, Brace & Company.

Blackburn, S. (1996). *Oxford dictionary of philosophy*. Oxford: Oxford University Press.

Cahn, S. M. (1997). *Classic and contemporary readings in the philosophy of education*. New York: McGraw-Hill.

Darling-Hammond, L., French, J., & Garcia-Lopez, S. (2002). *Learning to teach for social justice*. New York: Teachers College Press.

Davies, J. (1998). The dialectic of freedom. In W. F. Pinar (Ed.), *The passionate mind of Maxine Greene*. London: Falmer Press.

Dewey, J. (1916/1944). *Democracy and education*. New York, NY: The Free Press.

Durant, W. (1961). *The story of philosophy*. New York: Washington Square Press.

Freire, P. (1970/2004). *Pedagogy of the oppressed*. New York: Continuum Press.

Freire, P. (1973). *Pedagogy of freedom*. New York: Continuum Press.

Fromm, E. (1941/1965). *Escape from freedom*. New York: Avon Books.

Gandhi, M. K. (1951). *Non-violent resistance (satyagraha)*. New York: Schocken Books.

Giroux, H. (1983a). Theories of reproduction and resistance in the new sociology of education. *Harvard Educational Review, 53*, 257–293.

Giroux, H. (1983b). *Theory and resistance in education: A pedagogy for the opposition*. Hadley, MA: Bergin & Garvey.

Giroux, H. (1997). Crossing the boundaries of educational discourse: Modernism, postmodernism, and feminism. In A. H. Halsey, H. Lauder, P. Brown, & A. S. Wells (Eds.), *Education: Culture, economy, society* (pp. 113–130). New York: Oxford University Press.

Greene, M. (1988). *The dialectic of freedom*. New York: Teachers College Press.

Karier, C. J. (1986). *The individual, society, and education: A history of American educational ideas*. Urbana, IL: University of Illinois Press.

King, M. L. (1958). Stride toward freedom.

Kohn, A. (1999). *The schools our children deserve: Moving beyond traditional classrooms and "tougher standards."* Boston: Houghton Mifflin.

Kozol, J. (1967). *Death at an early age*. Boston: Houghton Mifflin.

Kozol, J. (1992). *Savage inequalities*. New York: Crown Publishers.

Marshall, C. (1997). Dismantling and reconstructing policy analysis. In C. Marshall (Ed.), *Feminist critical policy analysis* (pp. 1–40). London: Falmer Press.

McLaren, P. (1989). *Life in schools: An introduction to critical pedagogy in the foundations of education*. New York: Longman.

Merchant, B. M., & Shoho, A. R. (2006). Bridge people: Civic and educational leaders for social justice. In C. Marshall & M. Oliva (Eds.), *Leadership for social justice: Making revolutions in education* (pp. 85–109). Boston: Pearson Education.

Merrill, J. C. (1990). *The imperative of freedom: A philosophy of journalistic autonomy*. Latham, MD: Freedom House.

Merrill, J. C., Gade, P. J., & Blevens, F. R. (2001). *Twilight of press freedom: The rise of people's journalism*. Mahwah, NJ: Lawrence Erlbaum Associates, Inc.

Postman, N., & Weingartner, C. (2000). *Teaching as a subversive activity*. New York: Dell Publishing.

Postman, N., & Weingartner, C. (1971). *The soft revolution*. New York: Dell Publishing.

Pulliam, J. D., & Van Patten, J. (1995). *History of education in America*. Englewood Cliffs, NJ: Merrill.

Schmitt, R. (2003). *Alienation and freedom*. Cambridge, MA: Westview Press.

Smith, A. (1991). *Wealth of nations*. New York: Prometheus.

Spring, J. H. (1995). *The intersection of cultures: Multicultural education in the United States*. Boston: McGraw Hill.

Spring, J. H. (2001). *The American school: 1642–2000*. Boston: McGraw Hill.

Spring, J. H. (1988). *Conflict of interests: The politics of American education*. New York: Longman.

Thoreau, H. D. (1993). *Civil disobedience and other essays*. New York: Dover.

Urban, W., & Wagoner, J. (1996). *American education: A history*. New York: McGraw-Hill.

Tucker, R. W., & Hendrickson, D. C. (1990). Thomas Jefferson and American foreign policy. *Foreign Affairs, 69*(2), 135–156.

West, C. (1997). The new politics of difference. In A. H. Halsey, H. Lauder, P. Brown, & A. S. Wells (Eds.), *Education: Culture, economy, society* (pp. 509–519). New York: Oxford University Press.

Chapter 4 References: Social Justice as an Educational Construct: Problems and Possibilities

Appiah, K. A. (2006). *Cosmopolitanism: Ethics in a world of strangers*. New York: W.W. Norton & Co.

Apple, M. (1979). *Ideology and curriculum*. New York: Routledge.

Biesta, 2006, p. 2) Prologue, Biesta, (2006). *Beyond learning: democratic education for a human future*. Boulder, CO: Paradigm Publishers.

Blunden, A. (2003). *For ethical politics: Part Four: The fight for justice in the 21st century*. Victoria, Australia: Heidelberg Press. Retrieved May 2, 2006, from http://www.werple.net.au/~andy/blackwood/fep/ch04.htm

Bogotch, I. (2006). Biographical entries: Horace Mann, William Maxwell, Angelo Patri. In F. English (ed.), *Encyclopedia of educational leadership and administration*. Thousand Oaks, CA: Sage Publications.

Bogotch, I. (2005). A history of public school leadership: The first century, 1837–1942. In F. English (Ed.), *The Sage handbook of educational leadership* (pp. 7–33). Thousand Oaks, CA: Sage Publications.

Bogotch, I. (2002). Educational leadership and social justice: Practice into theory. *Journal of School Leadership, 12*(2), 138–156.

Bogotch, I., & Roy, C. (1996). The contexts of partial truths: An analysis of principal's discourse. *Journal of Educational Administration, 35*(3), 234–252.

Bogotch, I., & Taylor, D. (1993). Discretionary assessment practices: Professional judgments and principals' actions. *Urban Review, 25*(4), 289–306.

Bojer, J. (2000). Children and theories of social justice. *Feminists Economics, 6*(2).

REFERENCES

Bourdieu, P., & Passaron, J. C. (1977). *Reproduction in education, society and culture*. Beverly Hills, CA: Sage Publications.

Bowles, S., & Gintis, H. (1976). *Schooling in capitalist America*. New York: Basic Books.

Britzman, D. (2007). Teacher education as uneven development: Toward a psychology of uncertainty. *The International Journal of Leadership in Education, 10*(1), 1–12. Retrieved from http://www. informaworld.com/smpp/title~content=t713693371~db=all~tab=issueslist~branches=10-v10

Bruner, J. G. (1966). *On knowing*. New York: Atheneum.

Bruner, J. (1990). *Acts of meaning*. Cambridge, MA: Harvard University Press.

Bush, K., & Saltarelli, D. (2000, August). *The two faces of education in ethnic conflict. Towards a peacebuilding education for children*. Florence: Innocenti Research Center UNESCO.

Carr, W. G. (1942). *Community life in a democracy*. Washington, DC: National Congress of Parents and Teachers.

Cochran-Smith, M. (2004). *Walking the road: Race, diversity, and social justice in teacher education*. New York: Teachers College Press.

Constable, P. (2006, September 24). Afghan girls' study at risk. *Sun-Sentinel International*, 21A, 26A.

Constitutionfinder. http://confinder.richmond.edu/

Deutsch, M. (1975). Equity, equality, and need: What determines which value will be used as the basis for distributive justice? *Journal of Social Issues, 31*, 137–149.

Deutsch, M. (1985). *Distributive justice: A psychological perspective*. New Haven, CT: Yale Press.

Dewey, J. (1927/1954). *The public and its problems*. Athens, OH: Swallow Press, Ohio University Press.

Dewey, J. (1939). *Freedom and culture*. G. P. Putnam's Sons.

Diamond, J. (1999). *Guns, germs and steel*. New York: W.W. Norton & Co.

Elster, J. (1995). The empirical study of justice. In D. Miller & M. Walzer (Eds.), *Pluralism, justice, and equality* (pp. 81–98). New York: Oxford University Press.

Erickson, E. (1963). *Childhood and society*. New York: W.W. Norton & Co.

Fanon, F. (1968). *The wretched of the earth*. New York: Grove Press, Inc.

Fine, M. (2004, September). The power of the Brown v. Board of education decision: Theorizing threats to sustainability. *American Psychologist American Psychological Association, 59*(6), 502–510.

Foster, W. (1986). *Paradigms and promises: New approaches to educational administration*. Amherst, NY: Prometheus books.

Freedom House. (2005). http://www.breitbart.com/news/2005/12/20/051220134942.8w8uaqyp.html

Freud, S. (1962). *Civilization and its discontents*. New York: W.W. Norton & Co.

Garrison, J. (1999, November 10). *"John Dewey" Encyclopedia of philosophy of education*. Retrieved May 3, 2005, from http/www.vusst.hr/Encyclopeadia.john_dewey.htm. http://www.vusst.hr/ENCYCLOPAEDIA/john_dewey.htm

Giroux, H. (1988). *Teachers as intellectuals*. Grabby, MA: Bergin & Garvey.

Goodlad, J. (2004). *Romances with schools*. New York: McGraw-Hill.

Harrison, L. (2006, Spring). The culture club: Exploring the central liberal truth. *The National Interest*, 94–100.

Hayden, P. (2002). *John Rawls: Towards a just world order*. Cardiff: University of Wales Press.

Hayek, F. (1976). *Law, legislating and liberty: The mirage of social justice* (Vol. 2). Chicago: University of Chicago Press.

Hume, D. (1777/1952). *An enquiry concerning human understanding*. LaSalle, IL: The Open Court Publishing Company.

Illich, I. (1971). *Deschooling society*. New York: Harper & Row.

James, W. (1968). The one and the many. In *Pragmaticism* (pp. 57–72). New York: Washington Square Press.

Johnson, G. (1907). *Education by plays and games*. Washington, DC: McGrath Publishing Co.

Kagan, J. (1989). *Unstable ideas: Temperament, cognition and self*. Cambridge, MA: Harvard University Press.

Kemmis, S. (1996). Emancipatory aspirations in a postmodern world. In O. Zuber- Skerritt (Ed.), *New directions in action reseach* (pp. 199–242). London: The Falmer Press.

King, M. L. K. (1963, April 16). *Letter from a Birmingham jail.* Atlanta, GA: King Center.

Laing, R. D. (1972). *The politics of experience.* New York: Ballantine Books.

Maritain, J. (1943/1960). *Education at the crossroads.* New Haven, CT: Yale University Press.

Marcuse, H. (1970). The end of Utopia. In *Five lectures* (pp. 62–82). Boston: Beacon Press.

Marshall, C., & Oliva, M. (2006). *Leadership for social justice: Making revolutions in education.* Boston: Pearson Education.

Meier, D. (1995). *The power of their ideas.* Boston: Beacon Press.

Miron, L. (2006). *A conception of performative ethnography.* (Unpublished manuscript).

Nafisi, A. (2004). *Reading Lolita in Teheran.* New York: Random House.

Neuhaus, R. (1988, June). Traditions of inquiry: Whose justice? Which rationality? by A. MacIntyre. *Book Review. Commentary, 85*(6), 64–68.

Noguera, P. (2003). *City schools and the American dream.* New York: Teachers College Press.

Novak, M. (2000). Defining social justice. *First Things, 108*(December), 11–13.

Patri, A. (1917). *A schoolmaster in the Great City.* New York: MacMillan Company.

Plato, Apology. In E. Hamilton & H. Cairns (Eds.), *The collected dialogues* (pp. 3–26). Princeton: Princeton University Press.

Popper, K. (1945/1959/1963). *Open scociety and its enemies* (Vols. 1 & 2).

Poster, M. (2001). *What the matter with the internet?* Minneapolis, MN: University of Minnesota Press.

Rawls, J. (1971, 1999). *A theory of justice.* Cambridge, MA: Harvard University Press.

Rehnquist, W. (2004). *The supreme court.* New York: Alfred Knopf.

Roberts, R. (2005). *Injustice and rectification.* New York: Peter Lang.

Rorty, R. (1998). *Achieving our country.* Cambridge, MA: Harvard University Press.

Rossman, M. (1972). *On learning and social change.* New York: Vintage Books.

Rousseau, J. J. (1978/1943). *Emile.* New York: E. P. Dutton & Co.

Rusk, R. (1929). *The philosophical bases of education.* Boston: Houghton Mifflin Company.

Sergiovanni, T. (1989). Value-Driven schools: The Amoeba theory. In H. Walberg & J. Lane (Eds.), *Organizing for learning toward the 21st century* (pp. 31–40). Reston, VA: NASSP.

Shklar, J. (1990). *The faces of injustice.* New Haven: Yale University Press.

Schudel, M., & Bernstein, A. (2006, April 14). *Washington Post,* W.S. Coffin Jr., activist chaplain, obiturary4/'14/06) p. 8b in Sun-Sentinel.

Silberman, S. (2006, June). Don't try this at home. *Wired,* 192–197, 200.

Sizer, T., & Sizer, N. (1999). *The students are watching.* Boston: Beacon Press.

Stack, S. (2004). *Elsie Ripley Clapp (1879–1965): Her life and the community school.* Peter Lang: New York.

Stone, C. (1929). *Supervision of the elementary school.* Boston: Houghton Mifflin.

Strike, K. (1989).

Strong, E. (1968). Searches for agreement by persuasion. In C. Moore (Ed.), *The status of the individual in east and west* (pp. 377–387). Honolulu, HI: University of Hawaii Press.

Theoharis, G. (2004). *At no small cost: Social justice leaders and their response to resistance* (UMI No. 3143016). Unpublished doctoral dissertation. University of Wisconsin at Madison.

Toulmin, S. (1990). *Cosmopolis: The hidden agenda of modernity.* New York: the Free Press.

Tyack, D. (1974). *The one best system: A history of American urban education.* Cambridge: Harvard University Press.

Usher, R., & Edwards, R. (1996). *Postmodernism and education.* London: Routlege.

Van Dijk, T. (1998). *Ideology: A multidisciplinary approach.* London: Sage Publications.

Wu, J. (1968). The individual in Chinese political traditions. In C. Moore (Ed.), *The status of the individual in east and west* (pp. 381–410). Honolulu: University of Hawaii Press.

Young, I. (1990). *Justice and the politics of different.* Princeton, NJ: Princeton University Press.

Chapter 5 References: Towards a Theory of Social Justice/Injustice:
Learning to Lead in the Social Cage

Allen, W. (2005, October). A forward glance in a mirror: Diversity challenged—access, equity, and success in higher education. *Educational Researcher, 34*(7), 18–23.

Andrus, T. (2005–2006). A national study and analysis of poverty and African American incarceration. *National Forum of Educational Administration and Supervision Journal, 23*(1), 4–80.

Bartee, R., Beckham, J., Gill, C., Graves, C., Jackson, K., Land, R., et al. (2000, April). Race, discipline, and educational leadership: African-American student perspectives on the Decatur, Illinois, incident. *Journal of Special Education Leadership, 13*(1), 19–29.

Bem, S. (1993). *The lenses of gender: Transforming the debate on sexual inequality.* New Haven, CT: Yale University Press.

Blount, J. (1998). *Destined to rule the schools: Women and the superintendency, 1873–1995.* Albany, NY: SUNY Press.

Blount, J. (2005). *Fit to teach: Same-sex desire, gender, and school work in the twentieth century.* Albany, NY: SUNY Press.

Borja, R. (2005, October 12). Bennett quits k12 Inc. under fire. *Education Week, 25*(7), 6.

Brunner, C., Grogan, M., & Prince, C. (2003, October). *The American Association of School Administrators' national study of women superintendents and central office administrators: Early findings* (An occasional paper). Arlington, VA: AASA.

Bowles, S., & Gintis, H. (1976). *Schooling in capitalist America.* New York: Basic Books.

The Broad Foundation & Thomas B. Fordham Institute. (2003). *Better leaders for America's schools: A manifesto.* Retrieved February 11, 2004, from http://www.edexcellence.net/doc/Manifesto.pdf

Brock, D. (2004). *The republican noise machine: Right wing media and how it corrupts democracy.* New York: Three Rivers Press.

Brunner, C. (1999). Power, gender, and superintendent selection. In C. C. Brunner (Ed.), *Sacred dreams: Women and the superintendency* (pp. 63–78). Albany: SUNY Press.

Characteristics of recipients of earned doctorates, 2002. (2003, December 12). *The Chronicle of Higher Education*, p. A10.

Chen, J. (1980). *The Chinese of America.* New York: Harper & Row.

Collins, C., & Yeskel, F. (2005). *Economic apartheid in America.* New York: The New Press.

Conason, J. (2003). *Big lies.* New York: Thomas Dunn Books.

Cortina, R., & Gendreau, M. (2003). *Immigrants and schooling: Mexicans in New York.* New York: Center for Migration Studies.

Daniels, R. (1974). *The politics of prejudice: The anti-Japanese movement in California and the struggle for Japanese exclusion.* New York: Atheneum.

Davis, A. (1983). *Women, race, and class.* New York: Vintage Books.

Davis, D. (1966). *The problem of slavery in western culture.* Ithaca, NY: Cornell University Press.

Davis, D. (1975). *The problem of slavery in the age of revolution 1770–1823.* Ithaca, NY: Cornell University Press.

Davis, D. B. (2006). *Inhuman bondage: The rise and fall of slavery in the new world.* Oxford, UK: Oxford University Press.

Dewey, J. (1929). *The sources of a science of education.* New York: Horace Liveright.

Diamond, J. (1999). *Guns, germs and steel.* New York: W.W. Norton & Co.

Dyson, M. (2004). *The Michael Eric Dyson reader.* New York: Basic Books.

English, F. (2002, May). On the intractability of the achievement gap in urban schools and the discursive practice of continuing racial discrimination. *Education and Urban Society, 34*(3), 298–311.

English, F. (2005). Educational leadership for sale: Social justice, the ISLLC standards, and the corporate assault on public schools. In T. Creighton, S. Harris, & J. Coleman (Eds.), *Crediting the past, challenging the present, creating the future* (pp. 83–106). NCPEA.

English, F. (2004, Spring). Undoing the 'done deal': Reductionism, a historicity, and pseudo-science in the knowledge base and standards for educational administration. *UCEA Review, 46*(2), 5–7.

English, F. (2003). Cookie-cutter leaders for cookie-cutter schools: The teleology of standardization and the de-legitimization of the university in educational leadership preparation. *Leadership and Policy in Schools, 2,* 27–46.

Foucault, M. (1983). *The order of things: An archaeology of the human sciences.* New York: Vintage Books.

Foucault, M. (1985). *The use of pleasure: The history of sexuality* (Vol. 2). New York: Vintage Books.

Foucault, M. (1986). *The care of the self. The history of sexuality* (Vol. 3). New York: Vintage Books.

Foucault, M. (1990). *The history of sexuality* (Vol. 1). New York: Vintage Books.

Genovese, E. (1976). *Roll, Jordan, roll: The world the slaves made.* New York: Vintage Books.

Gould, S. (1981). *The mismeasure of man.* New York: W.W. Norton & Company.

Gonzales, G. (2003). Segregation and the education of Mexican children, 1900–1940. In J. Moreno (Ed.), *The elusive quest for equality* (pp. 53–76). Cambridge, MA: Harvard Educational Review.

Grant, M. (1985). *The roman emperors.* New York: Barnes & Noble.

Guttentag, M., & Secord, P. (1983). *Too many women: The sex ratio question.* Beverly Hills, CA: SAGE.

Hall, D. (2003). *Queer theories.* New York: Macmillan.

Hart, W. (2004). *Evil: A primer.* New York: St. Martin's Press.

Hernstein, R., & Murray, C. (1994). *The bell curve: Intelligence and class structure in American life.* New York: The Free Press.

Hessel, K., & Holloway, J. (2002). *A framework for school leaders: Linking the ISLLC standards to practice.* Princeton, NJ: ETS.

Highwater, J. (1990). *Myth and sexuality.* New York: Harper & Row.

Hine, D., Hine, W., & Harrold, S. (2006). *The African-American odyssey.* Upper Saddle River, NJ: Pearson.

Jensen, A. (1979). *Bias in mental testing.* New York: The Free Press.

Jones, D. (2003, December 30). 2003: Year of the woman among the 'Fortune' 500? *USA Today,* p. 1B.

Jordan, W. (1968). *White over black: American attitudes toward the negro, 1550–1812.* Chapel Hill, NC: University of North Carolina Press.

Kellner, D. (1989). *Critical theory, Marxism, and modernity.* Baltimore, MD: The Johns Hopkins University Press.

Kevles, D. (1995). *In the name of eugenics.* Cambridge, MA: Harvard University Press.

Kluger, R. (1977). *Simple justice.* New York: Random House.

Kohn, A. (2000). *The case against standardized testing: Raising the scores, ruining the schools.* Westport, CT: Heinemann.

Koschoreck, J., & Slattery, P. (2006). Meeting all students' needs: Transforming the unjust normativity of heterosexism. In C. Marshall & M. Oliva (Eds.), *Leadership for social justice: Making revolutions in education* (pp. 151–165). Boston: Pearson.

Kowalski, T., & Brunner, C. (2005). The school superintendent: Roles, challenges, and issues. In F. English (Ed.), *The SAGE handbook of educational leadership* (pp. 142–167). Thousand Oaks, CA: SAGE.

Kuhn, T. (1996). *The structure of scientific revolutions* (3rd ed.). Chicago: University of Chicago Press.

Kumashiro, K. (2002). *Troubling education: Queer activisim and antiopressive pedagogy.* New York: RoutledgeFalmer.

Lemann, N. (1999). *The big test: The secret history of the American meritocracy.* New York: Farrar, Straus & Giroux.

Levine, A. (2005). *Educating school leaders.* New York City.

Lewin, R. (1993, October). Shock of the past for modern medicine. *New Scientist, 23,* 28–32.

Lucas, S. (1999). *Tracking inequality: Stratification and mobility in American high schools.* New York: Teachers College Press.

REFERENCES

Lugg, C. (2003). Our strait-laced administrators: The law, lesbian, gay, bisexual, and transgendered administrators, and the assimilationist imperative. *Journal of School Leadership, 13*(1), 51–85.

Mann, M. (2003). *The sources of social power: A history of power from the beginning to A.D. 1760.* New York: Cambridge University Press.

Mann, M. (2004). *Fascists.* Cambridge, UK: Cambridge University Press.

Marshall, C., & Oliva, M. (2006). *Leadership for social justice: Making revolutions in education.* Boston: Pearson.

Marshall, C., & Gerstl-Pepin, C. (2005). *Reframing educational politics of social justice.* Boston: Allyn & Bacon.

Mayer, E. (2001). *What evolution is.* New York: Basic Books.

Mayer, H. (1998). *All on fire: William Lloyd Garrison and the abolition of slavery.* New York: St. Martin's Press.

McCarthy, C., & Dimitriadis, G. (2005). Governmentality and the sociology of education. In C. McCarthy, W. Crichlow, G. Dimitriadis, & N. Dolby (Eds.), *Race, identity, and representation in education* (2nd ed., pp. 321–335). New York: Routledge.

McDonald, M. (2005, November/December). The integration of social justice in teacher education: Dimensions of prospective teachers' opportunities to learn. *Journal of Teacher Education, 56*(5), 418–435.

McLaren, P. (1986). *Schooling as a ritual performance.* London: Routledge & Kegan Paul.

McLaren, P. (1994). *Life in schools.* New York: Longman.

McNeill, J. (1993). *The church and the homosexual.* Boston: Beacon Press.

Mehler, B. (1999, Winter). *Race and 'reason': Academic ideas a pillar of racist thought* (Intelligence Report, 93). Montgomery, Alabama: Southern Poverty Law Center.

Mohawk, J. (2000). *Utopian legacies: A history of conquest and oppression in the western world.* Santa Fe, New Mexico: Clear Light Publishers.

Morowitz, H., Hazen, R., & Trefil, J. (2005, September 2). Intelligent design has no place in the science curriculum. *The Chronicle Review,* pp. B6–B14.

Murphy, J. (1999). *The quest for a center: Notes on the state of the profession of educational leadership.* Columbia, MO: UCEA.

Murray, C. (2005, September 29). The hallmark of the underclass. *Wall St. Journal,* p. A.18.

Niethammer, C. (1977). *Daughters of the earth: The lives and legends of American Indian women.* New York: Simon & Schuster.

Nietzsche, F. (1966). The natural history of morals. In W. Kaufman (Trans.), *Beyond good and evil* (pp. 95–118). New York: Vintage Books.

Oakes, J., Gamoran, A., & Page, R. (1992). Curriculum differentiation: opportunities, outcomes, and meanings. In P. Jackson (Ed.), *Handbook of research on curriculum* (pp. 570–608). New York: Macmillan.

Osofsky, G. (1967). *The burden of race.* New York: Harper and Row.

Palmer, B. (1967). Slavery as a divine trust: Duty of the South to preserve and perpetuate it. In G. Osofsky (Ed.), *The burden of race: A documentary history of negro-white relations in America* (pp. 90–93). New York: Harper and Row.

Parker, L. (1998). "Race is…race ain't;" an exploration of the utility of critical race theory in qualitative research in education. *Qualitative Studies in Education, 11*(1), 43–55.

Parker, L. (2001). Statewide assessment triggers urban school reform: But how high the stakes for urban minorities. *Education and Urban Society, 33*(3), 313–319.

Parker, L., Kelly, M., & Sanford, J. (1998, Winter). The urban context of schools and education: community, commitment, and change. *Educational Theory, 48*(1), 123–137.

Parker, L., & Lynn, M. (2002). What's race got to do with it? Critical race theory's conflicts with and connections to qualitative research methodology and epistemology. *Qualitative Inquiry, 8*(1), 7–22.

Report of the National Advisory Commission on Civil Disorders. (1968). New York: E.P. Dutton & Co., Inc.

Samier, E. (2002, January). Weber on education and its administrative prospects for leadership in a rationalized world. *Educational Management and Administration, 30*(1), 27–46.

Sapon-Shevin, M. (1994). *Playing favorites: Gifted education and the disruption of Community.* Albany, NY: SUNY Press.

Schaefer, S. (2003, September 29). Income gap steady, poverty spreads. *Wall St. Journal,* p. A14.

Sellers, P. (2003, October 13). Power: Do women really want it? *Fortune, 148*(8), 80–82, 86, 88, 92, 100.

Shields, C. (2004, February). Dialogic leadership for social justice: Overcoming pathologies of silence. *Educational Administration Quarterly, 40*(1), 109–132.

Simonton, D. (1994). *Greatness.* New York: The Guilford Press.

Skocpol, T. (1979). *States and social revolutions. A comparative analysis of France, Russia and China.* Cambridge: Cambridge University Press.

Semali, L. (1997). In the name of science and of genetics and of the bell curve: White supremacy in American schools. In J. Kincheloe, S. Steinberg, & A. Gresson (Eds.), *Measured lies: The bell curve examined* (pp. 161–175). New York: St. Martin's Press.

Shakeshaft, C. (1989). *Women in educational administration.* Newbury Park, CA: SAGE.

Shakeshaft, C. (1999). The struggle to create a more gender-inclusive profession. In J. Murphy & K. Seashore Louis (Eds.), *Handbook of research on educational administration* (2nd ed., pp. 99–118). San Francisco: Jossey-Bass.

Shoho, A., Merchant, B., & Lugg, C. (2005). Social justice: Seeking a common language. In F. English (Ed.), *The SAGE handbook of educational leadership* (pp. 47–67). Thousand Oaks, CA: SAGE.

Sizemore, B. (2005). *Walking in circles: The black struggle for school reform.* Chicago: Third World Press.

Smith, M. (2006, February 17). Sense and segregation. *The Chronicle Review,* pp. B8–B10.

Tannahill, R. (1982). *Sex in history.* New York: Stein and Day Publishers.

Taylor, T. (1996). *The prehistory of sex: Four million years of human sexual culture.* New York: Bantam Books.

The Economist. (2005, June 11). Minding the gap, p. 32.

The Economist. (2005, July 16). Middle of the class. Equality of opportunity is under threat, pp. 9, 12.

The Economist. (2005, October 29). They stooped to conquer. In R. J. Evans (Ed.), *The third reich in power: 1933–1939* (pp. 87–88). New York: Penguin. (Book Review).

Tillman, C. (2004). African American principals and the legacy of Brown. In R. Floden (Ed.), *Review of research in education* (pp. 101–146). Washington, DC: AERA.

Walker, B. (1983). *The woman's encyclopedia of myths and secrets.* San Francisco, CA: Harper Collins.

Weber, M. (1946). The social psychology of world religions. In *From Max Weber: Essays in sociology* (pp. 267–301). New York: Oxford University Press.

Weinberg, G. (1972). *Society and the healthy homosexual.* Alyson Publications. (Reprinted in 1983 by St. Martin Press).

West, C. (1999). Race and modernity. In C. West (Ed.), *The Cornel West reader.* New York: Perseus Books.

West, C. (2004). *Democracy matters.* New York: The Penguin Press.

White, R. (2002). *Lincoln's greatest speech: The second inaugural address.* New York: Simon and Schuster.

Woodward, C. (1974). *The strange career of Jim Crow.* New York: Oxford University Press.

Young, I. (1990). *Justice and the politics of different.* Princeton, NJ: Princeton University Press.

Young, J. (2003, October 10). Researchers charge racial bias on the SAT. *The Chronicle of Higher Education, 50*(7), 34–35.

Young, M., & Lopez, G. (2005). The nature of inquiry in educational leadership. In F. English (Ed.), *The SAGE handbook of educational leadership* (pp. 337–361). Thousand Oaks, CA: SAGE.

AUTHOR INDEX

SUBJECT INDEX

A

administration/administrator, xi, 5, 17, 18, 24, 28–32, 34, 35, 39, 49, 58, 61, 71, 74, 80, 88, 89, 93, 94, 96, 98, 102, 104, 110, 116, 132, 151

African-American, 46, 62, 144

anthropology, 1, 9, 107, 128, 148

autonomy, 12, 54, 81, 101, 103, 136

B

balance, 23, 59, 70, 72, 82, 83, 85, 87, 88, 91, 92, 109, 111, 151

C

child/children, 3, 7, 10, 12–14, 25, 26, 33, 36, 49, 58, 60, 65, 75, 76, 80–82, 86–88, 90–93, 96–98, 100, 102, 105–108, 110, 117, 123, 127, 147, 137, 153–155

Christian/Christianity, 33, 65, 72, 73, 123, 127, 134–136, 138, 142, 144, 145

classicism, 63

complexity theory, 22, 23

constitution, 14, 62, 69, 71, 79, 88–91, 99, 114, 125

critical theory, 5, 6, 117, 155

curriculum/curricula, 6, 9, 18, 19, 25, 47, 53, 92, 94, 98, 105, 113, 114, 117, 118, 124, 148–152

D

democracy/democratic, xi, 14, 20, 25–27, 40, 61, 64, 69–71, 75–77, 81, 86, 88, 90, 99, 101, 111, 112, 152, 155

decision-making, 7, 20

developmental, 6, 10, 118, 141

distributive justice, 2, 3, 5, 6, 84

E

economics, 1, 3, 9, 49, 64, 87, 89, 104, 131, 148

emergent virtues, 40, 59, 60

empirical/empiricism, ix, 2, 7, 9, 49, 64, 67, 71, 84, 85, 87, 95, 102, 103, 109, 117, 121, 124, 136

enlightenment, 67–69, 71, 78, 88, 123, 127, 128, 142

epistemological/epistemology, 2, 7, 9, 41, 42, 63

equal/equality, 1–3, 6, 19, 20, 25, 36, 40, 43, 44, 46–48, 51, 53, 54, 57, 60, 62, 63, 71, 73, 75, 78, 101, 117, 134, 137

equity, 1–3, 6, 8, 10, 13, 31, 36, 41, 51, 57, 78, 91, 114

F

fear, 1, 29, 35, 54, 87, 88, 94, 99, 111, 138

feminism, 47, 50

freedom, 2, 4, 9, 10, 12, 14, 36, 51, 61–78, 82–85, 87, 88, 91, 97, 101, 102, 111, 125, 129, 145

G

gender, 6, 8, 19, 29–36, 47, 48, 53, 58–64, 71, 82, 114, 123, 125, 135, 137–139, 142, 145, 146

H

hegemony, 3, 6, 64, 71

historical/history, x, xi, 9, 11, 12, 14, 17–32, 34–37, 40, 41, 44–46, 49, 50, 54, 56, 58, 60, 66, 67, 72, 82, 85–87, 89, 91–95, 102, 104, 106, 111, 113, 115, 117, 119–125, 128, 129, 131, 132, 136, 139, 141, 144–146